MUSINGS OF THE OLD PROFESSOR

THE MEANING OF KOHELES

A new translation of and commentary
on the Book of Ecclesiastes

by

DAVID MAX EICHHORN, D.D.

JONATHAN DAVID
Publishers   ●   New York

CONTENTS

INTRODUCTION

How the Book of Koheles, known to the non-Jewish world as the Book of Ecclesiastes, ever managed to get included in the Biblical canon is one of the great enigmas of Biblical research. It is the one book of the Bible which bases its case on pure reason. The only other Biblical book which is as severely critical of the orthodox theology of the time is the Book of Job. There are many sections of the Bible which attempt to interpret life rationally. But no other Biblical book examines reality with the candor and the clarity that mark the words of Koheles, the old retired professor who lived and wrote in Jerusalem about the beginning of the second pre-Christian century. In addition, the Book of Koheles is not written in classically Biblical Hebrew. Its style and many of its word-meanings are more closely akin to the Mishna than to the Bible. This makes the task of translating and interpreting the book properly a quite difficult one.

The sages of the Talmud and of the Middle Ages approached the Book of Koheles in two very different ways. Some of them were sure that no book which dared to deviate from the conventional Pharisaic theological norm would have been given a place in the Biblical canon. So these scholars took it for granted that the unconventional language of Koheles was merely some sort of "Aesopian" language which masked a complete acceptance of the traditional theology. They tried desperately to make the rational words of Koheles fit the more mystical music of Pharisaic Judaism. But the words, the work of an unreconstructed forerunner of the Sadducees, just would not fit this music. Their efforts produced only spiritual disso-

1

nances, nonsensical noises, as, for example, when they tried to use the words of Koheles to substantiate the notion of the survival of the personal ego, an idea which is as far from the thinking of Koheles as black is from white. These sages either did not understand Koheles or they did not want to understand. They contributed little to a genuine comprehension and appreciation of the words of Koheles.

Fortunately, there were other Jewish sages who not only tried to understand the words of Koheles but who did understand them quite well and were not shocked by them. On the contrary, they were moved by a profound feeling that they were in the spiritual presence of one who had ventured to face Truth fearlessly and honestly. They, too, wanted to face Truth fearlessly and honestly. So it is to their thoughts, their reactions, their interpretations, that we shall direct our attention. Not to the nonsense-writers, the archaic conformists, the purblind antiquarians, for whom Koheles was and probably will ever be a nasty and a naughty word, shall we go for enlightenment. To those among our classical sages and scholars who were not afraid to look at life as closely as Koheles had looked at it shall we turn for a rational interpretation of the musings of the old professor.

1

(Chapter One, Verse One, "The words of Koheles, the son of David, king of Jerusalem," and Chapter One, Verse Twelve, "I Koheles was king over Israel in Jerusalem" are editorial notes based on the belief that King Solomon and Koheles were one and the same. Since King Solomon ruled from 973 to 933 BCE and the Book of Koheles was written about 200 BCE, this editorial presumption is without foundation in historical fact. Therefore, these two verses could not possibly have been part of the original text. The original text of the Book of Koheles begins (1:2) and ends (12:8) with identical words, "Vapor of vapors, everything is vapor.")

Koheles says, Chapter One, Verse Two,

"Vapor of vapors, vapor of vapors, everything is vapor."

Before beginning our commentary, two terms which will be used very often, Tanna and Amora, must be defined for those readers who may not be familiar with these words. A Tanna is a sage who taught in the yeshivos of Palestine during the period when the Mishna was being compiled, c.10-c.200 CE. An Amora is a sage who taught in the yeshivos of either Palestine or Babylon during the period when the Gemarra was being compiled, c.200-c.500 CE.

Rabbi Samuel ben Isaac, a Palestinian amora of the latter part of the third century, stated in the name of Rabbi Simon ben Eleazar, a tanna of the latter part of the second century: In Koheles 1:2, the word "vapor" is used seven times to symbolize the seven worlds in which man finds himself during his

3

lifetime. (Rabbi Simon ben Eleazar arrived at the figure of seven by giving the word "vapor" the numerical value of one and the word "vapors" the numerical value of two.) When one is a year old, he is like a king; he is kept in a special, fancy bed; everybody inquires concerning his health; everybody wants to look at him; everybody wants to hug him and kiss him. When he is two and three years old, he is like a pig; he dabbles in all manner of filth and pokes his fingers into every dirty hole. When he is ten years old, he is like a goat, jumping up and down aimlessly, frolicking and playing before his parents, amusing the passers-by. When he is eighteen years old, he is like a race horse, neighing and preening himself, enjoying the thrills of the race and the hunt, especially those connected with the race and the hunt for a pretty woman. Then he captures a woman and, shortly thereafter, finds himself saddled and bridled and loaded down like a jackass. Then his woman produces sons and daughters and he has to be on the move continually to support his family and he becomes like a dog, for he is full of "chutspa" (boldness) and he takes from here and from there and everywhere without scruple and without shame. Finally, he becomes old and looks and acts like a monkey. His appearance changes, his mind wanders, he eats and drinks in an offensive manner, his actions become infantile, he regains his youthful sexual powers in imagination but not in actuality and even his children mock him and belittle him. When he says or does anything, they tell their friends, "Do not pay any attention to him. He is an old fool." This is true only of an ordinary old man. The genuinely religious and the genuinely wise old men are different. That is what the Bible points out when it states, I Kings 1:1, "King David was old." Even though he was old, David still had the bearing, the mentality and the power of a king.

Rabbi Huna, probably Rabbi Huna ben Joshua, Babylonian amora who taught at Nares Yeshiva, c.335-370, wealthy owner of a brewery which made beer from dates, taught in the name of Rabbi Acha ben Jacob, Babylonian amora who worked for the Exilarch and probably was also on the faculty of Pumbedita Yeshiva, c.310-335: King David made a statement and did not explain it; but Solomon his son explained it. King Solomon made a statement and did not explain it; but David his father explained it.

David said, Psalm 144:4, "Man is like vapor." What kind of vapor? The vapor of an oven? Such vapor has substance. The vapor of a stove? Such vapor has substance. Solomon explained what David meant. Solomon explained that man is like the vapor of vapor, completely without substance and permanently impermanent. (This observation is based, of course, on the previously mentioned erroneous assumption that Koheles and King Solomon were one and the same.)

Solomon said, Koheles 6:12, "Man's days are as insubstantial as a shadow." What kind of shadow? The shadow of a wall? Such a shadow has substance. The shadow of a palm tree? Such a shadow has substance. David explained what Solomon meant. David said, Psalm 144:4, "Man's days are as a passing shadow," a shadow which is without substance. David meant that man's days are as the shadow of a passing bird. When the bird flies away, its shadow flies away with it.

An earlier authority, Mar Samuel, c.180-257, Babylonian amora, founder of the Nehardea Yeshiva, explained David's words in even more vivid fashion. He taught: David meant that man's days are like the shadow of a swiftly flying bee, which has practically no shadow at all.

Koheles says, Chapter One, Verse Three,

"What does a man gain from all his labor that he puts forth beneath the sun?"

Rabbi Benjamin stated: Some of the sages tried to keep the Book of Koheles out of the Bible because it contains sentiments which may lead one to heresy. They said, Is it possible that, at the height of his wisdom, Solomon believed that man gains no advantage from any labor of any kind? Is it possible that Solomon would have included in this belief the labor of studying Torah? No, it is not possible. Solomon speaks only of the kind of labor which man labors "beneath the sun," i.e., labor for material ends. Solomon does not include the labor which man puts forth for spiritual ends, i.e., the labor involved in studying Torah.

Rabbi Huna and Rabbi Acha declared in the name of Rabbi Chilfai, another Babylonian amora: Man's labor is beneath the sun but his treasure, i.e., the Torah, is above the sun.

Rabbi Yudan, Palestinian amora who taught from c.310-335, said: Beneath the sun, man has nothing; beyond the sun, man has everything, i.e., the Torah.

Rabbi David Luria, also known as Redal, Lithuanian Midrashic commentator, 1798-1855, explains: Rabbi Huna and Rabbi Acha and Rabbi Yudan are all saying that the pious man lives in two worlds at the same time, the world beneath the sun, i.e., the everyday world, and the world beyond the sun, i.e., the world of the Torah.

Rabbi Abraham ben Meir ibn Ezra, 1092-1167, Spanish poet, philologist, philosopher and Biblical exegete, writes: The phrase "beneath the sun" means "in the span of a human lifetime" because earthly time is measured through the sun. Daytime lasts from the rising to the setting of the sun and nighttime lasts from the setting to the rising of the sun, whether the moon and the stars are seen or not. Also sowing time and harvest, cold and heat, summer and winter are measured by the relationship of the earth to the sun.

Koheles says, Chapter One, Verse Four,

> "One generation goes and another comes; but the earth endures forever."

"One generation goes and another comes."

Rabbi Jochanan bar Napacha, 199-279, was a Palestinian amora. He was very handsome. He was the principal assistant of Patriarch Judah II and the most esteemed and productive amora of his time. He taught at the Tiberias Yeshiva, which was less conservative than the Babylonian yeshivos. He permitted the study of Greek and considered Greek philosophy to be on an intellectual par with Jewish religious teachings. Simon ben Lakish, also known as Rish Lakish, 200-275, was his brother-in-law and his closest friend and co-worker. Rabbi Joshua ben Levi, Rabbi Jochanan bar Napacha, and Rish Lakish formed an intellectual triumverate whose liberal influence had a lasting effect upon the development of Jewish religious thought. Rabbi Jochanan stated: The Bible teaches that the Bes Din (the law-making and law-enforcing agency) of Gideon was as important in the sight of God as the Bes Din of Moses; the Bes Din of Samson as important as the Bes Din of Aaron; and the Best Din of Jephthah as important as the Bes Din of Samuel—to teach us that anyone who is chosen to be leader of his community, even though previously he may have been an insignificant person, becomes, by virtue of assuming leadership, as worthy of respect as the mightiest of the mighty of former times, as it says, Deuteronomy 17:9, "And you shall go to the priests the Levites and the judge who shall be in those days." You are to go to the judge who sits in judgment in your own generation. This shows that, in the opinion of Moses, the judge who judges in your generation has the same stature in your generation as the judges of former generations had in theirs. Therefore do not say that the former times were more worthy of respect than the present time.

His colleague, Rish Lakish, added: Obey none except the judge in your own generation.

Rabbi Abba bar Kahana, Palestinian amora of the late third century, said: Let the present generation be as important to you as the past generations. Do not say, "If Rabbi Akiba were still alive, I would study Bible with him. If Rabbi Zeira and Rabbi Jochanan were still alive, I would study Mishna with them." Give as much credence to the scholars and teachers of your own time as you do to the scholars and teachers of former times.

Rashi, Rabbi Solomon Isaac, 1040-1105, famous French Biblical commentator, says: It is not possible to make an accurate comparison between sages of former generations and sages of the present generation because conditions vary from generation to generation.

"But the earth endures forever."

Ibn Ezra comments: All living things are composed of four elements: fire, air, water and earth. From these they were made and, when their period of life is finished, to these they will return. So the Bible says, Genesis 3:19, "You are made of earth and to earth you will return." This is also the meaning of Koheles 1:4. Living creatures appear and disappear but the earth, from which all living creatures are made, endures.

Koheles says, Chapter One, Verse Five,

"The sun rises and the sun sets and hastens to the place from which he rose."

Rabbi Levi bar Sissi, who taught from c.200-220, was among the last of the Tannaim and a favorite disciple of Rabbi Judah the Prince who sent him to Simonias, south of Sepphoris, "to give public lectures, decide questions of law, superintend the synagogue, prepare copies of authentic writings, teach the children and generally supply all the religious wants of the community." He was the father of Rabbi Joshua ben Levi. Rabbi Levi bar Sissi taught: What benefit does God provide for human beings who obey His commandments and do good deeds in order to store up future rewards for themselves? For such it is enough of a reward that God condescends to let His light, i.e., the sun, shine upon them. And what benefit does God provide for the righteous who obey His commandments and do good deeds without thought of storing up future rewards for themselves? For such, in the future, God will continually renew their influence as He now daily renews the circuit of the sun.

Rabbi Berachya Ha-kohen, Palestinian amora who taught from c.335-370, said: Before the sun of one righteous person sets, the sun of another righteous person rises. No righteous man departs from this world before another righteous man is born to take his place. On the day that Rabbi Akiba died, Rabbi Judah the Prince was born. On the day that Rabbi Adda bar Ahava died, his son Rav Hamnuna was born. On the day that Rav Hamnuna did, his son Rabbi Abbin was born. On the day Rabbi Abbin died, his son Rabbi Abbin II was born. So it is in every generation. There is no indispensable person.

Koheles says, Chapter One, Verses Six and Seven,

> "The wind goes toward the south and turns around toward the north; it turns around and around all the time. All the rivers run into the sea and yet the sea is never full; the rivers flow ceaselessly to their appointed destination."

The most important medieval compilation of comments on

the Book of Koheles is Midrash Koheles Rabba. It dates from the eighth century or later. Neither the name of the compiler nor the country in which it was first published is known. The following comments of Midrash Koheles Rabba on Verse Seven are taken from the sections indicated:

Koheles Rabba 1:7, Section Four: All man's wisdom is lodged in his heart. Yet, no matter how much wisdom man pours into his heart, he is never able to fill it. Would you say that, if a man brings forth some of the wisdom which is in his heart, it will never return to his heart? No. Koheles says, "The rivers flow ceaselessly to their appointed destination." The wise man never ceases giving of his knowledge. Through teaching others, he relearns that which he has already learned. Thus he is replenishing his own store of knowledge continuously.

Koheles Rabba 1:7, Section Five: All Torah which a pious man learns is lodged in his heart. Yet his heart never gets enough Torah nor is his spiritual hunger ever satisfied. A Roman noblewoman once asked Rabbi Jose bar Chalafta, second century tanna, pupil of Rabbi Akiba and founder of the Sepphoris Yeshiva, "Your Bible says, Daniel 2:21, 'God gives wisdom to the wise and knowledge to them that have understanding.' Would it not be better if the Scripture said that God gives wisdom to fools and knowledge to those who are not already learned?" Rabbi Jose replied, "My dear lady, if two people came to you, the one poor and the other rich, and they wanted to borrow money from you, to whom would you lend money, to the poor man or the rich man?" She answered, "To the rich one." He said to her, "Why?" She answered, "Because the rich will always have money with which to repay me, but the poor man, if he loses my money, with what will he repay me?" Rabbi Jose said, "Let your ears hear what your mouth has declared. If God were to give of His wisdom to fools, they would sit and meditate upon it in privies and theatres and bathhouses (In Rome in the second century what went on in theatres and bathhouses was quite like that which goes on in the United States in the twentieth century in night clubs and motels) ; but God gives His wisdom only to the wise and they sit and meditate upon it in the schools and the houses of worship." That is to say, the wise make good use of God's wisdom; fools would fritter it away.

Koheles says, Chapter One, Verse Eight,

> "All stories are tiresome; yet the story tellers never cease; and the eyes never seem to get enough of seeing the story tellers and the ears of hearing them tell their stories."

This will sound so very timely to those readers whose families are afflicted with "the curse of the box" that it underscores the truth of the next statement of Koheles, "There is nothing new under the sun," even though, in his time, the circle of mesmerized and largely moronic watching listeners had not yet been expanded immeasurably by the sorcery of television.

Samuel bar Nachman, Palestinian amora who taught from c.280-310, said: The blessings and the consolations brought by religious thinkers like the prophets must be excluded from this blanket condemnation of story tellers, because the message of a truly religious teacher is fresh and inspiring and produces deeds of goodness and kindness. It is not that any human being, including the great religious teachers, can explain away the secrets of the universe. Such knowledge is for God alone.

At the same time, it is not correct to say that the great religious teachers have no insight at all into the secrets of the universe. Rabbi Levi, a Palestinian contemporary of Samuel bar Nachman, said: The true religious prophet is able to see the way in which evil will be punished but not the way in which goodness will be rewarded. Rabbi Berachya Ha-kohen said: He is like one who is permitted to look in through the crack of a door.

Koheles says, Chapter One, Verses Nine and Ten,

"That which has been is that which will be; that which has been done is that which will be done; there is nothing new under the sun. Is there something of which it is said, 'See, this is new?' It has been here already in the ages that were before us."

Joseph Albo, c.1380-c.1445, Spanish philosopher, states, in his *Sefer Ha-ikkarim,* Book Three, Chapter Sixteen: From these verses and others like them, some have tried to prove the eternality of the Mosaic law. These expressions do not have any such meaning. The Bible does not seek to legislate for eternity. It seeks only to provide instruction for that portion of eternity which began with the creation of man. The word "l'olamim" used in Koheles 1:10 means a long time but it certainly does not mean eternally. All the terms in the Bible which some have taken to mean eternity are not meant to refer to infinity. We may never be in a position to change the order of things as set forth in the Torah, but certainly God has the power to do so. To believe otherwise is to limit the power of God. There is no evidence that any law is either unchangeable or irreplaceable. There is no necessity for making immutability a fundamental principle of any divine law in general or of the law of Moses in particular.

Koheles says, Chapter One, Verse Eleven,

"We have no remembrance of those who lived a long time ago, neither shall there be any remembrance of those who live a long time after us by those who will live a long time after them."

There is a golden thread that runs through most Semitic religions, and particularly the Jewish religion, which carries with it the belief that immortality belongs to the idea, the family and/or the nation but not to the individual person who spreads the idea, strengthens the family and serves the nation. The concept of personal survival after death is very attractive because it appeals to the basic urge for self-preservation which is instinctive in every living being. When the concept began to be promoted forcefully by religions originating in Persia and Greece, certain Jewish teachers and writers picked it up eagerly and adapted it to the Messianic thinking of their time, because it fitted in admirably with their own narrow and egotistical apocalyptic theories. While historic Judaism has not repudiated completely the idea of personal immortality (for who can say with absolute assurance that there is or that there is not life after death?), historic Judaism has repudiated the kind of religious thinking which puts a major emphasis on the after-life and which makes of this present world a place of secondary importance. If the other world exists, fine and dandy. If there be eternal life for earthly creatures and if a just and good God grants such eternal life to those who have done good because they were too frightened to do otherwise, He will most certainly also grant eternal life to those who, without the least regard for reward or punishment, have done good because they felt it is right to do good. The Jew who is true to the finest in his religious tradition will dismiss with contempt any concern over "what's in it for me, either now or later?" Let those who derive satisfaction from harboring and promoting such a selfish and unworthy concern continue to do so. The good Jew has not and will not.

(Koheles 1:12, "I, Koheles, was king over Israel in Jerusalem," is, obviously, an editorial insertion. It is an additional attempt, probably by the same editor who concocted Koheles 1:1, to indicate that King Solomon wrote the Book of Koheles. Beyond introducing an historical absurdity and disturbing the author's train of thought, Koheles 1:12 adds nothing. It should, therefore, be omitted from any reconstruction of the original text.)

Koheles says, Chapter One, Verses Thirteen to Fifteen,

"I set to work to examine and to investigate logically everything which is being done beneath the heavens; what a miserable and troublesome notion this is for those to whom God has given it! I have seen everything which is done beneath the sun; and, indeed, it is all evanescent and like grasping at the wind. That which is crooked cannot be made straight and that which is defective cannot be trusted."

Ibn Ezra comments: That which has a crooked nature can never be made straight. One who has within him a built-in deficiency can never be numbered with those who are not so encumbered. Another possible interpretation of Verse Fifteen is that the nature and knowledge of ordinary people are so imperfect that it is useless for them to try to comprehend the innermost secrets of the universe. Most of the doings of the nations testify eloquently to the truth of this statement.

Obadiah ben Jacob of Sforno, Italy, c.1475-1550, an exegete usually referred to simply as Sforno, comments: What is the meaning of "That which is crooked cannot be made straight?" Everything earthly keeps growing until it reaches full maturity; but the road to full growth is not a straight one. The way to maturity follows a winding and crooked path. And, once one has matured, he cannot go back and change the pattern of his growth nor can he then achieve the fuller stature he would have achieved had his way been less winding and less crooked.

Koheles says, Chapter One, Verses Sixteen to Eighteen,

"I said to myself: I have gathered together a greater store of wisdom than any other who ever lived in Jerusalem; I have considered much thought and knowledge. I have gotten for myself information on prudence and information on madness and folly; and now I know that all this is likewise grasping at the wind. The more wisdom, the more vexation; to increase one's knowledge is to increase one's pain."

Rabbi Ishmael ben Elisha, a tanna of the early part of the second century, taught by means of the following proverb: The larger the camel, the greater the load, i.e., the more intelligent a man is and the more wisdom he acquires, the greater the measure of his personal and social responsibility.

Rabbi Meir, renowned Palestinian scholar and expounder of Torah, who taught from c.140 to 165, interpreted Koheles 1:18 by means of the following Biblical analogy: The Bible states, Genesis 3:1, that the serpent was the most clever of all the animals. Because of this, his punishment for tempting Eve to transgress was more severe than if he had not been so very intelligent. Greater knowledge brings not only greater responsibility but also greater pain if one proves unworthy of the responsibility with which he has been entrusted.

Rav, also known as Abba Aricka, c.175-247, Babylonian amora and founder of the Sura Yeshiva, said: It is a principle of Jewish law that a Talmid Chacham, a learned sage, does not need to be warned before he is punished. A Talmid Chacham is expected to understand all the risks he is taking both in the world of learning and in the world of doing.

Samuel bar Nachman said: If the finely knit linen garments which are woven at Bet Shean in the Galil get stained, they become worthless, i.e., if an eminent scholar becomes involved in wrongdoing, his reputation is ruined; if the coarsely knit garments which are made at Arbel in the Galil become stained, it makes no difference in their value, i.e., if an ignoramus does wrong, his reputation is not affected. To what may the matter be compared? To two men who went into a restaurant to eat. One said, "Give me white bread and roasted meat and good wine." The other said, "Give me black bread and beans." The one who ate the expensive food got sick. The one who ate the cheap food felt fine. It should have been the other way around; but the one who ate the fine food was a scholar and the one who ate the cheap food was an ignoramus. The scholar was tense, nervous; he had a delicate stomach; he got sick. The ignoramus was in a good mood; he was as strong as an ox; he had a tough stomach; he did not get sick. The moral should be obvious; but, if it is not, let me ask you: Did you ever see a jack-ass overcome by spasms of vomiting and fever because it had a nervous stomach? No, you have not and you never will. Only thinking man has such spasms because only thinking man has a nervous stomach. And the more thinking the man, the more nervous the stomach.

If one follows this line of thought to its logical conclusion, one must recognize, as Abraham ibn Ezra recognizes, that it will discourage men from seeking to increase their knowledge, because such a course seems to lead to nothing but misery and dissatisfaction. Ibn Ezra writes: After Koheles had acquired great knowledge, he realized that one who has gained a thorough understanding of the way of the world has gotten for himself nothing but trouble and pain. He finds no happiness in a good wife or in gifted children because he is ever mindful that they are fated to die either during his lifetime or after his death. He takes no pleasure in the acquisition of property or wealth because he knows that these are insubstantial and transitory. In a period of misfortune, he has no hope; and, on the day of death, he does not feel that life has been worth the living. These are the gloomy thoughts which such a knowing one has on his mind continually.

There were those among the sages who interpreted Koheles 1:18 somewhat differently.

Raba bar Joseph, c.280-352, Babylonian amora, president of the Machoza Yeshiva, said: A brilliant young man whose being has become inflamed by the burning fire of scholarship is like a seed under the earth; when he begins to sprout, he grows fast. If such a young scholar is hot tempered, it is the fire of Torah which has heated him up, for so Scripture states, Jeremiah 23:29, "Is not My word like fire? says the Lord."

Rav Ashi, 354-427, the legendary editor of the Babylonian Talmud, continued the thought: Is it not true also that the genuine scholar must be hard as iron, for does not this same verse in Jeremiah conclude "And like a hammer that breaks the rock into pieces?"

Rabbina commented: Even though the prophet Jeremiah said this, the true scholar must understand that it is his responsibility to conduct himself calmly and with mildness of manner, for so says Koheles, Koheles 11:10, "Let unhappiness be absent from your thoughts."

Isaac Alfasi, known also as Ha-rif, 1013-1103, Moroccan exegete, explains that the passage in Jeremiah does not really refer to a young scholar getting angry but rather to his becoming highly excited and highly zealous, because his mind is working so much faster and penetrating so much farther than that of the normal person that he gets extremely agitated.

This mood, which borders sometimes almost upon hysteria, must be understood and treated with forbearance.

Samuel ben Isaac Ashkenazi Jaffe, also known as Yafe Toar, Midrashic exegete who lived in Italy in the sixteenth century, takes these comments on Jeremiah 23:29 and relates them to Koheles 1:18: Now we can understand what Koheles meant when he said, "The more wisdom, the more vexation; to increase one's knowledge is to increase one's pain." He did not mean that added wisdom brings added anger or that increased knowledge causes increased pain. Wisdom and knowledge add to the enlightenment and the joy of mankind. Koheles was referring to the fiery ardor of creative scholarship which sometimes gives temporary pain to him who is possessed by it and temporary vexation to those who work with such a one.

This thought has been developed further by two sages who have lived, comparatively speaking, in our own time.

Zev ben Israel Einhorn, also known as Maharzu, who lived in Russia in the nineteenth century, says: The wise man understands that mankind does not conduct its affairs in an intelligent manner and that mankind is corrupted by its own ignorance; and he wants to improve mankind, in accordance with the wisdom which he possesses, and mankind pays no attention to him; and this causes him vexation and pain.

Enoch ben Joseph Zundel, who also lived in Russia in the nineteenth century, writes: Rav Ashi's comment must not be taken literally, for there is a well-known statement by Rabbi Simon ben Eleazar which says exactly the opposite, "A scholar must always be as pliable as is the reed and never unyielding as is the cedar." It is for this reason that the pens with which Sifrey Torah, Tefillin and Mezzuzos are written are made from the reed. Hard, unyielding pens are never used for this holy purpose. What Rav Ashi meant to say is that a scholar whose understanding is not as sharp as iron has no right to be called a scholar. Immoderate zeal and anger are undesirable characteristics in anyone and are most certainly to be avoided. The intelligent man is the man whose mind and spirit are under complete control. He conducts himself in all matters with calm deliberation, with humility and with compassion, because of his deep understanding of the ways of nature and of man. As Raba bar Joseph said, he will understand that there are some young scholars in whom the spiritual force of Torah generates great heat. When such a young scholar becomes filled with Torah, he is set aflame and sometimes he says and does things which the more mature and level headed scholar would not say or do. Sometimes the sparks of truth ignite the fires of anger. And there are some scholars who just never grow up. Yes, there are some men of intelligence and learning who, no matter how long they live, just never grow up. It may be that Koheles had them in mind when he wrote, "The more wisdom, the more vexation; to increase one's knowledge is to increase one's pain."

2

In the second chapter, Koheles comes to a conclusion in the first part of the chapter which he contradicts completely in the concluding portion of the chapter. In the first thirteen verses, he tells how he has examined the various approaches to life, "the way of the intellectual and the way of the sensualist and the way of the materialist," and has decided that "the gulf separating wisdom and materialism is as great as the difference between light and darkness." He decides to write a poem in praise of the way of wisdom. Verse Fourteen begins with the words: "The eyes of the wise are in his head but the fool walks in darkness"—and then his train of thought stops abruptly, as though he does not fully believe what he is writing. He reveals what is really on his mind, as he continues: "And both of them suffer a common fate." The wise man and the fool both die; they are both forgotten; the fruits of one's labors are eaten by the unworthy and the undeserving; life is without justice and without reward; man is in constant trouble and in constant pain. "There is no genuine enjoyment in life except that which comes from eating and drinking and getting what satisfaction one may from his work." And, the chapter concludes, the belief that God rewards the righteous and penalizes the wicked, "this, too, is vapor and a grasping after wind."

This was strong medicine, even for the most rationalistic of the medieval Jewish sages. They tried diligently to comprehend the rugged realism of Koheles' teachings. Some passages they understood very well. Others were quite beyond their intellectual grasp. They just could not bring themselves to admit that there is a book in the Bible which contains such iconoclastic sentiments. With the exception of Midrash Koheles Rabba, the Talmudic and Midrashic writings ignored this second chapter almost completely, except for the use of a few verses as "proof texts" in settings which give no indication of the extreme rationalism of their Biblical source. And even Koheles Rabba approaches the latter half of the chapter in gingerly fashion, exhibiting but occasionally that boldness of thought so characteristic of Midrashic literature. Only the medieval exegetes, ibn Ezra and Sforno and, to a lesser extent, Rashi, ventured to come to grips with what Koheles was trying to say. They struggled very earnestly but they did not fully succeed.

Koheles says, Chapter Two, Verses One and Two,

> "I said to myself: Let me try merriment and take a look at enjoyment; these, too, are nothing but vapor. Of laughter I said: It is to be scorned; and concerning merriment I said: Of what use is it?"

Having reached the opinion, at the end of Chapter One, that the possession of wisdom is no guarantee of happiness, that "to increase one's knowledge is to increase one's pain," Koheles searched for other ways of getting pleasure out of life. He decided that he would begin by getting away from anything that was either intellectual or practical and would spend his time doing nothing but just having fun, being gay, joking, laughing, gallivanting around the night-spots of Jerusalem. He soon tired of this. It becomes boring soon enough when one is young; when one is old, the effect can be devastating. The realization comes all too quickly that the unctuous bow, the friendly greeting, the flirtatious glance are not centered about what one may have on his mind or in his heart

but are fastened upon the coins of the realm which he is carrying in his pocket. This is a dulling, a crushing realization. It
can turn a greying cavalier into a depressed, weary, apprehen-
sive oldster in less time than it takes to tell.

"Of laughter I said: It is to be scorned." Koheles was not
speaking of every kind of laughter. He was speaking, say the
sages, of the laughter of stupidity, the laughter of idiocy, the
laughter of cruelty, the raucous laughter of those who get enjoyment from the sight and sound of abuse and of pain. This
kind of laughter, says Rashi, is the rowdy-dowdy companion
of weeping and sighing; it accompanies a merriment which
brings grief to others and may end in grief for oneself.

Rabbi Abba bar Kahana said: How childish, how idiotic
is the manner in which the pagans behave at their chariot races
and their gladiatorial combats! Concerning such merriment,
one should ask: Of what use is it? What would ever tempt
a truly religious, a truly intelligent person to want to witness
such imbecilic spectacles? (Nearly seventeen hundred years have
passed since you asked this question, Rabbi. The pagans still
behave in the same idiotic and childish manner at the modern
chariot races and gladiatorial combats. The more blood, the
louder the screams of excitement; the more pain, the greater
the merriment.)

Koheles says, Chapter Two, Verses Three to Nine,

"I sought to measure the pleasures of the flesh, to balance
against each other the way of the intellect and the way of
the world, so that I might decide which way is best for human beings to follow during their brief earthly lives. I concentrated upon worldly matters: I built houses; I planted
vineyards; I created gardens and parks; I planted in them
every kind of tree; I made water-ponds with which to nourish
the growing forests; I bought male slaves and female slaves

who produced for me even more slaves; I had larger herds
of big animals and little animals than any man of Jerusalem
had ever owned; I gathered together silver and gold, precious
stones and merchandise; I surrounded myself with the kinds of
pleasures in which men especially delight, male singers, female
singers and large numbers of big-bosomed beauties. I kept on
building and acquiring until my possessions exceeded those of
any who had been before me in Jerusalem; but at no time did
I cease to ponder upon the meaning of it all."

Ibn Ezra says that when Koheles discovered that having
wisdom as one's only companion is like being accompanied
wherever one goes by a stern father and that to have merriment as one's sole companion is to live completely aimlessly,
he decided to find some other companion who would not have
the shortcomings of wisdom and of merriment and through
whom he might obtain pleasurable yet intelligent stimulation.
Sforno expands on this thought by explaining that, at first,
Koheles was so engrossed in philosophic studies that he took
no interest in worldly affairs except in the most general way.
After becoming convinced that neither philosophy nor the pursuit of pleasure holds the complete answer to man's desire for
happiness, he decided to try the method used by those who
aspire to community leadership, i.e., he would take a deep
interest in affairs of business and in the affairs of the community. However, he determined that he would not allow
himself to become so deeply involved in these worldly matters
that he would forget the chief purpose of his quest, which
was to find an answer to the question: Which way of life
gives a man the deepest inner satisfaction? Even though he
became eminently successful as a businessman, acquiring greater
wealth than any who had ever lived before him in Jerusalem,
and even though he carried through many schemes which were
of great benefit to the community, such as planting public

gardens and designing irrigation projects, he kept in mind continually the reason for his undertaking this experiment in practical affairs: "At no time did I cease to ponder upon the meaning of it all."

Koheles says, Chapter Two, Verses Ten and Eleven,

"I tried to find an answer for every question which came to my mind; I did not evade any mental problem; on the contrary, the more difficult the problem, the more my mind rejoiced; my reward for this mental labor was found in the labor itself. When I finally compared the value of all the material things which my hands had gathered and the value of my mental efforts, I recognized that the quest for material things is a vapor and a grasping after wind which has no lasting advantage."

Sforno says: Those whose minds and hearts are occupied completely with material things suffer when some harm comes to these material things or when their material ambitions are not fulfilled; but Koheles, who was interested in material things only as a scientist is interested in the substance which he is analyzing, derived greater genuine pleasure from his mental analysis than is obtained by those who ignore the world of the mind and concern themselves completely with the material world. Having finished his experiment, Koheles came to the conclusion that the quest after material things, like the quest after pleasure, has no lasting meaning or value.

Koheles says, Chapter Two, Verses Twelve and Thirteen,

"When I took a good look at the way of the intellectual and the way of the sensualist and the way of the materialist, I said to myself: How useless it is for lowly man to challenge Superior Authority, to question that which was decided long ago. I realized then that the gulf separating wisdom and materialism is as great as the difference between light and darkness."

When Rabbi Jochanan bar Napacha, famed Palestinian amora mentioned in the comment on Chapter One, Verse Four, died, he was succeeded at the Tiberias Yeshiva by a number of Babylonian instructors who were less liberal in their attitudes than he had been. Unlike Jochanan, they tried in every way to keep their pupils from studying Greek and from being influenced by Greek culture. One of these Babylonians, Rabbi Simon bar Abba, who taught at the Tiberias Yeshiva from about 280 to 310, discussed the meaning of Chapter Two, Verse Twelve, with his contemporary, Rabbi Chanina bar Pappa. Typically, Rabbi Simon saw in this verse a condemnation of Greek culture. "The way of the sensualist," he said, refers to the pagan religion of the Greeks, "the way of the materialist" refers to atheistic Greek philosophy, and "the way of the intellectual" is, of course, Judaism. Rabbi Chanina does not seem to have agreed that Koheles was castigating the Greeks and praising the Jews. He seems to have felt that the statement has universal application. Chanina said that "the way of the sensualist" is the pattern of life of anyone who is filled with an overwhelming desire to dominate. "The way of the materialist" is marked by an uncontrollable desire for worldly goods, a desire sparked by an irrational sense of personal insecurity. Were Rabbi Simon alive today, he would probably be a professional anti-Communist; and his colleague, Rabbi Chanina, would, undoubtedly, be a psychiatrist, a very good psychiatrist.

"How useless it is for lowly man to challenge Supreme Authority, to question that which was decided long ago."

Midrash Koheles Rabba states: If anyone says to you, "I know all the secrets of the universe; I can explain to you just why everything is the way it is"; say to him, "You miserable creature, you who lack the courage to challenge the authority of any earthly king, you have the 'chutspa,' the insolence to make such a statement as this in the presence of the King of kings, the Holy One, blessed be He!"

Rabbi Simon ben Yochai was an outstanding tanna of the second century CE, disciple of Rabbi Akiba, founder of a yeshiva at Meron in Galilee, and, in Jewish folklore, a worker of miracles. Because of the latter reputation, he is the legendary author of the famous mystical work, the *Zohar,* which was actually written by Moses de Leon in Spain in the thirteenth century. But legends do not die easily. Every year the mystics of Israel make a pilgrimage to Meron to the grave of their great hero, Rabbi Simon ben Yochai, on the eighteenth day of Iyar, the holy day of Lag b'Omer, the day on which he died. Rabbi Simon was blessed with a rich imagination and he may have been something of a mystic. He was also blessed with good common sense. Commenting on Koheles 2:12, Rabbi Simon said: It is quite in order to criticize anything which has been built by the hands of man but it is not proper to criticize that which has been ordained by God. When an earthly king builds a palace, people come to look at it and they say, "How much more beautiful this palace would be if the columns were thicker or the walls were wider or the ceiling was higher!" But have you ever heard anyone say, "How much more handsome would I be if I had three hands or three eyes or three feet?" Koheles said rightly that one must never "question that which was decided long ago."

Rabbi Levi bar Chayasa, whose time and place are unknown, said: When an earthly king builds a palace, would he consider putting a waterspout directly over the main entrance? This would not be considered practical or aesthetically attractive. Yet, when God made man, He put a waterspout directly over the main entrance to man's body. How so? He put the nose over the mouth and humanity has found this arrangement to be neither impractical nor aesthetically unattractive. So, as Koheles said, there is little purpose in questioning that which was decided long ago.

Rabbi Nachman bar Isaac, c.280-c.356, Babylonian amora and head of the yeshiva of Pumbeditha, was concerned that this attitude of Rabbi Simon ben Yochai and Rabbi Levi bar Chayasa, if carried too far, might hamper the freedom of scientific inquiry. Therefore he modified their statements somewhat by declaring: It is possible for a wise man to discover some of the secrets of the universe, just as it is possible to cut a path through the densest thicket of reeds or, by means of a guide rope, to lead a person in and out of the most intricate maze of rooms in the biggest house.

These words of caution from Rabbi Nachman prompted later Jewish commentators to advise their readers to exercise additional caution in interpreting the words of Rabbi Nachamn. Rashi declares: Rabbi Nachman is saying that, with a great amount of effort, a wise man may be able to piece together a little bit of the riddle of the universe; but to understand fully the pattern of creation and the laws of the universe is completely beyond the power or comprehension of mortal man and is a wisdom reserved for God alone.

Redal interprets the similes of Rabbi Nachman as follows: The wise man must first seek to remove the common errors which are held by the masses and which are as thorns and thistles to them as they seek to find their way to the house of truth. But even after the wise man has helped his generation to pass through the thickets of error and to arrive with him at the house of truth, he must carefully map out a plan for walking through the house, lest those with him now become confused and lost because of the complexity of the corridors that lead to the various rooms in the house.

Maharzu comments: No matter how hard one may try, it is impossible to comprehend completely the mind of an earthly ruler. How much more impossible is it to comprehend the mind of the King of kings, the Holy One, blessed be He. Rabbi Nachman wanted to let us know that, even among those secrets of the universe which through extraordinary mental effort we shall be able to unravel, there will be gradations of difficulty in comprehension. Some of them, after discovery, will be easy to understand, just as easy as looking into the rooms of a house. Others will require a depth of understanding that will be as difficult to reach as cutting through the undergrowth of an almost impenetrable jungle.

Sforno asks: How can limited man hope to improve upon the labors of Him Whose work is perfect? How can something created from mere matter hope to improve upon the plan or the product of its Spiritual Creator?

"The gulf separating wisdom and materialism is as great as the difference between light and darkness."

Rabbi Meir said: The gulf between Judaism and paganism is as great as the gap between light and darkness.

Ibn Ezra says: Just as, by means of light, one may see clearly those material objects which are near and become aware of those which are distant and may discern the distinguishing characteristics of these objects and evaluate everything appropriately in accordance with its proper perspective, so also, by means of wisdom, may one make evaluative judgments with the mechanism of the mind.

Sforno says: What a great difference there is between one who concentrates upon improving his mind and another who devotes himself solely to sensory experiences without giving thought to their significance! Just as darkness is the complete absence of light, so, too, is absolute sensuality completely devoid of wisdom.

Koheles says, Chapter Two, Verse Fourteen,

> "The eyes of the wise are in his head but the fool walks
> in darkness;—and both of them suffer a common fate."

Koheles Rabba comments: So the eyes of the wise are in his head? And where, pray, are the eyes of the fool? In his feet? Koheles means to say that the wise man is able, at the very beginning of a matter, to sense its outcome. Rabbi Meir used to say that the end of a matter is really at its beginning, i.e., the way in which a person estimates the significance of a matter at its beginning determines, in large measure, the manner in which the matter will end.

Ibn Ezra: The wise man is compared to an alert person who is able to select the right path and to avoid the wrong; the fool is compared to one who walks unsurely and unheedingly in the darkness and knows not when he may stumble and fall.

Sforno: The wise is able to foresee what may possibly happen in the future so that, at times, he will shun present benefit or pleasure in order to avoid future pain. To have this kind of wisdom one must be able to withstand material temptation. The fool does not have the will to turn away from present temptation nor the insight to foresee future consequences and so, inevitably, he gets himself into trouble.

"And both of them suffer a common fate."
All the commentators agree that this means that the careers of both wise man and fool end in death.

Koheles says, Chapter Two, Verses Fifteen to Seventeen,

> "I said to myself: That which will happen to the fool will
> happen to me. Why have I been so anxious to become wise?
> I decided that this, too, is vapor. For there is no eternal re-

membrance of either wise man or fool. It is clear from past
experience that, in the days to come, everyone now existing
will be forgotten. Alas, the wise man dies as does the fool. So
I came to hate life itself for I saw no good in anything which
is done under the sun; for it is all evanescent and like grasping
after wind."

One would think that the meaning of these verses is pain-
fully plain: Life is worthless. Life is without meaning or value.
Life is not worth the living. The wise man is no better off
than the fool. The dead are soon forgotten. For everyone, no
matter how good or how wise he may be, death is the end.

So one would think. But even the most scrupulous of the
Talmudic and medieval rationalists refused to recognize the
obvious import of Koheles, Chapter Two, Verses Fourteen and
following. It would have been difficult enough for these Jewish thinkers to admit that, in these verses, Koheles was denying,
with absolute finality, all hope of personal immortality. But
to admit that he was also saying here that study, knowledge,
wisdom are without worth or significance, this, for these dedicated scholars, was completely impossible. The ideal of learning, the ideal which they held most precious, would be
destroyed. They could not grant that this was the meaning of
these words of Koheles.

But there it was, right there in the Bible where it had been
placed by decision of the Tannaitic sages in the second century of the Common Era. And so the passage could not be
disregarded. The commentators had to say something about
it. Their weavings and bobbings to avoid direct contact with
the literal meaning of the text would do credit to the most
agile mental pugilist. What follows now is what they say about
these verses. It will be quite clear to the reader that what they
say the text says is not what the text really says.

Koheles Rabba contains two interesting passages that deal with these verses. Each passage begins with a comment on Verse Fourteen.

Koheles Rabba 2:15—Section Four: "The eyes of the wise are in his head"—This is a man who, when famine threatens, lays in a supply of food for three years. "But the fool walks in darkness"—This is a man who lays in a supply of food for only one year. "And both of them suffer a common fate. I said to myself: That which will happen to the fool will happen to me."—The wise man says to himself: I shall have food to eat and he will have food to eat. "Why have I been so anxious to become wise?"—Why did I pawn my very cooking pots in order to get money to buy food to store up for the time of famine? "There is no eternal remembrance of either wise man or fool. . . . In the days to come, everyone now existing will be forgotten."—That is what the wise man said to himself; but that is not what happened. When the years of drought and famine came, the wise man had plenty to eat and the fool almost starved. Indeed, it is not always true that "the wise man dies as does the fool."

Koheles Rabba 2:15—Section Five: "The eyes of the wise are in his head"—This refers to the Talmid Chacham, the sage who studies continually. "But the fool walks in darkness"— This refers to the come-day-go-day student of the Torah. That one is called Rabbi and this one is called Rabbi. That one is called "Chacham" and this one is called "Chacham." That one has the privilege of leading the congregation in prayer and this one has the privilege of leading the congregation in prayer. Therefore, "why have I been so anxious to become wise?" Why have I made such sacrifices of health and of strength to improve my store of knowledge? And I said to myself that "there is no eternal remembrance of wise man or fool." Ah, but this is not so. On the morrow the two Rabbis will enter a gathering of scholars or a similar gathering and each of them will be asked a scholarly question. One will be asked and will answer; and the other will be asked and will not be able to answer. Therefore, do not think that "the wise man dies as does the fool," for the wise man lives on through his learning and his teaching and the fool does not. Rabbi Chiyya bar Nehemiah, an amora of uncertain time and place, said: If a pupil, when he cites an opinion, is not required to give the name of the teacher from whom he got the opinion, the name of the teacher will soon be forgotten. How can a teacher be expected to devote himself wholeheartedly to his pupils, if such a breach of scholarly good manners is allowed to become the fashion?

Rashi read into the words of Koheles just exactly what he wanted to read into them. Rashi interprets these verses as follows: I said to myself, "If that which will happen to the fool will happen to me, why have I been so anxious to become wise?" Then I decided that this kind of thinking was vapor. Since both the wise and the fool die, I might imagine that the same fate awaits both the wise and the fool; and, therefore, I might ask myself: "Why should I be overly concerned about righteousness?" Then I said to myself that to think in this fashion is also vapor; for the memory of the righteous and of the wicked are not equal after death. One leaves behind him a good remembrance and the other leaves behind an evil remembrance. In the days to come, the evil ones now existing will be forgotten. I know this because the wicked ones who lived in former times, no matter how strong and how successful they were, have been forgotten. Does the wise man die as does the fool? He most assuredly does not. Even after they are dead, the wise are triumphant and bring blessing to their descendants.

Sforno, in his interpretation, comes to the defense of the belief in personal immortality: Even though the wise man dies as does the fool, it is impossible to believe that the wise, like the fool, does not achieve immortality. The ability possessed by the wise of predicting the future, a quality mentioned in Verse Fourteen, is generated by an immaterial source of power; for there is no material source of power which can generate a non-sensory capability. It follows, therefore, that this immaterial source of power which gives supersensory strength to the wise will not be destroyed as are the sensory powers of the fool. "So I came to hate life"—When I came to realize that there exists a power which is not destroyed but which is, of necessity, of an everlasting nature, I came to hate all worldly matters which have importance only "under the sun," i.e., which are material and transient in nature; and I decided that all such worldly matters are "vapor."

While ibn Ezra did not fully understand these verses of Koheles (or, perhaps, he did understand but, surrounded by narrow-minded and intolerant contemporaries, he did not dare to show that he understood), he comes somewhat closer to the true meaning of the verses than do the other exegetes: The same fate meets all who come into the world, whether they are good or bad. Why, therefore, have I busied myself with worldly things and tried to gain as much earthly knowledge as I could? I have now decided that this striving after earthly knowledge is vapor. (The inference is, of course, that striving after spiritual knowledge is very much worth-while.) Since everything earthly eventually changes and is eventually forgotten, everything earthly is valueless. There is no more remembrance on earth of the wise than of the fool. Even if the wise man is remembered for a year or a few years, eventually he is forgotten completely. Therefore, the wicked ones of earth are hardened in their wickedness because they see that death and earthly oblivion come to the wise as quickly and as inevitably as they come to the fool.

Koheles says, Chapter Two, Verses Eighteen to Twenty-one,

> "And I detested all the material possessions for which I had labored under the sun, since I would have to leave them to a man who would live after I was gone. And who knows whether this man will be a wise man or a fool? Yet he will have power over the wealth for which I sweated and schemed under the sun. This, too, is vapor. My heart began to despair concerning all my labor under the sun. There are those who conduct their affairs with wisdom and knowledge and expertness and yet have to turn their fortune over to others who have contributed nothing toward it. This is vapor and very unjust."

Koheles was distressed because a later generation would enjoy the fruits of his labor and because he would have no control over the manner in which his property would be used after his death. The sages felt that this was an extremely selfish point of view and quite contrary to the generally accepted Jewish principle that one lives in order to serve and strengthen his family and society rather than himself. It is as though Koheles were saying, "I shall be concerned about others only if I am sure that those others are concerned about me. I shall help only those who think as I think and who act as I desire them to act." In order to indicate that this kind of attitude is at complete variance with the teachings of Judaism, Koheles Rabba tells the following story, a story which is also found in Vayikra Rabba and in Tanchuma Kedoshim:

The Roman emperor Hadrian, while travelling on a road near the city of Tiberias, saw an old man planting fig trees. He said to him, "You foolish old man! If you were a youth and engaged in such work in the morning of your life, it would make sense; but why, in the time of old age, as the darkness of the grave approaches, do you spend your time on a task from which you will never benefit?" The old man replied, "This was the task to which I devoted myself in the morning of my life and this is the task to which I continue to devote myself in the evening of my life; and that which seems good in the sight of the Master of Heaven to do to me, He will do." Hadrian asked, "How old are you?" The man answered, "I have lived one hundred years." The emperor continued, "Do you really think that you will ever eat any of the fruit of these trees?" "If it be God's will, I shall eat," the old man said, "and, if not, my children will eat. Just as my fathers labored for me, so must I labor for my children." As Hadrian took his leave, he said, "Old man, if you live to eat the fruit of these trees, let me know."

Some years later, when the trees bore their first ripe fruit, the old man was still alive. He said, "I must do as the emperor requested." He filled a basket with figs and took it to the gate of Hadrian's palace. The guards asked him, "What do you want, old man?" "Take me to the king," the old man said. When he came into the royal presence, Hadrian also asked, "What do you want?" He said, "I am the old man whom you saw planting fig trees several years ago on the road near Tiberias. You asked me to bring you some of the figs from these trees after they would begin to bear fruit. Here is a basket of those figs." Hadrian arose from his throne and commanded the old man to sit and await his return. He took the basket of figs from the room. When he returned, he was still carrying the basket; but the figs had been removed and the basket was now filled with gold coins. "Take your basket and return home, old man," commanded the emperor, "and live out the rest of your days in the manner which you so well deserve." After the old man had departed, Hadrian's courtiers said to him, "Why have you shown such great honor to an old Jew?"

Hadrian replied, "His Creator has honored him. Therefore, should not I also honor him?"

The old man had a neighbor who had a very grasping and selfish wife. She said to her husband: "See what the emperor has done. He loves figs so much that he has given a basket of gold in exchange for a basket of figs." She persuaded her husband to fill a great sack with figs and take them to the palace. The guards said to him, "What do you want?" He said, "I hear that the emperor is so fond of figs that he pays a gold piece for every fig that is brought to him." When this was reported to Hadrian, he became very angry. He commanded that the man should be forced to stand at the gate of the palace and all who passed by should be invited to pelt him with his own figs. That evening the man returned home, bespattered and disgusted. He said to his wife, "For this misfortune I have you and your advice to thank." His wife's rather unsympathetic response was, "You are fortunate that your basket contained soft, cooked figs and not tough, raw figs; and you are even more fortunate that the fruit you brought to the palace was figs and not lemons."

. . . By means of this story, Koheles Rabba records its disagreement with Koheles 2:18-21 and supports the traditional Jewish position that unselfishness is noble and selfishness is a sin.

Koheles says, Chapter Two, Verses Twenty-two to Twenty-six,

> "What a misfortune for man is all his labor and his ambition with which he concerns himself under the sun. He is unhappy all his life; trouble is his constant concern; at night he cannot rest. This, too, is vapor. There is no genuine enjoyment in life except that which comes from eating and drinking and getting what satisfaction one may from his work. This is my understanding of the way that God has handled this

matter. For who has more right than I to eat and to enjoy the fruit of my labors? And as for the belief that to the good man God gives wisdom and knowledge and joy and to the sinner He gives the task of satisfying the material wants of the good man, this, too, is vapor and a grasping after wind."

On the meaning of these concluding verses of Chapter Two, the Talmud and the Midrash maintain a discreet silence. The medieval commentators make a few innocuous and rather cautious remarks about the lesser iconoclasms in these statements; but there is no determined effort to come to grips with or to answer the deep, pessimistic cynicism that undergirds these bitter words. Perhaps in this almost total silence lies an indication of a measure of agreement. Perhaps there are times when even the wisest and the kindest and the best cannot help saying to themselves: Who knows? Perhaps it would have been better never to have been born. Perhaps life is without meaning, purpose, hope. Perhaps those to whom nothing is important except the pleasurable employment of bodily entrances and exits are right. Perhaps this is the way whatever God there is meant it to be. Perhaps there is no relationship between so-called goodness and Reality. Perhaps the universe is just one great big laugh; and the endlessly spawning Earth-worms who think themselves important and immortal are the victims of an incomprehensible Practical Joker. Who of Earth has the right answers? Nobody, said Koheles. Many have opinions. Many have beliefs. Many cling firmly to a faith in Divine wisdom and goodness and justice. But, said Koheles, nobody of Earth really knows.

3

The key thoughts of Chapter Three of Koheles are expressed in language strong and clear: "There is an appointed time for everything that happens under the sun. . . . Everything God has made fulfills its purpose at the appropriate time. . . . The wheel of life revolves eternally. . . . Man has no advantage over the beast. . . . Everything comes from mud and returns to mud."

Again there seems to be a reluctance on the part of the Talmud to deal straightforwardly with these challenging statements, expressed so very forthrightly; again the Talmud mentions only some of them and then in a very superficial way; again it is the Midrashists and a few of the medieval commentators who have the courage to come to grips with the point of view of Koheles and, in some instances, to substantiate it and, in others, to attempt to refute it. Again, too, there are efforts to twist and to misinterpret, to avoid and to evade, to bring this Biblical rebel into line with the generally accepted theology, which was and still is the theology of the Pharisees, as that theology has been recorded in every Pharisaically oriented exposition of Jewish belief and law from the Mishna to the Shulchan Aruch.

Koheles says, Chapter Three, Verse One,

> "Everything is transient; but there is an appointed time for everything that happens under the sun."

Ibn Ezra comments: There are well-meaning men who believe that this verse teaches that humanity is obligated to do everything at the proper time. But the poem which follows immediately after does not bear out this interpretation. It begins with the words, "There is a time for birth and a time to die." Everyone will certainly agree that a human being has no control over the circumstances surrounding his own birth and, in most instances, over the timing or manner of his death. The words of Verse Eleven, "Everything He, i.e., God, has made fulfills its purpose at the appropriate time," also indicates how little man has to do with the process which is being described. If God has made everything and God controls everything, how can mankind be held responsible for what happens on earth?

The correct interpretation, continues ibn Ezra, is: The whole life process is a predetermined process. In each period of his life, a person acts and reacts in the manner which accords with the inner nature which he has developed in this particular period of his gradually maturing, gradually unfolding span of years. There is a proper and, in a certain sense, a preordained time for every important earthly act. Because of the predetermined character of human nature, one's actions and reactions are quite largely mechanical. As Psalm 39:7 says, "Man moves along like an automaton; therefore man's ambitions are as vapor." The Psalmist refers primarily to man's ambition to acquire wealth. This also explains the significance of Psalm 37:16, "Better is the little that the righteous has than the riches of many wicked." The concluding words of Psalm 39:7 agree with the sentiment expressed so forcefully by Koheles in the latter half of Chapter Two, "Man heaps up riches and does not know who will haul them away."

It has been mentioned already that Koheles was probably a forerunner of the Sadducees. This surmise is based on the broad generalization that the Sadducees were inclined to be more intensely rationalistic in their approach to theology than were the Pharisees. The Pharisees tended toward the mystical and the other-worldly. Therefore, Koheles fits into the Sadducaic rather than the Pharisaic mood. However, on the matter of freedom of the will versus predestination, Koheles espouses a position condemned by the Sadducees and upheld by the Pharisees. The Sadducees seem to have believed that man has complete freedom of will, while the Pharisees maintained that human destiny is quite rigidly regulated. "Everything is completely under God's control," one Pharisee wrote, "except man's capability of fearing God." Another said, "God foresees everything but gives man the right, in limited circumstances, to choose between the good and the evil." The Pharisees were not absolute determinists but the area of freedom of action and decision which they believed God has granted to man does not leave man very much terrestrial or philosophic space in which to maneuver.

Koheles says, Chapter Three, Verses Two to Eight,

"There is a time for birth and a time to die;
There is a time to plant and a time to uproot that which has been planted.
There is a time to kill and a time to heal;
There is a time to tear down and a time to build.
There is a time to weep and a time to laugh;
There is a time to mourn and a time to dance.
There is a time to cast stones and a time to gather stones;
There is a time to embrace and a time to refrain from embracing.
There is a time to seek to save and a time to give up as lost;
There is a time to keep and a time to throw away.
There is a time to tear and a time to mend;
There is a time to keep silent and a time to speak.
There is a time to love and a time to hate;
There is a time for war and a time for peace."

This is, obviously, a poem. It is written in the typical style of Biblical poetry. That is, it is written in the form known technically as "parallelism" in which clause is balanced with clause and sentence with sentence. One of the forms of parallelistic poetry, in which the second line reinforces the first by repeating the same thought but in different words, is known as synonymous parallelism. Another kind of parallelism is antithetic parallelism, in which a clause or a sentence is followed by another clause or sentence that repeats the same thought in reverse. An example of antithetic parallelism is Psalm 1:6, "The Lord knows the way of the righteous; but the way of the wicked will perish." A study of this poem of Koheles indicates that each verse is written as an antithetic parallel and each two-verse stanza is written as a synonymous parallel. This was recognized by all the commentators. Let us examine the poem, stanza by stanza, and consider the manner in which each stanza has been interpreted.

"There is a time for birth and a time to die;
There is a time to plant and a time to uproot that which has been planted."

Koheles Rabba: From the time a man is born he begins to die. From the time a man is born, it has been decreed how many years he will live. If he lives righteously, he is permitted to live out the full number of his years. If he does not, some of the allotted years are taken away from him. This is the opinion of the famed tanna, Rabbi Akiba ben Joseph, c.45-135. The majority opinion is that, if he is righteous, years are added to his life; if he is not righteous, years are taken away.

Rashi: Every individual, every nation and every people has a time at which it is destined to appear on the pages of history and a time at which it is destined to disappear from those pages.

Ibn Ezra: Just as there is a time fixed for the appearance and disappearance of every individual human being, so, in nature, there is a time fixed for the appearance and disappearance of every individual plant and tree.

Sforno: Death is as necessary as life for, if there were no death, the life cycle would not be possible and life would be reduced to a completely static condition.

"There is a time to kill and a time to heal;
There is a time to tear down and a time to build."

This contrasts conditions in time of war to those in time of peace. Rashi explains: There is a time to destroy a nation when it deserves destruction and, later, there is a time to be helpful to the survivors of a nation after its national structure has been destroyed. There is a time to tear down the walls of a city in order to render it defenseless; and there is a time to build up the walls to make a city safer against its enemies.

"There is a time to weep and a time to laugh;
There is a time to mourn and a time to dance."

During a period of sorrow, one weeps and mourns; when the period of sorrow is over, the time has come to laugh and to dance.

"There is a time to cast stones and a time to gather stones;
There is a time to embrace and a time to refrain from embracing."

This is a very difficult verse to interpret. In order to accord with Biblical parallelistic style and with the rest of the poem, there must be a relationship of synonymous parallelism between the first and the second lines; but what can it possibly be? What has the throwing and gathering of stones got to do with the act of embracing?

Koheles Rabba did a very strange thing, something for which there seems to be no rational explanation. It interpreted the first half of the stanza as referring to the sexual relationship between husband and wife and the second half as referring to the association of one righteous man with other righteous men. Koheles Rabba does not seem to have believed that there is any bond between the meanings of the two verses except that each describes a certain kind of relationship. And the seemingly obvious purport of each verse is completely inverted. The first verse, which has no readily discernible sexual denotation, is given a sexual interpretation; and the second verse, which seems to have a sexual denotation, is given a quite non-sexual interpretation. Koheles Rabba explains this stanza as follows: "There is a time to cast stones"—This refers to the period of the month when one's wife is ritually clean, i.e., available for sexual use; "and a time to gather stones"— This refers to the period of the month when one's wife is ritually unclean, i.e., unavailable for sexual use. "There is a time to embrace"—If you see a group of righteous people gathered together, join them, embrace them, hug them, kiss them, i.e., become as much a part of the group as you can; "and a time to refrain from embracing"—If you see a group of wicked people, keep away from them and anyone like them.

None of the other commentators seems to have agreed with Koheles Rabba.

Ibn Ezra also saw no direct relationship between the matters discussed in each line of the stanza but he tried to find a rational explanation for their juxtaposition. He says that Koheles is pointing out in this stanza that, even for common everyday occurrences, there is an appropriate time. In the first verse he states that there is a time when it is appropriate to remove stones that are causing damage to one's property and there is another time when it is appropriate to go out to gather stones which one may use to improve his property. The second verse means that the fulfilling of human sexual impulses also has its appropriate times; there are times when a man will grasp in ardent embrace the woman who snuggles up to him and there are times when he will push her away.

Matnos Kehuna, written by Baer Ashkenazi of Poland, c.1550-c.1610, is convinced that both parts of the verse refer to the sexual act. The casting of stones is a euphemism for the emission of semen, he writes. He does not indicate the manner in which he interprets the reference to the gathering of stones.

Maharzu (Zev ben Israel Einhorn, Russia, nineteenth century) bases his explanation on a passage in Midrash Sh'mos Rabba which interprets Exodus 1:16. This verse in Exodus tells how Pharaoh commanded the Hebrew midwives, present at the birth of a Hebrew child, to look at the "avnaim," which is generally translated as "birthstool," the low chair on which the midwife sat while she was assisting with the birth. The midwife was to do this in order to discover if the child just born was male or female. This translation obviously makes no sense. The midwife could hardly be expected to determine the sex of the child by looking at the seat on which she was seated. What the text really means is that the midwife, immediately after the birth and while still on her low chair beside the mother, is to determine by sight or by touch whether the newborn infant is male or female. Midrash Sh'mos Rabba 1:14 translates "avnaim" as "womb," i.e., the place or the direction toward which the midwife is to direct her gaze at the moment of birth. This meaning of "avnaim" is derived from the Hebrew word "binyan," which means "building" or "development." The womb is regarded, according to this interpretation, as the place where the foetus is formed, developed, built up. On the basis of this translation of "avnaim" in Midrash Sh'mos Rabba, Maharzu makes the following comment on Koheles

3:5: One cannot regard this verse as referring literally to the casting of stones or the gathering of stones. The word "avanim" used in Koheles 3:5 does not mean "stones." It means "womb," just as the Hebrew word "avnaim" in Exodus 1:16 means "womb." The verse refers to the casting of the seed into the womb by the male and the gathering of the seed in the womb by the female.

There are other interpretations which are too mystical to merit serious consideration. Rashi, for example, states that the verse refers to the removal of the stones of the Bes Hamikdash to Babylon after the destruction of the Holy Temple and the return of the stones to Jerusalem after the Exile. Yafe Toar (Samuel ben Isaac Ashkenazi Jaffe, Italy, sixteenth century) says it refers to the breaking by Moses of the first set of Sinaitic Tablets and to God's command to Moses to return for a second set of Tablets.

The plain fact is that commentators ancient and modern have been puzzled by Koheles 3:5. What its precise meaning may be is anybody's guess.

"There is a time to seek to save and a time to give up as lost;
There is a time to keep and a time to throw away."

Sometimes, in periods of distress, one must give up that which he has gathered together in periods of prosperity. Koheles Rabba illustrates this interpretation by means of the following story:

A certain merchant and his son went on a journey by ship to Caesarea Maritima to buy some merchandise. They took with them a bag of gold with which to pay for the merchandise. As they carried their belongings onto the ship, the sailors heard the sound made by the clinking coins in the bag. While the merchant and his son were sitting in a dark corner of the ship, unobserved and undetected, they heard one sailor say to another, "When we get well out on the Mediterranean, we shall throw those two overboard and take their gold." What did the merchant and his son do? They pretended to have a violent argument and, at the height of the argument, in a simulated fit of rage, the merchant picked up the bag of gold coins and hurled it into the sea. When the ship arrived at Caesarea Maritima, the merchant went to the local magistrate and lodged a complaint against the sailors. The sailors were thrown into the city jail and told that they would be kept there until the merchant was repaid for the loss of his bag of gold. The sailors argued, "What legal basis is there for requiring us to pay back the merchant for the loss of his money? Did he not of his own free will cast the money into the sea?" The magistrate's reply was, "The legal basis for this was established by the wisest of men in Koheles 3:6, when he stated, 'There is a time to keep and a time to throw away.' "

"There is a time to tear and a time to mend;
There is a time to keep silent and a time to speak."
So is it written in Koheles Rabba: The wife of Rabbi Mana died in Sepphoris. His colleague, Rabbi Abin, a Palestinian amora who taught from about 335 to 370, came to pay a condolence call. Rabbi Mana said to Rabbi Abin, "Are there any words of Torah you would like to offer us in our time of grief?" Rabbi Abin replied, "At times like this the Torah takes refuge in silence," i.e., the best and wisest consolation one may give a mourner is the consolation of wordless sympathy and silent understanding. Truly, there are times when silence is more harmonious than the greatest of symphonies and more eloquent than the grandest of orations.

"There is a time to love and a time to hate;
There is a time for war and a time for peace."
Koheles Rabba says: "There is a time to love"—in time of peace; "and a time to hate"—in time of war.

Ibn Ezra says: Whether one will love or will hate depends not so much upon one's inner nature as it does upon the time of life and upon the accompanying circumstance.

Koheles says, Chapter Three, Verse Nine,

"So what does one gain from his wearisome labor?"

Koheles Rabba and ibn Ezra agree: If there is a fixed time for everything to happen, why should an artisan be concerned about the perfection of his product or why should an industrious person work so hard?

Maharzu carries the argument over into the moral realm: If mankind were to agree with the proposition that everything is preordained and nothing that a person does can effect any sort of change in anything, it would certainly follow that there is no reason for a man to try to do that which is right or to refrain from doing that which is wrong. If mankind were to hold to the belief that absolutely everything lies in God's power and that God does in all things exactly as He wishes, men could then say that they have no responsibility for anything and, in practical consequence, could then proceed to act as they wished without believing that they would be held accountable for the results of their actions.

Another interpretation of this verse is also found in Koheles Rabba: "What does one gain from his wearisome labor?" He has the satisfaction of working with others who are interested in the same kind of activity as is he and, if one does his work well, he has the further satisfaction of gaining the approval and respect of his colleagues. There are those who go a step further and say that, even in one's social life, he should associate primarily with those who follow the same occupation as does he. Rabbi Isaac said in the name of his father, Rabbi Marion: This additional point is based on a clever interpretation of Habbakuk 2:4 "V'tsaddik be'emunaso yichye" which is usually translated to mean "A righteous man shall live by his faith" but, to fit the present situation, must be translated as "A sensible man will associate only with persons of his own trade or profession." This switch from a spiritual to a material interpretation is accomplished by translating the Hebrew word "emuna" by its derived meaning of "occupation" rather than its primary meaning of "faith." Some who believe in an after-life say that Rabbi Isaac's twist applies to the world-to-come rather than to this world, i.e., it is quite alright in this world for persons of different occupations to associate with each other but, in the world-to-come, there will be a strict segregation of individuals according to trade and profession.

Koheles says, Chapter Three, Verse Ten,

"I have examined the pattern of life which God has established for mankind."

Rashi and ibn Ezra agree with this translation but Koheles Rabba does not. Koheles Rabba translates this verse as follows: "I have discovered the most troublesome matter which God has made a part of human life." A number of eminent Talmudic sages also believed that this was the correct meaning of the verse. They pondered over the question: What is this "most troublesome matter" discovered by Koheles "which God has made a part of human life?"

Rabbi Jochanan bar Napacha said: This refers to the folly of theft. Rabbi Simon ben Lakish said in the name of Rabbi Jochanan: If one were guilty of a large variety of crimes, the one which would stand forth first to accuse him would be the epithet "Thief." Rabbi Pinchas, probably Rabbi Pinchas bar Chama, a Palestinian amora who taught from about 310 to about 355, said, also in the name of Rabbi Jochanan: People are so greedy by nature that the temptation to steal is harder for most persons to resist than is the temptation to commit the more heinous crimes of idolatry, incest and murder.

Rabbi Ibbu, a Palestinian amora who taught from about 280 to about 310, said: This refers to the folly of lust for wealth. Rabbi Yudan said in the name of Rabbi Ibbu: No one dies with even half his lust for wealth satisfied. If he has one hundred, he works hard to make it two hundred; if he has two hundred, he works hard to make it four hundred.

Rabbi Abbahu, a contemporary of Rabbi Ibbu, said: This refers to the folly of study. What is the use of study? One learns and then soon forgets. Rabbi Isaac Nappacha, another contemporary, took issue with Rabbi Abbahu. In Palestine, Rabbi Tobias stated in the name of Rabbi Isaac and, in Babylon, the scholars stated, also in the name of Rabbi Isaac: It is good that a man learns and then forgets. If a man remembered everything he learns, he would study Torah for only two or three years and then he would devote his time completely to worldly affairs. But, since he learns Torah and then forgets it, he is compelled to devote at least a part of his time, for the rest of his life, to the study and restudy of Torah.

Koheles says, Chapter Three, Verse Eleven,

> "Everything He has made fulfills its purpose at the appropriate time; He has also put the hope of eternity in their heart, which makes it impossible for mankind to comprehend what God has done or will do from the beginning to the end."

This is one of the most profound sentences in the entire Bible. Yet it is a sentence whose full import has escaped almost every translator and commentator, ancient and modern. When the verse is translated correctly, its meaning is very clear. In Verse Ten, Koheles notes that he has found "the pattern of life which God has established for mankind." In Verse Eleven, he describes the pattern. It is set forth simply: Everything in creation fulfills its purpose at the appropriate time and then disappears. Absolutely nothing on or of Earth exists permanently. Mankind foolishly clings to the idea that there is immortality of one kind or another for the human animal. This idea, this hope "makes it impossible for mankind to comprehend what God has done or will do from the beginning to the end" of Earth and of Time. A profound concept simply put, a brave, honest, rational concept. How long will it be before mankind acquires the courage and the honesty and the intelligence necessary to understand and to accept this concept? Mankind is presently much too busy playing with electronic and atomic toys to concern itself with such a trifle as Truth.

What does the Talmud have to say about this profound statement? The Talmud has this to say in Tractate Berachos 43b: What is the meaning of Koheles 3:11 "Everything He has made fulfills its purpose at the appropriate time?" Rabbi Chisda, 217-309, head of the yeshiva at Sura, Babylonia, said in the name of his teacher, Rav: This verse teaches that God approves of every human occupation. Rav Papa bar Chanan, c.300-375, who, together with Rabbi Huna ben Joshua, operated a very lucrative brewery which manufactured beer from dates and, as an avocation, taught in the yeshiva of Nares, said: Now one may understand the meaning of the popular proverb, "Hang the edible heart of a cabbage palm around the neck of a pig and, instead of eating it while it is clean, the pig will first drag it through the dirt," i.e., human beings, like pigs, carry on their work in unchangeable ways,, fortified by habits approved by God.

Commenting on Berachos 43b, Rashi says: God even approves of tanners, because He knows that unpleasant occupations fulfill a useful purpose in the world. Commenting on Rashi's comment, Polish Rabbi Samuel Edels, 1551-1631, known as Maharshaw, says: Every occupation has its place and its use. It is impossible to get along without perfumers and it is impossible to get along without tanners. The rest of the statement of Koheles bears this out, "He has put the world (Maharshaw translates the Hebrew word *olam* as *world,* which is its usual meaning but not in Koheles 3:11) in their heart," i.e., God convinces every person that he is best fitted for the occupation in which he is engaged. "It is impossible for mankind to discover what God has done or will do from the beginning to the end," i.e., it is not good for a person to attempt to follow any other occupation than that to which God has led him because it is God's will that he should follow this occupation from the beginning to the end of his working days.

That is what the Talmud has to say about the significance of Koheles 3:11. Do we find here any glimmer of understanding of the real meaning of the verse? No.

The Midrash contains a much more accurate and adequate explanation of the thoughts that went through the mind of Koheles. There are lengthy comments on Koheles 3:11 in three of the classical Midrashic compilations: Bereshis Rabba, compiled in Palestine between the fourth and sixth centuries; Koheles Rabba, compiled somewhere in the Jewish world in the eighth century or later; and Midrash Tehillim, compiled in Palestine about the eleventh or twelfth centuries. The names of the compilers are not known. Much of the material to be cited is found in almost identical language in all three sources.

Every one of the sages who is definitely identifiable in these Midrashic passages is Palestinian. It is reasonable, therefore, to assume that the others who are quoted but who cannot be identified precisely were also from Palestine. At any rate, not a single authority quoted is positively Babylonian. What is the significance of this? It might be explained very simply by saying that, since the passages in Koheles Rabba and Midrash Tehillim were presumably copied from the older source, i.e., Bereshis Rabba, and since Bereshis Rabba was probably written in Palestine at a time when the Babylonian Talmud was not yet completed and Babylonian scholarship had not yet gained acknowledged mastery over the Jewish world, it is only natural that, in these passages, only Palestinian sages should be quoted. One might explain it that way; but such an explanation would not settle the matter. Koheles Rabba and Midrash Tehillim were written hundreds of years after the completion of the Babylonian Talmud and long after Babylonia had become the recognized world center of Jewish scholarship. Why, then, in addition to quoting from Bereshis Rabba, did not Koheles Rabba or Midrash Tehillim also quote thought-provoking comments on Koheles 3:11 by Babylonian sages? The answer to this question may, indeed, be stated in simple fashion: In all likelihood, such comments were not available because they did not exist.

Their lack would seem to indicate that the Palestinian sages were more willing than were their Babylonian colleagues to probe deeply into the writings of the old professor from Jerusalem. There are indications elsewhere as well that the Palestinian Tannaim and Amoraim were more liberal and rational in their approach to theological problems than were their Babylonian contemporaries. Perhaps this may be attributed to the impact of a number of historical factors: The climate of open discussion and debate created in Palestine by the ideological conflicts of the Essenes, Pharisees and Sadducees; the infiltration into Palestine of challenging foreign theological and philosophic ideas, especially those emanating from Greek sources;

the unhealthy influence upon the Babylonian Jewish community of the non-Jewish ruling classes: at first, the crudeness and parochialism of the well-meaning but illiterate Parthians and, later, the religious fanaticism of the learned but narrow-minded Sassanian Persians; the gradual acceptance by Babylonian Jewry of the myth that the Bible may be understood only through study of a Pharisaically oriented body of law, i.e., the Babylonian Talmud. If this explanation makes sense, it points the way toward a fitting answer to the following present-day puzzler: Why do those Jews who venerate the dry-as-dust, casuistic, legalistic approach to the essentially Babylonian Talmud look with scorn upon those Jews who prefer the down-to-earth, unfettered, inquisitive, challenging manner of the essentially Palestinian Midrash?

For the sake of clarity, let us now split Koheles 3:11 into three parts and discuss separately the interpretations of each part that we find in the Midrash and in the writings of the later Biblical exegetes. Let us subdivide the verse as follows: (1) "Everything (God) has made fulfills its purpose at the appropriate time; (2) He has also put 'ha-olam' (This word is translated by the interpreters in a number of ways) in (man's) heart; (3) which makes it impossible for mankind to comprehend what God has done or will do from the beginning to the end."

"Everything (God) has made fulfills its purpose at the appropriate time."

Rabbi Eleazar ben Pedas, a Palestinian amora who died in Tiberias in 279 CE after having served as judge in that city and also as principal of its yeshiva, said: There is no doubt that this statement in Koheles is absolutely true, for so Scripture says, Genesis 1:31, "And God saw all that He had made

and, behold, it was very good." Redal explains: Rabbi Eleazar
is saying that there is nothing in the world which does not
have its proper time and place in which it is good and appropriate. In the final analysis, there is nothing in Creation which
is absolutely evil. The Biblical expression "very good" includes
all things which man regards as evil, such as death, suffering
and so forth.

Redal was absolutely right. Rabbi Eleazar was probably
giving professional support to the famous interpretation of
Genesis 1:31 by his Palestinian contemporary, Rav Samuel
bar Nachman. Rav Samuel said: God called the sixth day of
Creation "very good" because on that day the Evil Inclination
was created. Good by itself is only good but the combination
of Good and Evil is very good. How is it possible to call the
Evil Inclination good? Because, were it not for the Evil Inclination, mankind would not marry and have children and
the human race would not be able to continue.

Rabbi Abbahu, another Palestinian contemporary of Rabbi
Eleazar, fashioned a folk tale: For two thousand years before
it was time for the world to be created, God kept on making
and destroying worlds, in order that, when the time would
come to make the final and definitive product, He would have
exactly the kind of world He wanted. As God threw aside the
unsatisfactory experimental worlds, one after the other, He
kept muttering to Himself: "This one does not please Me.
This one does not please Me." When God, at long last, finished making the world which pleased Him, "God saw all
that He had made and, behold, it was very good."

Another interpretation: Rabbi Judah the Prince, c.135-
c.205, scholar-diplomat, redactor of the Mishna, so outstanding
that he is often referred to in our classical literature simply
as "Rabbi," said: To be a sin, the sin must be committed at
the appropriate time. What did he mean? Maharzu explains:

Every act is judged on the basis of the time and circumstances which accompany it. For example, an unmarried man who would rape a virgin on an ordinary day and while under the influence of liquor would not be in the same criminal category as a married man who would commit the same crime on Yom Kippur. A young bride who would be unfaithful to her husband on their wedding night would be judged differently from a woman who would commit an act of infidelity after many years of separation from her husband. When the people of Israel made the golden calf immediately after Moses had received the Torah, it was a greater sin than if the people of Israel had done this many years after being given the Torah. And so one could give many more examples to prove this point.

A final interpretation: To prove that "everything God has made fulfills its purpose at the appropriate time," Midrash Tehillim told the following story about King David: David once said to the Holy One, blessed be He, "Master of the universe, everything which You have created is proof of Your eternal wisdom, except the torment of insanity. What benefit can there possibly be in this distortion of body and mind? A man walks in the street tearing at his garments; the children run after him and make sport of him; how can this possibly be pleasing to You?" God replied, "Since you complain because I have created insanity, you have My word that you shall have need of this phenomenon before you die. You will be placed in a situation in which you will plead with Me to give you the ability to feign insanity." The predicted situation develops in the course of the incident described in the Bible in I Samuel 21:11-16.

David flees from Saul to the hoped for protection of the Philistine Achish, king of Gath. In Gath he discovers that the bodyguard of Achish is the brother of Goliath, whom he has killed in combat. He is filled with fear. He prays to God, "Master of the universe, help me." God asks, "What do you want Me to do?" David replies, "Teach me to act as though I have become insane." God gives David the necessary instructions. David begins to act the fool. He goes about writing on doors, "Achish king of Gath owes me a million and his wife owes me a half-million." For some years, the wife and daughter of Achish have both been demented. They run around, screaming and raging, inside the palace while David screams and rages outside the palace. Achish yells to his servants, "Do I lack madmen, that you allow this fellow to act like a madman before my house? Send him away from here." David leaves with all possible haste, happy that his ruse has saved his life. God says to him, "Now you know that at times even insanity serves a useful purpose. There is a time for wisdom and there is also a time for insanity." And, concludes Midrash Tehillim, now you know also the meaning of Genesis 1:31 "God saw all that He had made and, behold, it was very good," and now you understand Koheles 3:11 "Everything God has made fulfills its purpose at the appropriate time."

"He has also put 'ha-olam' in man's heart."

Rabbi Jonathan, probably Rabbi Jonathan ben Eleazar, a Palestinian amora who taught from about 250 to 280, interterpreted this phrase in two ways: (1) Do not read "ha-olam" "the world" but "ha-elem" "the youth." The text refers to the love for children which God puts into the hearts of parents. (2) Do not read "ha-olam" "the world" but "ha-elem" "the secret." God has put into the heart of man the knowledge that God conceals from His creatures the time and manner of their deaths. Therefore, man lives in constant fear of the angel of death. Redal comments as follows: Rabbi Jonathan's premise may be correct and his conclusion incorrect. There are many men who are not afraid to die and yet their actions are conditioned by the knowledge that death may come upon them at any moment. Because of this knowledge, man knows that his time on earth is limited and, therefore, he should not be wasting it on non-essential activities. So he labors zealously for the benefit of humanity and studies Torah and keeps his affairs in proper order and never takes a long vacation. This is the right way to live and this is why the Bible says, in the first chapter of Genesis, that life is good but life and death together are very good. Because of the thought that death is always imminent, man labors for the good of the present world in an attempt to win for himself life and remembrance in the world-of-the-future.

Rabbi Benjamin, in the name of Rabbi Levi, probably Rabbi Levi bar Sissi, comes closer than any other Midrashist to grasping the full significance of the phrase: God has put into the heart of man the thought of eternity, a love for eternal life and eternal values, so that man tries in every way within his power to preserve and to improve the human race and the world order.

In his Biblical commentary, Rashi makes the following observations about this passage: God has put a measure of worldly wisdom into the hearts of humanity. He has not given anyone complete knowledge, so that no one knows just when God is going to test him or exactly what his weak points are, but He has given us sufficient understanding to know that our hearts should always be in a humble and repentent mood because of the thought, "Tomorrow, tonight, five minutes from now, I may be dead." The word "ha-olam" as used here has the connotation of "world" and also of "secret." The significance of this: The day of man's departure from the world is a secret. If a man knew the exact date of his death, he would never build a house or plant a vineyard. But because there is a possibility that the day of death is far off, man continues to plant and to build. It is, indeed, fortunate that earthly creatures do not know just when they are going to die.

"He has also put the hope of eternity in man's heart, which makes it impossible for mankind to comprehend what God has done or will do from the beginning to the end."

With regard to the meaning of the closing phrase of Koheles 3:11, both Talmud and Midrash maintain a complete silence. Just as, in dealing with the ignorant, one must be suspicious of endless garrulousness, so, too, in dealing with the wise, one must be equally suspicious of excessive silence. One has the feeling that, among the Tannaim and Amoraim, there must have been those who understood the final words of Koheles 3:11 but would not, perhaps dared not, explain.

Among the Bible commentators, there were at least two, Abraham ibn Ezra and Obadiah ben Jacob of Sforno, who understood, and there was at least one who dared to explain.

Sforno said that the use of the word "ha-olam" indicates that God has given man the power of innate reason with which to comprehend eternal principles. While this power is strong enough to recognize the existence of the principles, it is not strong enough to go beyond the principles and to fathom the details of God's plan for the world.

Ibn Ezra put the whole matter plainly and bluntly: Some say that "ha-olam" means "worldly temptations" and that the phrase means that God has placed worldly temptations in man's heart. This is not what "ha-olam" means here. In this instance it means man's "hope of immortality." "B'nay adam mis'askim k'ilu yich'yu l'olam uba-avur his-askam lo yavinu ma-aseh ha-Elohim may-rosh v'ad sof." These are the exact words of ibn Ezra as they stand in the Hebrew text. Their meaning: Human beings act as if they are going to live forever. Because of this delusion, they are unable to comprehend any aspect of God's plan for the world and for man.

Koheles says, Chapter Three, Verses Twelve to Fourteen,

> "I concluded that there is nothing worth-while in any of life's endeavors, except to be happy and to enjoy life. Indeed, any man who is able to eat and drink and to get satisfaction out of his work is enjoying a privilege which only God can grant. I understood that everything which God has ordained is eternally unchangeable; nothing will ever be added to it or taken from it; and God has ordained that mankind shall live in fear of Him."

Joseph Albo, in his philosophic work, *Sefer ha-Ikkarim, The Book of Principles,* written in Spain in the first half of the fifteenth century, proves to his own satisfaction that Koheles 3:9-14 states that it is man's fear of God which causes man to become immortal. This unique interpretation of this passage in Koheles is found in *Sefer ha-Ikkarim,* Book Three, at the beginning of Chapter Thirty-one:

The goal which the soul seeks to reach while it is in the body, by means of observing the commandments of the Torah, is to gain for itself the character of being a fearer of God. When the soul has attained this quality, it is exalted and is prepared for immortality, which is the good stored up for the righteous and the soul's happiest state. The Bible says, Psalm 31:20, "How great is the goodness which Thou hast stored up for those who fear Thee." This is made more clear by what the Bible says about the heavy punishment which will be inflicted on the people of Israel if their souls do not obtain for themselves the quality of fearing God through observance of the commands of the Torah. The Bible says, Deuteronomy 28:58ff., "If you do not keep all the words of this Law written in this Book, to fear the honored and dread name of the Lord your God, then God will send upon you and your seed powerful plagues, etc."

One may ask: How is it possible for the fear of God to bring a person to the exalted status of achieving immortality? Would it not be more logical for this status to be obtained through the possession of a superior intellect? The answer is that Solomon proved in the book of Koheles that fear and nothing but fear is the cause of immortality. God in His wisdom has decreed that this shall be so and one should not seek to determine the reason why. Koheles is seeking to discover by what means immortality is acquired. He asks, Koheles 3:9, "What does one gain from his wearisome labor?" Then he says, Koheles 3:10, "I have seen the pattern of life which God has established for mankind." This means, "I have seen the tasks which God has given to mankind to keep mankind busy," that is to say, man's trades and professions, all of which are "appropriate for their time," that is to say, for the time being, in order that knowledge of each of the crafts may not disappear. He says, Koheles 3:11, "He also has put the world in their heart, which makes it impossible for mankind to comprehend what God has done or will do from the beginning to the end." This means that God has put into the human heart a desire to acquire knowledge of natural causes. Even though it is not possible for man to understand these fully, because it is "impossible for mankind to comprehend what God has done or will do from the beginning to the end," nevertheless this desire is also "appropriate in its time," in order that the study of science may not cease but not because, as some people think, it may lead to the attainment of immortality. Sometimes scientists think they have discovered the truth when they have not. Therefore, Koheles now says, Koheles 3:12, "I have concluded that there is nothing worth-while in any of life's endeavors, except to be happy and enjoy life," which means that, in all these earthly endeavors, including knowledge, there is no other good except that of pleasure, for every man gets pleasure from doing what he wants to do and in the way that he wants to do it. This sometimes brings benefit to him, in that, if, for example, he is a philosopher, philosophy shows him how to live a good and useful life on earth, although it does not have much use besides this. This leads to the next statement of Koheles, Koheles 3:13, "Indeed, any man who is able to eat and drink and to get satisfaction out of his work is enjoying a privilege which only God can grant." All of this is in explanation of Koheles 3:10, "I have seen the pattern of life which God has established for mankind"; and there is nothing in this pattern, as it has been expounded so far, that will help man attain immortality.

Then he says, Koheles 3:14, "I understand that everything which God has ordained is eternally unchangeable; nothing will ever be added to it or taken from it; and God has ordained that mankind shall live in fear of Him." This means that anything which God has created outside of the natural order, outside of the realm of growth and decay, as, for example, the galaxies of the universe, will live forever, as David said, Psalm 148:6, "He has established them forever and ever." God has ordained, therefore, that, if the truly intelligent part of man is to be preserved eternally, man must stand in fear of Him. It appears that this fear is the true mean to which nothing may be added and from which nothing can be taken away, because it is by additions and subtractions that a true balance is lost and destructive influences set in. Or the words "God has ordained that mankind shall live in fear of Him" may indicate that the Torah and the commandments are the true means through which the fear of God is acquired and, through this fear, the soul achieves immortality.

Koheles says, Chapter Three, Verse Fifteen,

> "That which has been was even before that and that which is to be has already been; and the wheel of life revolves eternally."

The concluding phrase means literally "God seeks that which has already gone by." This is the symbolic language the author uses to express the idea that "the wheel of life revolves eternally," as we shall learn when we consider the comment of ibn Ezra on this verse. Vayikra Rabba, the Midrash to the Book of Leviticus, translates the concluding phrase as "God seeks that which is pursued." The Talmudic sages also translated this phrase in this way and, using this translation, made the following comments:

Rabbi Huna said in the name of Rav Joseph: God is always on the side of the persecuted. Whether it be one righteous man who is trying to cause trouble for another righteous man or a wicked man who is trying to cause trouble for a righteous man or a wicked man who is trying to cause trouble for another wicked man, God is always on the side of the persecuted. Even when a righteous man tries to cause trouble for a wicked man, God is quite likely to aid the wicked man.

Rabbi Judah bar Simon, a Palestinian amora who taught from about 310 to 335, said in the name of Rabbi Jose ben Nehurai: God always holds the pursuer accountable for any harm he does to the pursued. This is proved by the Bible. Abel was pursued by Cain and God showed favor to Abel, Genesis 4:4 "God looked with favor upon Abel and upon his offering." Noah was persecuted by his generation and God showed favor only to Noah, Genesis 7:1 "You only do I consider righteous before Me in this generation." Abraham fled before Nimrod and God showed favor to Abraham, Nehemiah 9:7 "Thou art the Lord, the God Who chose Abram."

Isaac fled before the Philistines and God showed favor to Isaac, Genesis 26:28 "We saw plainly that the Lord was with you." Jacob fled before Esau and God chose Jacob, Psalm 135:4 "The Lord has chosen Jacob for Himself." Joseph fled before his brothers and God chose Joseph, Psalm 81:6 "He appointed it in Joseph as a testimony." Moses fled before Pharaoh and God chose Moses, Psalm 106:23 "Moses His chosen one." David fled before Saul and God chose David, Psalm 78:70 "He chose David as His servant." Saul fled from the Philistines and God chose Saul, I Samuel 10:24 "See him whom the Lord has chosen." Israel fled from the nations and God chose Israel, Deuteronomy 14:2 "The Lord has chosen you to be His own treasure out of all peoples that are upon the face of the earth."

Rabbi Eliezar ben Jose ben Zimra said: This principle was also applied in the selection of animals that are considered worthy to be sacrificed. The ox flees before the lion. The goat flees before the leopard. The sheep flees before the wolf. None of the pursuing animals is considered worthy of being offered up as a sacrifice; but of the pursued it is written, Leviticus 22:27 "An ox or a sheep or a goat . . . may be accepted for an offering made by fire unto the Lord."

As has been noted, ibn Ezra believes that the concluding phrase of Koheles 3:15 means "The wheel of life revolves eternally." Ibn Ezra says: God lives in a timeless world. For God, past, present and future do not exist. The division of time into past, present and future is a man-made device which the plan of God does not recognize. God's idea of time may be compared to a wheel in which each part is continually following every other part and in which the part which is peripheral, i.e., the world, is continually revolving around the motionless central point, i.e., God. That part of the wheel which is now on the east of the central point will eventually be on the west of it and vice versa. There is no beginning or end to the motion of the wheel or to any part of its orbit. Only God is eternally motionless. His creation moves in an endless round, endlessly the same.

Koheles says, Chapter Three, Verse Sixteen,

> "Furthermore, I saw under the sun that instead of justice there is injustice and instead of righteousness there is unrighteousness."

Sforno comments: Koheles is referring to the manner in which judges and lawmakers may be bribed to pervert justice and to enact bad laws.

(Chapter Three, Verse Seventeen, states: "I said to myself: God will judge the righteous and the wicked; for there is an appointed time in the Divine plan for every thing and every deed." This verse could not possibly have been written by Koheles. The idea that God rewards the righteous and punishes the wicked is completely foreign to the thinking of Koheles. This verse must have been inserted by a later editor, who felt very self-righteous about planting a bit of Pharisaic theology in the midst of a quite un-Pharisaic exposition. This is the way of many editors, ancient and modern: To try to make the text say what the editor wants it to say, rather than what the author wants it to say.)

Koheles says, Chapter Three, Verse Eighteen,

> "I said to myself concerning mankind: God tests them and shows that they are beasts."

Rashi explains: When I saw the injustice there is in the world, in that arrogant men impose their authority by force upon those who are too weak to resist, I also understood that God will let such wicked men know that tyranny cannot endure and God will prove to them and to the princes and the kings that they have no more lasting importance than have cattle or wild beasts.

Koheles says, Chapter Three, Verse Nineteen,

> "Man and beast share a common fate; as one dies, so dies the other; they have much the same nature; man has no advantage over the beast; for everything that is is vapor."

There are two attempts in the classical writings to contest the statement of Koheles that "man has no advantage over the beast." One is found in Albo's *Sefer 'ha-Ikkarim*, Book Three, Chapter Two. Professor Isaac Husik translated this passage as follows: Koheles says, "The advantage of man over the beast is nothing; for everything that is is vapor." The meaning is that the advantage of man above the beast is something whose existence is weak. If the passage read, "There is no advantage of man over the beast," it would have the meaning of a purely negative proposition. But since he says, "The advantage of man over the beast is nothing," the judgment is affirmative, equivalent to the statement that man has advantage over the beast, but this advantage is weak, i.e., something whose existence is weak, because it is mere potentiality. The student of logic will understand that this judgment has the value of an affirmative proposition rather than a negative. . . . Translator Husik added a footnote: What a peculiar interpretation! . . . A footnote to the footnote: I agree.

Koheles Rabba also takes issue with the statement that "man has no advantage over the beast" but does so in a manner which suggests that the sages are not really serious but are indulging in a rather sly form of sardonic humor:

Man does have certain advantages over the beast, says Koheles Rabba. What are these advantages? Rav Nachman says in the name of his father, Rabbi Isaac: God has given human beings instruments for procreation and excretion which are more aesthetic in appearance than those which he has given to the beast.

Rabbi Jannai and Rabbi Yudan discussed the matter. Rabbi Jannai said: Man is held in higher esteem than the beast because man wears shoes and puts a cloth over his buttocks. . . . Yafe Toar comments that Rabbi Jannai is speaking euphemistically. He is referring to the clever way in which the urinary and deficatory orifices are built into and covered over by the flesh of the human body. . . . Rabbi Yudan said: Man is privileged because his buttocks have a thick covering of flesh and he is able to sit down, a posture denied to most of the animal kingdom.

Rabbi Levi and Rabbi Ammi, disciple and successor of Rabbi Jochanan bar Nappacha, discussed the matter. Rabbi Levi said: Man's advantage over the beast is that man is given the privilege of burial and the beast is not. Rabbi Ammi said: Not only is man buried but he is given the privilege of being buried in a coffin, which the beast is not. To this Rabbi Levi responded: Not only is man buried in a coffin but he is given the privilege of being wrapped in a shroud before he is placed in the coffin, a further privilege which the beast does not have.

It seems highly likely that our Amoraic forbears were gently pulling our legs. The excellencies and advantages which they mention are hardly those which would be set down by scholars who took at face value the statement in Psalm 8:6, "Thou hast made man but little lower than the angels."

Koheles says, Chapter Three, Verse Twenty,

> "All go to one place; everything comes from mud and everything returns to mud."

None of the commentators has any comment to make on this. What is there for them to say? The sentence speaks for itself. Stripped of all the pretty words and all the wishful thinking, this is what Life is. This is The Truth.

Koheles says, Chapter Three, Verse Twenty-One,

"What rational basis is there for believing, as some believe, that the anima, the living spirit of a man, ascends unchanged into Heaven while the life-spirit of a beast is reabsorbed into the undifferentiated mass of earthly life-energy?"

The commentators twist the meaning of this verse to try to make it appear that Koheles said that the righteous go to Heaven and the wicked go to Hell. Koheles, obviously, said nothing of the sort.

Koheles says, Chapter Three, Verse Twenty-Two,

"I have come to the conclusion that there is nothing better than that a man should find satisfaction in what he is doing; this is his appointed destiny; there is none who will reveal to him what the future years hold in store."

Rashi comments: A person should be satisfied with achieving whatever lies within the range of his capabilities. He should be satisfied if he is happy in his work and has enough to eat. He should not overreach himself by coveting the possessions of others or by trying to become rich or famous, especially if the attainment of these objectives lie beyond the range of his capabilities and/or his prospects.

4

Having set forth his conviction, in Chapter Three, that man and beast share a common origin and a common destiny and that man has little or no advantage over the beast, Koheles continues, in the first twelve verses of Chapter Four, to reflect upon the manner in which human beings treat each other during their earthly sojourn: There is so much injustice in the world that the dead are better off than the living. Most fortunate of all are those who may never be born. Excessive ambition and excessive idleness are both bad. Success creates jealousy; idleness brings on poverty. It is good to work just hard enough to satisfy one's basic needs and to secure tranquility of mind. To work only by oneself and for oneself is stupid. Everyone should have at least one companion who will be a help and a comfort to him in good times and bad.

The next four verses of the chapter, verses 13 to 16, are very difficult. They are couched in mysterious language and depart completely from the straight-forward, clear manner in which Koheles has been expounding his point of view. Exactly what the meaning of these verses may be and whether they were written by Koheles or inserted by a later writer are matters for individual conjecture.

The final verse of this chapter, verse 17, begins a discussion that is continued in Chapter Five. Therefore, its significance will be considered at the beginning of the next chapter.

Koheles says, Chapter Four, Verse One,

"Once again I reflected upon all the wrongs which are committed under the sun; behold the tears of the oppressed—

and no one offers them consolation; their oppressors handle them violently—and no one offers them help."

Ibn Ezra: Koheles concludes Chapter Three by saying that the best way for a person to live is to be satisfied and happy with what he has. Then he begins to think about the harsh realities of existence: There is cruelty and oppression in the world. Men's money and possessions are taken away from them pitilessly and by force. Judges and rulers are corrupt and evil. The judge takes a bribe and then finds the innocent guilty; the ruler robs his people of their hard earned wages. Those who are wronged are defenseless; they can only weep. They are in an even worse situation than a person who loses a loved one in death. When the mourner weeps, someone is sure to come to give him comfort; but, when one stands helpless before the crushing might of a dictator or of organized society, he weeps and no one comes to comfort him.

Koheles says, Chapter Four, Verse Two,

"And I felt that those who are already dead are better off than those who are yet alive."

Ibn Ezra: Those who are oppressed are better off dead than alive. A human being is able to endure without flinching whatever unpleasant experiences come to him through the powers of nature over which he has no control. But a human being is not able to endure cruel and oppressive treatment to which he is subjected as a result of the decisions or actions of other human beings like himself. When he is mistreated by those who are also creatures of earth, who share the same humble origin and destiny as his own, and who, in consequence, should be kindly and understanding in their relations with their fellowmen, his spirit breaks and he chooses to die rather than to go on living in such an inhuman world.

Koheles says, Chapter Four, Verse Three,

> "More fortunate than both of them is he who has not yet
> been, who has not seen the evil deeds which have been done
> under the sun."

There is a Talmudic tradition that God originally intended
to give the Torah to mankind in the one thousandth genera-
ation after Creation. But He changed His mind and gave the
Torah to the generation of Moses, which was only the 26th generation after Creation. There had been ten generations from
Adam to Noah, ten from Noah to Abraham and six from Abraham to Moses. What caused God to change His mind? There are
some who say that He realized that the human race would not
be able to continue for a thousand generations without the wisdom contained in the Torah. Others say that, at the time of Creation, 974 generations rushed into His presence and insisted on
being created before God created the world. Some say that God
was so outraged by the ill-mannered conduct of these impatient
generations that He destroyed them; others say that God punished them by decreeing that their coming into being should
be delayed beyond the previously ordained time and that they
should be fed into the stream of humanity gradually, so that
not too many insolent ones would appear in the world at any
one time. Those who adhere to the latter theory believe that
the "chutspa-niks," the arrogant ignoramuses who are present
in every generation, were members of this 974-generation group.
According to Koheles Rabba, it is to these 974 generations that
Koheles refers when he says, "More fortunate than he who
exists or who has already existed is he who has not yet existed."
It is not that Koheles feels that being a "chutspa-nik" is a
good thing or that those who will live in the future will live
in a better world than those who lived in the past. It is that
Koheles believes that those who have not had to undergo the

experience of living are better off than those who have had this experience. Koheles is saying that the 974 generations were very foolish in trying to push forward the moment of their birth. He is saying that it would have been better for them if they had not been created at all.

The Talmud also reports that, for two and one-half years, Bes Hillel and Bes Shammai debated the question as to whether man would be better off if he had never been created. Bes Hillel maintained that it would have been better for man if he had never been created. Bes Shammai argued that it is better for man that he has been created. After two and a half years of debate, they took a vote. Bes Hillel won. The majority voted that it would have been better for man if he had not been created; but, they decided, now that he has been created, he has no choice but to conduct himself properly.

Joseph Albo, in discussing this debate in his *Sefer ha-Ikkarim,* Book Four, Chapter 29, says: The debate between Bes Shammai and Bes Hillel really had to do with a difference of opinion over whether the soul is a material or a spiritual substance. Bes Shammai, which maintained that it is good that man was created, was moved by a conception of the soul which accords with that of Aristotle, i.e., that the soul is a material substance, part and parcel of the same earth-stuff from which the body of man is made. This point of view holds that existence is to be preferred to non-existence, for, when one exists, he always has the possibility of reaching a higher state of perfection by means of the intellect. On the other hand, Bes Hillel maintained that it would have been better if man had not been created, because Bes Hillel regarded the soul as being a spiritual substance with an independent entity, entirely separate and distinct from the earth-stuff of which the body of man is made. Since, as a result of being in existence, i.e., being put in the body, the soul is placed in jeopardy of being damaged or punished, Bes Hillel declared that it would be better for the soul if it never comes into existence, i.e., never enters a human body at all. That is what is meant in Koheles 4:3, "More fortunate than the living and the dead is he who has not yet existed." If the soul were a material substance, this statement would make no sense, because, for a material substance, existence is certainly better than non-existence. Is not all existence good, as the Scripture testifies, Gen. 1:31, "God saw everything which He had made and, indeed, it was very good"? There is no question but that Koheles regarded the soul as a spiritual and not a material substance. Since this is the correct point of view and that which accords with the Torah, Bes Hillel and Bes Shammai finally agreed that it would have been better if man had not been created. They also agreed that, since he has been created, he must conduct himself properly, in order to prevent his soul from being damaged or punished.

Albo's interpretation of Koheles is very interesting and clever but not very accurate. One who wrote, as Koheles wrote, "Man and beast share a common fate; as one dies, so dies the other; they have much the same nature. . . . All go to one place; everything comes from mud and returns to mud. . . . What rational basis is there for believing (as some believe) that the anima, the living spirit of a man, ascends unchanged into Heaven while the life-spirit of a beast is reabsorbed into the undifferentiated mass of earthly life-energy?", one who writes like this can hardly be regarded as one who believes that man is a unique combination of mortal body and immortal soul. Nevertheless, it is also quite clear that, if Koheles had been present when that Talmudic vote was taken, he would have voted with Bes Hillel and against Bes Shammai.

Koheles says, Chapter Four, Verse Four,

> "I saw that every achievement and every successful accomplishment serves only to create jealousy between one man and another; this, too, is vapor and grasping at the wind."

Ibn Ezra: Most human accomplishments, including those which are done for the benefit of humanity, create jealousy between one person and another, because basic to any effort at accomplishment is the desire to lord it over one's fellowman or, at the very least, not to lack anything which the best people have, whether it be in the matter of housing, clothes, food, children, wisdom or reputation.

Sforno: This includes such accomplishments as giving charity and building synagogues and yeshivos and the like. When an individual uses his wealth to do good deeds of the kind just mentioned, he obtains communal favor and respect but he also earns for himself the jealousy of those who cannot match his wealth. In the opinion of Koheles, the using of one's money as the means through which one gains the respect and favor of the community is "vapor" and the joy which is felt as the result of using one's money in this way is "grasping at the wind."

Koheles says, Chapter Four, Verse Five,

"The fool folds his arms together and eats his own flesh."

Ibn Ezra: Jealousy is not an unmitigated evil. Every person must have in him a measure of jealousy if he is to achieve a measure of success. The man whose psychological makeup is completely devoid of jealousy is a fool. Such fools have no ambition and so they are without the urge to work for a living. They merely fold their arms together and exist on what they already have. Eventually they find themselves without any means of staying alive because they have consumed everything they possess without doing the work necessary to add to their present store. It is as if they were eating their own flesh because, if they pursue this course of action indefinitely, they will die of starvation.

Koheles says, Chapter Four, Verse Six,

"Better is a handful of tranquility than two handfuls of meaningless success."

Ibn Ezra: This is the answer of the fool to the statement in the preceding verse. The fool says, "I am more satisfied to have one handful of bread which I have come by easily than to have two handfuls of bread for which I had to work." Only a fool talks this way. An intelligent person thinks of the future and makes sure that he will have enough to eat on the morrow, for one never knows what change of fortune the rest of today may bring.

Rabbi Isaac, probably Rabbi Isaac Nappacha, interprets Koheles 3:6 differently in comments found in Vayikra Rabba and Koheles Rabba:

Better is he who teaches two sections of a chapter of ritual law and lives up to what he teaches than he who teaches a whole chapter of the ritual law and does not live up to it, because he just wants to be known as a scholar who has mastered many chapters of the ritual law. Better is he who teaches ritual law and lives up to what he teaches than he who teaches ritual law and Mishna and does not live up to them, because he just wants to be known as a scholar who has mastered many tractates of the ritual law and the Mishna. Better is he who teaches Mishna and lives up to it than he who teaches Mishna and Gemarra and does not live up to them, because he just wants to be known as a scholar who has mastered many tractates of the Talmud. As the popular proverb says: One caged bird has more value to the owner than a hundred birds flying through the air.

Better is he who has ten gold coins and goes into business on a modest scale and supports himself modestly than he who borrows the money of others in order to be known in business circles as "a big wheel" and in order to live luxuriously. The popular proverb says: He who borrows large sums of money in order to do business on a grand scale is likely to destroy that which is his and that which is not his.

Better is he who works and gives charity from his own money than he who exacts usury and commits robbery and gives charity from that which belongs to others. Such an unscrupulous individual acts as he does because he wants to have the "meaningless success" of being listed among "the big givers." The popular proverb says: The prostitute lies down on any man's bed in order to buy apples and pomegranates for the sick and to give charity to the poor.

Better is he who has one garden and tends it and get his living from it than he who buys the gardens of others for half their value. One who engages in this kind of sharp practice does so because he wants the "meaningless success" of being known as the owner of many estates. The popular proverb says: He who has one garden will eat the birds; but, if one has many gardens, the birds will eat him. Maharzu explains the meaning of the proverb: When the birds come to eat the crops of a man who has only one garden to guard, he kills the birds and eats them. When the birds come to eat the crops of a man who has many gardens to guard, he is not able to protect his crops against the raids of the birds and so the birds figuratively eat him up by eating up his crops.

As Rabbi Jacob, probably Rabbi Jacob ben Korshai, teacher of Rabbi Judah the Prince, says in the Mishna: Better one hour of repentance and good deeds in this world than all the life of the world to come; and better one hour of tranquility in the world to come than all the life of this world.

Sforno says: When one is able to obtain what he needs without exhausting all his energy, he has both time and energy left for study and contemplation. When one is filled with an unhealthy acquisitive desire, he keeps on working in order to get more than he needs, he spends his time on "meaningless success" and he opens the door to the kind of human jealousy which breeds trouble for himself and for his fellowmen.

Koheles says, Chapter Four, Verses Seven and Eight,

> "I continued my investigations and discovered another form of vapor beneath the sun. This is the predicament of the man who is completely alone in the world, who has neither son nor brother; yet there is no limit to his labors; his lust for wealth is insatiable. Does he never ask himself: 'For whom do I toil? For whom do I deny myself the comforts which I can well afford?' This, too, is vapor. It is a bad situation to be in."

Rashi: There are individuals who like to work only by themselves and for themselves. There are scholars who are not interested in having others share their studies and learning, in having scholarly companions who will be like brothers to them, disciples who will be like sons to them. If they are bachelors, they do not marry and get for themselves a life-companion who will enrich their lives, help them and bear them children. If they are in the mercantile business, they do not want any partners. There are many such "lone wolves." The scholar of this type spends his time storing up facts within himself. The merchant of this type does nothing but buy and sell. Since such as these do not raise up disciples or get married and have children, how empty are their achievements!

Ibn Ezra: In Verses Five and Six, Koheles has described for us one kind of fool. In Verses Seven and Eight, he brings to our attention a second kind of fool who is the exact opposite of the other fool. This is the miserly person who has no wife or companion or servant but who lives by himself. How is it possible for an individual to be so completely and blindly self-centered that he denies himself the pleasure of human association, the pleasure of sharing the happiness of others? The man who lives and labors only for himself and who does not seek to enjoy life himself and to bring enjoyment of life to others is just as much a fool as the man who is a loafer and a social parasite and who takes no heed of the needs of the morrow.

Sforno: The text describes the man who has no one who loves him and whom he may love in return, no one from whom he receives proofs of affection, no one through whom he is able to demonstrate his own goodness and worth. He is driven only by an unquenchable thirst for wealth, a wealth from which he derives no enjoyment of any kind. This is, indeed, completely foolish and meaningless. It offers no prospect of present happiness or of future good.

Koheles says, Chapter Four, Verses Nine to Twelve,

"Two are better than one; their joint efforts will be well rewarded. If one falls, the other will lift him up; unfortunate, indeed, is he who falls and has no one to pick him up. Two who lie down to sleep together keep warm; but how may one sleeping by himself hope to keep warm? One may be overpowered where two will triumph; a cord of three strands cannot be pulled apart quickly."

"Two are better than one."

One of the very earliest of the Midrashim, the Sifrey, completed before 200 CE, as quoted in the Yalkut Shemoni, a medieval compilation of Midrashim, commented: This means that a man should get himself a companion with whom he may study Bible and Mishna and may dine and may share his secret thoughts.

Koheles Rabba says: It is better for two students to study Torah together than for each to study by himself. "If one falls, the other will lift him up"—If one student forgets a certain law, the other will remind him of it. "A cord of three strands cannot be pulled apart quickly"—The third strand in the cord is a good teacher who will correct the mistakes of the students.

Another interpretation in Koheles Rabba: Two who are partners in business will be more successful than each one working for himself. "If one falls, the other will lift him up" —If each were working for himself, the two would not only not work together but they would work against each other as business competitors. But, as partners, if one gets into financial difficulties, the resources of the other will support him. "A cord of three strands cannot be pulled apart quickly"—A partnership of three is even stronger than a partnership of two.

Another interpretation in Koheles Rabba: Rabbi Jochanan bar Nappacha said: "Two are better than one" refers to the companionship of the sexes. A man and woman living together are better off and happier than is each one living by himself and herself. However, their house is not a home unless there is a third Person present. "A cord of three strands cannot be pulled apart quickly"—The third strand in the strong marriage bond is the Holy One, blessed be He, Who makes it possible for the couple to seal their union with children and to maintain a radiant atmosphere in their home.

A final interpretation from Koheles Rabba: Rabbi Meir said: If you see someone walking by himself along a public highway, greet him by saying, "May your journey be a peaceful one, O you who are in mortal danger." Two walking together are to be greeted with the words, "Peace be with you, O you who are likely to have a quarrel." Three walking together are given the greeting, "Peace be with you, O men of peace." Redal explains the meaning of Rabbi Meir's statement: One walking by himself on the public highway subjects himself to the possibility of being robbed and murdered. Two who journey together and become bored with each other's company and have an argument and separate are then in the same dangerous situation as he who travels alone. If three persons journey together and two of them have a quarrel, the third person may serve as peacemaker and keep the party from breaking up.

Ibn Ezra says, quite correctly, that these verses are an integral part of the discussion which began with Verse Seven. Koheles is still considering the plight of the fool who lives and works for and by himself. He would be much happier and healthier in mind and body if he had a companion. He would get more enjoyment from his labors and from his food. If he got sick or met with an accident, his companion would care for him. One of the obvious meanings of "Two are better than one" is that everyone should get married, and of the "cord of three strands" is that husband, wife and child are the indispensable elements of a home where God and peace and love abide.

"A cord of three strands cannot be pulled apart quickly."

The Talmud interprets this phrase in a number of other ways.

In Kesubos 62b, the phrase is said to refer to Rabbi Ushya and his father, Rabbi Chama, and his father, Rabbi Bisa, three amoraim who lived in Palestine in the third century. Why? Because they were all alive and studying and teaching in the same country at the same time. When Rabbi Ushya wanted to find out if his decision in a certain matter was correct, he would consult with his grandfather, Rabbi Bisa. When a man and his son and grandson study Torah together and teach Torah to the same generation, the Torah remains in their family as a permanent guest, i.e., it is considered that a scholarly rabbinic dynasty has been established. Indeed, the fortunate grandfather is declared to be the equal of Moses. So says Kiddushin 30a: Anyone who teaches Torah to his grandson is regarded as though he had received the Torah at Mount Sinai.

Mishna Kiddushin 1:10 declares: He who has knowledge of Scripture and Mishna and right conduct will not easily fall prey to sin, for so it is written, "A threefold cord is not broken quickly." Kiddushin 40b, commenting on this, states that he who has no knowledge of Scripture and Mishna and right conduct makes no contribution to the welfare of the community. Maimonides and Jacob ben Asher, in their law codes, go even further. They say that such a person is not qualified to serve as a witness in a court of law.

A passage in Menachos 43b is designed to strengthen the morale of those who cling to some of the ancient observances. It says: Anyone who wears Tephillin on his head and arm, Tsitsis (fringes) on his garment and has a Mezzuza on his door will be protected against sin, as Koheles 4:9 testifies, "A cord of three strands cannot be pulled apart quickly." Furthermore, it states that every time a Jew fulfills the mitsva of Tefillin, Tsitsis or Mezzuza he creates an angel who joins the host of angels which surrounds him and protects him. This is a good illustration of how Pharisaic mystics sometimes used the rationalistic statements of Koheles to support points of view which the old professor would have considered absurd.

Koheles says, Chapter Four, Verses Thirteen to Sixteen,

"A poor but wise young man is better than an old but foolish king, who is incapable of making sound decisions. From the prison-house he went forth to rule, even though he had been born in humble surroundings. I saw all the people who were walking about under the sun with the second young man who shall rise in his stead. The masses of people who helped bring them to power seemed to be infinite in number; yet a later generation will not be happy with their government; this, too, is vapor and a striving after wind."

As was stated in the introductory paragraphs of this chapter, the meaning and purpose of these verses are completely incomprehensible. Why and how they were included in Koheles has been part of the Biblical scholarly guessing game for many centuries. They seem to have no organic relationship to the sections which precede or follow. The mysteriousness of their language is completely out of harmony with the style and spirit of the rest of the book. It is better suited to an eschatological work of the type of the Book of Daniel than to a book which is boldly and furiously rationalistic. The traditional interpretation is that the wise young man is the Biblical Joseph and the foolish old king is Potiphar. An obvious difficulty with this interpretation is that Potiphar was not a king but only a court official. Some have tried to get around this by identifying the figures as Joseph and the Pharaoh who elevated him to power. Modern scholars have tried to make the sentences fit one or more of the Egyptian or Syrian rulers of the period. One theory is that it refers to the transfer of control over Palestine from the Egyptians to the Syrians in 198 BCE. Nowhere else in the book does Koheles seem to evince such a close and detailed interest in contemporary political happenings.

The simple fact is that thus far no completely satisfactory explanation has been offered as to why these verses are here or what they mean. Perhaps they were not written by Koheles at all but were put in by a later editor to confuse the reader, i.e., to weaken the conviction of the reader that Koheles was a hard hitting, straight thinking rationalist. Perhaps they were put in by an editor who was being influenced by the eschatological ferment of the Maccabean or post-Maccabean periods.

Perhaps they were written by Koheles himself to give a subtle slap to a political enemy or a ruler whom he disliked but could not openly attack. Perhaps he hoped that the wise reader would recognize the adversary and understand his meaning and help to initiate appropriate political or military action. Which of the proferred explanations is the most plausible? Some think they know but nobody really knows.

A few of the medieval comments on these verses are interesting in themselves, even though they do not reveal to us what was in the mind of Koheles.

Koheles Rabba translates the Hebrew word "yeled" as "child" rather than "young man" and proceeds to interpret the phrase "A poor but wise child is better than an old but foolish king" as follows: "A poor but wise child"—This is the Good Inclination. Why is it called a child? Because it exerts very little influence on a person during the first thirteen years of his life. Why is it called poor? Because the parts of the body pay no attention to it. Why is it called wise? Because it teaches mankind the right way to live. . . . "An old but foolish king"—This is the Evil Inclination. Why is it called a king? Because every part of the body pays homage to it. Why is it called old? Because it is part of everyone's life from the day he is born until the day he dies. And why is it called foolish? Because it teaches mankind the wrong way to live. And why is this king said to be incapable of making sound decisions? Because one who is moved only by the Evil Inclination does not realize how much misfortune and pain will come upon him as a result of his folly.

Continuing this train of thought, Midrash Tehillim makes the following comment on "From the prison-house he went forth to rule, even though he had been born in humble surroundings": The Good Inclination is born in the domain of the Evil Inclination, i.e., at birth the child leaves the womb and enters the world by travelling through that passageway where the sexual impulse holds sway. Even though in childhood he remains under the domination of the Evil Inclination, he may, through study of God's Law and upon reaching maturity, tear himself free from the bondage of the Evil Inclination and place himself under the guidance of the Good Inclination. Rashi adds the comment that, although human beings are "born in humble surroundings," i.e., from a part of the body which also houses filth and impurity and whose odor is sometimes offensive, Judaism insists that they are born in purity and completely free from sin.

5

The Book of Koheles has been described as a "notebook," as the random thoughts which a very wise man jotted down from time to time. It could well be that this was the way in which the material for this book was collected. Although the philosophy of the book is clear and consistent, it certainly is not presented sequentially or systematically. This lack of mathematical precision makes Koheles' writing more human and more attractive than the objective presentation of a Maimonides or a Spinoza. It is as though one were engaging a man of learning and of insight in conversation rather than absorbed in listening to him lecture. Koheles is always very positive but, despite the incisiveness of his reasoning and the disagreeable nature of some of his findings, his manner is never harsh nor dictatorial but remains, from beginning to end, pleasant and gracious. At times, his thoughts just seem to ramble about, without giving evidence of wanting to travel in any particular direction or reaching any predetermined point.

Chapter Five is a good example of this rambling tendency. It begins with a discussion of the way in which one should conduct himself in the house of God. Koheles' definition of "the house of God" differs profoundly from the conventional notion. It is not a place where one goes to offer sacrifices or to chant formalized prayers. It is a communal building where scholars gather for periods of study and meditation, where community business is transacted and where pledges to charity are made. This part of the chapter ends with Verse Five. Its spirit may be summed up in a short couplet:

"Let your words be few;
What you promise, do!"

84

Then follow a number of verses which seem to have no direct relation to one another. They express a variety of aphoristic opinions: Live in the world of reality and not in a world of dreams; the more political power, the more political corruption; everything in Creation has a useful purpose; the only real and lasting form of wealth is land.

Beginning with Verse Ten, Koheles describes the difficulties of the rich. The possession of wealth brings with it many weighty responsibilities and problems, social, personal, ethical. In Verse Fourteen, Koheles returns to a theme which has occupied his attention a number of times in the earlier chapters, i.e., the futility of material ambition. Man brings nothing with him when he comes into the world and takes nothing with him when he departs. His life is full of trouble and tension. Fame and fortune are worthless goals. The happy man is he who eats, drinks and enjoys his work, not because of the expectation of some ultimate reward but simply because he likes to do what he is doing. As for the rare individual who has acquired money and property, presumably without effort, and who is happy and enjoying life to the full, "such a one has received a special gift from God."

As was mentioned in the preceding chapter, the concluding verse of Chapter Four is misplaced. It should be in the text as the first verse of Chapter Five because it is closely related to the opening section of Chapter Five and is totally unrelated to the final section of Chapter Four. Therefore, our discussion of Chapter Five begins with the interpretation of Verse Seventeen of Chapter Four.

Koheles says, Chapter Four, Verse Seventeen,

"Be careful of your actions when you go to the house of God; to listen to the instruction given there is more worthwhile than the offering of sacrifices by fools, who have no understanding of the nature or will of God."

A person well grounded in Hebrew, who has been comparing this translation of the Book of Koheles with the Hebrew text on which it is based, will have discovered long ago that this is not a literal, word-for-word translation. It is not meant to be. It is an attempt to convey to the reader the thought and the spirit of Koheles, as well as the style and meaning of his language. No translator can achieve such an objective with a literal translation, especially if the document he is translating is more than two thousand years old. Since my work is meant primarily for interested Bible students, rather than for Biblical scholars, I have not endeavored to justify my translation, verse by verse, for the scholars. Yet it should be understood that whatever differences there may be between this and other translations are not the result of mere caprice or a deliberate desire to be different. This translation of Koheles is based on a careful study of the basic meanings of the Hebrew words, their usages in the time when the book was written and the ways in which the book was interpreted by those who lived only a few hundred years after its author.

I explain this now because, at this point, it is necessary to discuss a matter that does involve the meaning of a Hebrew word. The word in question is the Hebrew "rah," which is the last word of Koheles 4:17 and normally means "evil." It refers to the fools who offer sacrifices, who, according to practically every English translation, "do not know that what they do is evil." What sense does this translation make? Very little. Nowhere in his book does Koheles overtly attack the prevailing cult of Temple worship, Temple priesthood and Temple sacrifice. In his time, the Temple was, for the Jewish people, both sacred shrine and national capitol. The high priest, who

presided over the Temple sacrifices, was not only the spiritual
ruler of the people but, in very large measure, their earthly
ruler as well. The foreign overlords held him responsible for
the preservation of order and the collection of taxes. Therefore,
for Koheles to have declared that the offering of Temple sacrifices was evil would have subjected him immediately to the
charge of treasonable heresy and would have put his life in
jeopardy. Many of the Palestinian contemporaries of Koheles
shared his rationalistic views. Liberal Greek thought had made
a deep impression upon Jewish intellectuals. It was not at all
dangerous to state that to listen to the instruction of the wise
is more worthwhile than the offering of a sacrifice by a fool.
Even the Temple priests would have agreed with that sentiment,
at least the well-provided-for priests, the ones who did not
have to depend for a living upon their share of the animal
sacrifices. But, in Jerusalem in 200 BCE, to declare that the
Temple sacrifices were an evil! He who would have done
this would have been an even bigger fool than the fools of
whom Koheles wrote.

What does the word "rah" at the end of Koheles 4:17 really
mean? The answer is found in the commentary of ibn Ezra.
He writes, "There are those who say that the Hebrew word
'rah' at the end of this verse, a word which usually means
'bad' or 'evil,' in this case means 'ratson,' 'will,' (i.e., the will
of God.)" Franz Delitsch, 1813-1890, the famous Christian
Hebraist, in his commentary on Koheles, stoutly defends this
translation of "rah." According to this theory, the word is not
derived from the Hebrew root, Resh Ayin Ayin, meaning "to
do evil," but it is derived from an Aramaic root, Resh Ayin
Aleph, meaning "to desire," a verbal root which is the equivalent of the Hebrew root Resh Tsadi Heh. This is not surpris-
ing. There are many instances of Aramaic influence in later
Biblical Hebrew. The same Aramaic root forms the basis for

similar words meaning "desire" or "will" in other verses in Koheles and also in two verses of Psalm 139—Verse Two, "Thou, O Lord, understandest my desire from afar"; and Verse Seventeen, "How precious to me are Thy desires, O God!"

The purpose of this digression, then, is to explain to the reader who knows Hebrew that Koheles was too sensible to have said what most translators make him say, i.e., that fools who offer Temple sacrifices do not know that they do evil. What he did say, in all likelihood, was that to listen to the words of the wise is a more worthwhile activity than the offering of a sacrifice by a fool, who has no understanding whatsoever of the true nature of God or of what God really wants.

Now let us continue with the interpretations of Koheles 4:17 which are in our classical writings. Unfortunately, none of them indicates a complete understanding of what Koheles was trying to say; but some of the comments are very interesting and quite timely.

"Be careful of your actions when you go the house of God."

When Koheles spoke of the "house of God," he was not referring to the Temple that stood on Mount Zion in Jerusalem. He meant one of the meeting-houses which had come into being as the result of the efforts of Ezra the Scribe and his followers, meeting-houses which served the people as centers for social and political gatherings, for study and for prayer. It was in these "batey k'nesios," these "houses of assembly," rather than in Jerusalem's Holy Temple, that the modern synagogue had its genesis and early development. Koheles undoubtedly went often to his neighborhood's "house of assembly," his local "house of God," to teach and also to listen to the teachings of others. He probably did not attend the elaborate rituals at the Temple on Mount Zion more often than was absolutely necessary, i.e., whenever his wife insisted or on the main holy days, when everybody went.

But, to the Jewish sages of the Middle Ages, Koheles' "house of God" was no neighborhood "house of assembly." They believed it could only mean "the" Temple. They interpreted his statement accordingly. Mishna Berachos said that a man may not enter the Temple area bearing a staff or wearing his sandals or carrying any money or with dirty feet. He may not use the area as a shortcut and he may not spit in the area. Others said that one may not appear in the Temple clad only in one's underwear or in a bathing suit. Any person who was ritually unclean was, of course, not permitted to enter the Temple. Respect for the Temple continued even after its destruction. Disrespect and levity are forbidden when one visits the ruins of the Temple. God has said, in Leviticus 19:30, "My Sabbaths you shall observe and My sanctuary you shall respect." Respect for God's sanctuary is as important as the observance of the Sabbath. Rabbi Jose ben Jehudah said, "Since one would not enter the presence of an earthly king in unseemly manner, how much the more is he expected to be careful when he enters the presence of the King of kings, the Holy One, blessed be He." Ibn Ezra comments, "Although it is necessary to show God even more respect than one shows an earthly king, the Heavenly King does not keep His distance as does the earthly king. If His subjects come near to him in sincerity and in truth, He welcomes them and listens to them willingly."

A number of very practical Temple problems were discussed by the sages in a manner that would have caused Queen Victoria to blush and Anthony Comstock to telephone for the bluecoats. If one is in the Temple and just has to spit, what does he do? Some Talmudic authorities permit him to spit, provided that he can absorb the spit in his garments. But the post-Talmudic authorities, specifically the Rambam and the Semag, were not so kind. They declared that spitting was forbidden in the Temple under any and all circumstances whatsoever. And what if one discovers in the middle of the Temple service that he needs to go to the toilet? This should never have to happen, say the sages. Just as a little child should always be taken to the toilet before it is brought into the sanctuary, so, too, the well-mannered and well-trained adult will follow the same procedure. This is one of the meanings of the words of the prophet, Amos 4:12, "Be prepared to meet your God, O Israel." But what if one has neglected to make the proper preparations and there he is, right in the middle of the service, when, all of a sudden, he is reminded that he forgot to prepare? What does he do? He should complete the forgotten preparations before he continues his prayers. The Kabbalists say that Satan has no power over a man in the time of prayer if the man has the necessary spiritual strength to withstand Satan's blandishments. Such spiritual strength is possible only if, before one begins to pray, one has prepared. If one has forgotten to prepare, Satan will triumph.

Huna bar G'niva, an amora, translated the second part of the verse as follows: "To be present in the Temple when the Shema is recited is more worthwhile than the offering up of sacrifice by fools." He said: Better is the recitation of the Shema at the proper time than the thousand burnt offerings of a fool. In God's sight, prayer properly offered is of more importance than burnt offerings improperly offered. This was one of the favorite principles of the Pharisees. There are some who interpret this principle to mean that the Pharisees set up the system of private and synagogal prayers as a permanent substitute for the system of animal sacrifices. This is not so. If and when the Temple is rebuilt and rededicated, the Pharisees, ancient and modern, expect the system of animal sacrifices to be reinstituted and to continue as in the period before the destruction of the Second Temple.

"To listen to instruction is more worthwhile than the offering up of sacrifices by fools, who have no understanding of the nature or will of God."

Enoch ben Joseph Zundel, nineteenth century Russian sage, quotes from the ethical work *Me-eyn ha'Berachos* as follows: Fools have no understanding of the meaning of bringing sin offerings. Fools do not really repent, because they think that by bringing a sin offering they are paying in full for having sinned. A sin offering is effective only if it is accompanied by genuine repentence, by a firm resolve not to repeat the offense. This is, therefore, unlike the other commandments of God which the more one does them, the more worthy he becomes. A sin offering has worth only if the one making atonement sincerely regrets what he has done. Fools do not understand this. Fools think that offering God a sin offering gives them the right to go out and repeat the sin, provided, of course, that later on they bring another sin offering for the second sin. Such fools have no understanding of the nature or will of God.

In Book Three of *Sefer ha-Ikkarim,* the Spanish Jewish philosopher, Joseph Albo, uses Koheles 4:17 as the basis for presenting an excellent exposition of the concept of Freedom of the Will:

An act of absolute free will is one which a man does knowing that he may do the opposite without anyone or anything being able to hinder him and yet he chooses to do that which he does. But if a person does not know how or has not the power to choose to do the opposite of what he does and if he does what he does without having such knowledge or power, then what he does is not an act of absolute free will for which he should be praised if it is good or condemned if it is bad. Even the bringing of a sacrifice, which is a good act, is an act which is devoid of religious or ethical significance if it is brought from habit or custom, if its being brought does not involve the making of a decision to do that which is good and not to do that which is evil.

This is what is meant in Koheles 4:17, "Be careful of your actions when you go to the house of God." Be sure you are going there by choice and not because of habit or custom. Koheles says, "To listen to the instruction given there is more worthwhile than the offering up of sacrifices by fools, who have no understanding of what they are doing." For a man to listen to the words of the wise has more worth than the bringing of sacrifices by fools, because, through listening to the words of the wise, one may learn to distinguish good from evil and to choose good and avoid evil. This is something which fools cannot do. Even the sacrifices which they bring are accounted as nothing. Since they do not listen to the wise, they cannot distinguish between good and evil and, therefore, they cannot freely choose to do evil. So their doing good by bringing a sacrifice is not to their credit, since it has in it no element of choice. They do not bring it out of any other motive than that of habit and custom. For this they deserve no praise. A man is not to be praised merely for doing a good deed. He is to be praised only if, having it within his power to do an evil deed, he chooses, instead, to do a good deed.

Koheles says, Chapter Five, Verse One,

"Do not speak out impetuously; do not be hasty in speaking before God; for God is in the heavens and you are upon earth; therefore let your words be few."

The sages felt that this verse deals with two related theological matters, the problem of Good and Evil and the nature of prayer.

"Do not be hasty in speaking before God; for God is in the heavens and you are upon earth."

Rabbi Simon ben Chalafta, one of the last of the tannaim, who taught from about 200 to 220, said: If two men are fighting and one succeeds in getting on top of the other, who usually wins? The one who is on top. How much the more is this so when the One Who is always on top is the Eternal One and you are the one on the bottom. So when you start to argue with God, be careful. "Do not speak out impetuously. Let your words be few."

An earlier tanna, Rabbi Joshua ben Chananya, c.40-c.125, had explained the matter in a different way: Study well Isaiah 29:15-16, "Woe unto them that go very deep in order to hide their intentions from God, who work in the darkness; they say, 'Who sees us? Who knows us?'" The matter may be compared to the case of an architect who planned the fortifications for a certain city and later became the province's tax collector. When he came around to collect the taxes for this community, the people tried to evade him by hiding in the underground caves of the fortifications. He cried out to them: "How can you hope to hide yourself from me in this place? I planned it, remember?" So it is with those "that go very deep in order to hide their intentions from God, who work in the darkness." O you perverse people! Is the Potter no more wise than the clay with which He works? "That the thing made should say of Him that made it, 'He made me not'; or the thing formed say of Him Who formed it, 'He has no understanding.'" How dares that which has been created compare itself to its Creator, that which has been planted to its Planter?

"Do not be hasty in speaking before God." God knows exactly what He is doing and why. In Talmud Berachos is written: Rav Huna ben Joshua said that Rav said in the name of Rabbi Meir, and some say it was in the name of Rabbi Akiba: One should always be prepared to say that everything which God does is good. Rabbi Akiba once went on a journey to assist Bar Cochba in his rebellion against the Romans. He took with him a donkey on which to ride, a rooster to wake him in the morning and a lantern to light his way at night. One evening he arrived in a certain town and tried to get a room at the local inn; but all the rooms were already taken. Rabbi Akiba said to himself, "Everything which God does is good," and he went out into the fields to sleep. In the course of the night, a lion came and ate the donkey, a cat came and ate the rooster and a wind came and blew out the lantern. Each time a new trouble befell him, Rabbi Akiba repeated to himself, "Everything which God does is good." That same night, Roman soldiers came to the town looking for Rabbi Akiba. They went to the inn to arrest him but he was not there. They went out into the fields to search for him but they could not find him. They left with their mission unfulfilled. The next day Rabbi Akiba said to the people of the town, "It is just as I have always believed, 'Everything which God does is good.' If there had been a room for me at the inn, if my lamp had been lighted in the field, if the donkey had brayed or the rooster had crowed, the Roman soldiers would have found me."

Enoch ben Joseph Zundel explains that "good" and "evil" are man-made terms and that, in God's sight, everything is good because everything serves a useful purpose: There are two kinds of servants of God, one kind which serves Him through Nature (Man calls this the Evil Inclination) and another which serves Him in a way which is above Nature (Man calls this the Good Inclination). The second is one whose conduct is without blemish and who is controlled by his intellect. The temptations of the flesh are strong but the righteous and wise servants of God struggle mightily to overcome the temptations and they succeed. The war which every person wages within himself, the war between his instincts and his intellect, is the fiercest struggle there is. When two nations go to war and one conquers the other, the war stops. But not so the war of the senses. It goes on continually, day and night, within every individual. One may win a thousand battles but the war still continues. Most human beings are unable to stand the strain and they give in. They are the kind of servants who serve God through Nature, through the way directed by the senses. Those who serve in a supra-Natural manner are the superior type because they serve God through their intellect and through their love for Him and not because they follow the dictates of their senses. Nevertheless, it must be understood that to serve God through the senses is also considered service, although of an inferior and earthly sort, while to serve God intelligently and unselfishly is spiritual and eternal. What Man calls the Evil Inclination is not only a means of tempting some to do wrong; it is also an instrument which enables many to do good.

The sum and substance of the matter is: Refrain from criticism of God. In His infinite wisdom, He has decided that mankind shall never know nor understand why the world is the way it is. The only right way to live and the only happy way to live is to have complete and unquestioning faith in the goodness and wisdom of God.

Maharshaw comments: Even if God is punishing you and you are pleading with Him for mercy, "let your words be few," because God already knows anything you can tell Him and whatever He has decided to do is right and good.

"Do not speak out impetuously; do not be hasty in speaking before God."

The sages regarded prayer as being man's way of talking to God. Sforno says: Do not pray until you have properly prepared yourself to pray. It is recorded that, in former days, scholars would spend an hour in meditation before they began their formal prayers in order to make sure that their hearts and minds were properly prepared.

Albo, in *Sefer ha-Ikkarim*, reacts to Koheles 5:1 as follows: When praying, one is not allowed to say exactly what his emotions prompt him to say. An acceptable prayer must fulfill three requirements: 1. It must be brief and yet express adequately the intention of him who prays. It must not be verbose, for, as Koheles 5:2 says, "Too many words is the mark of the fool." 2. What is intended in one's heart must be consistent with what is said by one's mouth. As David said, Psalm 19:15, "May the words of my mouth and the meditations of my heart be acceptable to Thee." What one thinks and what one says must be consistent one with the other. 3. The voice must be subdued and indicate submission, in the manner of a man supplicating his master.

There are some people who fulfill the obligation of prayer by the right intentions of the heart. There are some in an even higher category who receive favors from God which they have not requested. There is an even higher category who are so filled with love of God that they are never expected to pray at all and yet God's Presence is with them always.

The best and wisest prayer is that of Rabbi Eliezer in Berachos 29b: "Master of the universe, do Thy will in Heaven above; give contentment of mind to those who revere Thee here below; do that which is good in Thine eyes." "Do that which is good in Thine eyes"—What did Rabbi Eliezer mean? He meant: "Anytime that I pray to You, do not be moved by my words or my request to do what I want You to do, for there are many times when I pray for something which would not be good for me, even though I think it would be good for me. You know much better than do I whether it would be good or bad for me. Therefore, the choice of what to do is Yours and not mine. Please do for me what You know will be for my good." This is why the Mishna says that one is obliged to thank God for the evil as well as for the good, because God decides everything and, from God's vantage point, all of God's decisions are good.

It is best for man, when he prays to God, to pray in general terms and not in specific terms or with specific requests. The man who prays in specific terms or with specific requests is trying to do the impossible; he is trying to bend God's will to his will, and he is showing an unwillingness to bend his will to God's will, an unwillingness which is the mark of an unbeliever. He is also seeking to limit God's wisdom and power of action. The implication is that God has no other way of setting matters aright except to do that desired by the suppliant. When one makes a request of an earthly being, it is often necessary to explain to him what he must do in order to fulfill the request; but with God this is not necessary. God knows much more about what is proper and improper than we do. So one must pray to God only in general terms and let the rest to Him. . . .

Koheles says, Chapter Five, Verse Two,

"Too much business causes one to have nightmares and too many words is the mark of the fool."

Rashi: This expands upon the thought with which the previous verse ended, "Let your words be few." Put a limit upon the number of matters in which you become involved and the number of words you speak. If you get wrapped up in too many matters, you will not sleep well at night; if you talk too much, you will be considered a fool and you will get into trouble.

Ibn Ezra: If one has a dream in which many unrelated things are mixed together in a crazy mess, it may be because he ate too much of a mixture of different kinds of food before going to sleep. (Ibn Ezra translates the Hebrew word "inyan" as "variety of food" rather than as "business matters.") Such a dream is not subject to interpretation; it has no lesson of good or evil; it is merely vapor. Of equal insignificance is the fool who talks too much. Whether he tries to impress God or man, he invariably ends by being worse off than when he began.

Sforno: A dream which is full of nonsense may be caused by one using his imagination too much during his waking hours. Likewise, when a fool prays, if he uses too many words, his imagination may get the better of him and he will depart from the spirit of unselfishness and humility that marks the true prayer.

Koheles says, Chapter Five, Verses Three and Four,

> "When you make a promise to God, do not delay its fulfillment, for God dislikes insincerity; whatever you promise Him to do, do. It is better not to promise than to promise and not do."

The sages taught: There are three circumstances under which God opens up an individual's Heavenly account book to see whether he is worthy of having a miracle performed in his behalf: When he goes on a journey alone, when he is sitting in a house that is about to cave in and when he makes a religious vow and does not fulfill it.

The sages also taught: Anyone who makes a promise to God and does not keep it may cause the sins of idolatry, immorality and murder to come into the world. Where do we learn this? From the story of Jacob.

When Jacob left his parents and started for the home of his uncle, he slept at night at a place he called Beth El, "the house of God." He set up a stone to mark the spot and he made a vow, saying, Genesis 28:20-22, "If God will be with me and will protect me as I journey along and will give me food to eat and a garment to wear, and if I return safely to the domain of my parents, then, indeed, Yahweh will be my God. And this stone which I have set up as a marker shall be changed into a house of God and, of everything which Thou wilt give me, I shall return a tenth unto Thee." God fulfilled His part of the bargain completely. Jacob got rich and established a household and returned safely to the territory of his parents; but he did not keep his promise to Yahweh.

So God sent Esau to Jacob to kill him and Jacob had to pay Esau a ransom for his life—but Jacob did not realize that he was being punished because he had committed a sin. Then God sent an angel to wrestle with Jacob and the angel crippled him—but Jacob still did not realize that he was being punished because he had committed a sin. Then Shechem the Chivite seduced Dinah, the daughter of Jacob, and the brothers of Dinah murdered Shechem and his brethren—and Jacob still did not realize that he was being punished because he had committed a sin.

God said, "How long will it be before this man realizes why he is being punished? The time has come to let him know." So He said to Jacob, Genesis 35:1, "Go up to Beth El and live there and set up an altar there to the God Who appeared to you when you were fleeing from your brother Esau." He said, "Go back to that place where you made the vow and do what you promised to do. All these troubles have come upon you because you have delayed the fulfillment of your promise. If you want the troubles to stop, go up to Beth El and build for Me there the house of worship which you promised to build. When you were in difficulty, you made a vow to Me but, as soon as everything went well with you, you forgot your vow; but I did not forget."

Immediately Jacob called his family together and said, Genesis 35:2, "Put aside your idols and take a bath and change your clothes. We are going to Beth El. There I shall erect an altar to the God Who answered me in the day of my distress and Who has been with me ever since."

Because Jacob did not carry through his part of the bargain which he had made with God, he caused the evils of idolatry, immorality and murder to come into the world. This teaches us what may happen when one fails to fulfill a promise made to God. "It is better not to promise than to promise and not do."

Rabbi Meir and Rabbi Judah the Prince had a difference of opinion on the matter of making promises to God. Rabbi Meir said: Better than he who promises God and does as he promised or he who promises and does not do as he promised is he who never promises God anything but who carries out his religious obligations quietly and faithfully at the appropriate time and in the appropriate manner. Rabbi Judah disagreed. He said: Best of all is he who makes promises to God and keeps his promises.

Sforno says: Just as he who thinks that God delights in a multiplicity of words in prayer is a fool and discovers eventually that just the opposite is true; so is one a fool who makes a pledge to God which he does not intend to pay promptly.

The pledger thinks that God is pleased with him for having pledged and will not care how long it takes him to pay the pledge. He will learn that this is not so. "God dislikes insincerity." A pledge to God must be made freely and paid promptly. The biggest fool of all is he who pledges and says to himself that he will not pay the pledge until God does for him exactly what he wants done.

Koheles says, Chapter Five, Verse Five,

> "Do not permit your mouth to get you into trouble; do not tell the charity collector that your charity pledge was not meant to be taken seriously. Why provoke the anger of God by your words? Why destroy whatever good reputation you may now have?"

"Do not permit your mouth to get you into trouble."

Rabbi Sama bar Raba, one of the last amoraim, who lived in Babylon between 430 and 500 and taught in the yeshiva of Pumbedita, said: Words are very valuable and must be used cautiously and carefully. Wise, indeed, is the saying of the great-grandson of Hillel, Simon ben Rabban Gamliel, a saying which is found in Mishna Avos 1:17, "All my days have I been among scholars and I have found nothing better for a man than to keep silent," i.e., the more one talks, the more one puts on display his ignorance and his weaknesses. Yafe Toar comments: When one sits among the wise who are discussing Torah, it is better to keep silent and to listen to what is being said and to gain understanding than to join in the discussion and raise questions and arguments. If this is true where one has the opportunity to speak in the course of a learned discussion and does not, how much more true is it that one should not waste his words on discussions that deal with unimportant and worthless matters!

Rabbi Joshua ben Chananya taught: There is a Palestinian proverb: Whenever words are being sold in the marketplace for one Sela per word, the ability to refrain from speaking is being sold there for two Selas per word.

Rabbi Judah of the village of Nibburaya, near Tiberias (and some say he was from the village of Nibbur Chayil), translated Psalm 65:2 as follows: "Silence is a way of praising Thee, O God." He said: Silence is the highest form of praise.

Rabbi Eleazar said in the name of Rabbi Jose ben Zimra: Man has two hundred and forty-eight limbs. Some of them lie flat and some stand erect. The tongue is one of them. It lies flat between the two cheeks and a stream of water passes under it and it is guarded by several folding doors, i.e., the teeth and the lips. Yet, despite all these safeguards, just see how often the tongue gets out of bounds and how many conflagrations it generates. If it were strong enough to stand erect and was not restrained by these protective devices, how much greater would be its power and its menace!

"Do not tell the charity collector that your charity pledge was not meant to be taken seriously. Why provoke the anger of God by your words? Why destroy whatever good reputation you may now have?"

Rabbi Joshua ben Levi, Palestinian amora, head of the yeshiva at Lydda during the first half of the third century, stated that this verse refers to one who makes a public pledge to charity and then refuses to pay. Do not tell the synagogue sexton who comes to collect the pledge: "I did not really mean what I said. My pledge was not meant to be taken in earnest. I only spoke out in order to avoid public embarrassment or so that others might pledge; but I did not and I do not intend to give any of my own money." Or perhaps you will say: "I did not know what I was doing." Or: "At the time I made the pledge I was confident that I would be able to pay but now I find that I am unable to pay." None of these excuses will be acceptable to God. God will be angry at you for not making good the words which came out of your mouth. God will take away from you the reward for any good deeds which you may already have to your credit.

Sforno says: Even if you intend to pay, do not make pledges hastily lest you bring sin and punishment upon yourself. It is better to pay freewill offerings right away than to run the risk of not being able to pay them when they come due. One who makes a vow to contribute money for a religious purpose and then does not pay transgresses the Biblical law against making improper use of sacred property, i.e., once his money is pledged, it is no longer his and belongs to the purpose for which it has been pledged.

The Hebrew word used for synagogue sexton in the statement of Rabbi Joshua ben Levi, quoted in the previous section, is "chazan," the word now used for the synagogue cantor. This word has had an interesting development. It comes from a Hebrew root meaning "to oversee," "to supervise." It first appears in the Mishna where it has the following usages: Children's religious school superintendent, sheriff, court crier, synagogue sexton. The modern meaning, i.e., one whose primary responsibility is to lead the congregation in prayer and chant the important parts of the service, does not appear until quite late in the post-Talmudic period. There are clear indications, however, that, even before the completion of the Mishna, the Chazan was also used as a "sh'liach tsibur," a "representative of the congregation," the term used for one who is designated to conduct public worship services.

Koheles says, Chapter Five, Verse Six,

> "Rather than become involved in a multiplicity of delusions and vain ambitions and other worldly matters, strive to fear God."

This is a very difficult verse to translate from the Hebrew. The original text is obviously ungrammatical and so we must assume that it has not come down to us in its original form. Some scholars have tried to guess what the original form may have been. Others have decided that it was inserted by a later editor and does not really belong in the book. I have tried to translate it in a way which does no immoderate violence to the Hebrew text and, at the same time, preserves the spirit of Koheles.

Neither Talmud nor Midrash made a worthy attempt to relate this verse to the rest of the book. The medieval commentators tried to do so but, if my translation mirrors the thought of Koheles, Rashi seems to be the only one who had some idea of what Koheles was trying to say. Rashi says that Koheles meant: Stay away from speculations and false prophets and strange interpretations. Stick to the paths of tradition and of the intellect; from them learn to respect and fear God. . . . The trouble with Rashi's explanation is that Koheles and he were tuned in on different theological wave lengths. Their definitions of what constitutes "tradition" would have been decidedly different. There is little reason to doubt that Koheles would have numbered Rashi among the "false prophets."

In spirit, ibn Ezra was much closer to being a fellow traveller of Koheles than was Rashi. But ibn Ezra does not get the thought of Koheles in this verse because he is determined to link it to the verses which preceded it. He says it means: It is not wrong to have dreams and speak of nonsensical things and of other worldly matters as long as, in the course of the

dreams and discussions, God's name is respected and not profaned. . . . This comment is not worthy of either Koheles or
ibn Ezra. Ibn Ezra was far too wise to believe that a human
being can completely control the thoughts and fantasies that
come to him in dreams about God or anyone or anything else.

Sforno takes a similar tack. He tries to link the verse to
the dreams, the long prayers and the unpaid vows discussed
in the previous verses. He says: Be careful of being too lengthy
in prayer and in making vows lest you be trapped in sin. They
are snares as are empty dreams, which are caused by too much
use of the deceitful imagination. One may dream that he is
able to escape the consequences of mistakes made in prayers
or vows and in other areas where the person has made errors
based on selfish desires. One must keep clear of these entangle-
ments because of his fear of being punished by God. . . .
Sforno's explanation may be described as both ingenious and
ingenuous.

The final phrase of the verse, "Strive to fear God," requires
special explanation. In the sense in which Koheles thought of
God, this is his figurative way of saying, "Try to live in accordance with the realities of existence." The sense of the
whole verse is: Do not live in a dream world or be overly
ambitious or concern yourself too much with worldly affairs
but live in a manner that accords with the facts of existence.
The concluding phrase is certainly not to be interpreted as
referring to the Personal God of the Pharisees. As a thorough-
going rationalist, Koheles would hardly have been likely to
believe in the sort of God Who personally keeps watch over
the actions of every individual creature in the universe. He gives
every indication of believing in a God Who is concerned about
the universe as a whole rather than about every action of every
individual in it. The God of Koheles does not control man-

kind by playing Policeman but through the exercise of His Will and His Law. One who believes in such a God respects and loves Him but does not literally fear Him.

Koheles says, Chapter Five, Verse Seven,

> "If you see that the poor in the land are oppressed and that justice and righteousness have been stealthily removed, do not be surprised at this state of affairs; for he who has power is being watched by one more powerful than he; and above them both are others even more powerful."

Rabbi Jose bar Chanina, a Palestinian amora who taught from about 250 to 280, stated that this verse referred to the Roman Empire. He said: Do not be surprised or dismayed because you now see the Roman Empire oppressing the poor and robbing the weak and yet, at the same time, it is enjoying great prosperity and its capital city, Rome, is the outstanding city of the world. You will live to see this great empire punished for its sins. "For he who has power is being watched by one more powerful than he" refers to the Roman hierarchy that begins with the military commanders and from there goes on up, through the governors of the provinces, to the officers of the royal court. Above all these is the Eternal King, most powerful Ruler of all, Who controls the destinies of men and of nations and Who will humble the pride of the great Empire. Rabbi Jose would not have dared to speak of Rome so boldly if, at the time of his speaking, he and his people were being ruled by the Romans. Therefore, it may be assumed that this interpretation of Koheles 5:7 was taught by Rabbi Jose at some time between the years 263 and 272, the years during which the Romans had to relinquish control of Palestine to King Odenathus and Queen Zenobia of Palmyra, a Syrian city north of Damascus.

However, it is very unlikely that Koheles was referring, in Koheles 5:7, to the Roman Empire and it is even more unlikely that he was making any reference to God. He obviously had in mind a tyrannical dictatorship, which had a number of characteristics common to all tyrannical dictatorships, including the most modern varieties, Fascism and Communism. A state of affairs in which "justice and righteousness have been stealthily removed" and "he who has power is being watched by one more powerful than he" is as truly descriptive of a twentieth century "Iron Curtain" satellite as it was of the ancient despotic systems known to Koheles. Koheles was alluding to either the Egyptian or Syrian Empires, probably the latter, since it was the more obnoxious of the two. In this period of Jewish history, these two empires were fighting each other almost continually for possession of Palestine. The Roman Empire did not begin to take an active interest in Palestinian affairs until about forty years later, in the time of Judah the Maccabee. And so far as God is concerned: It has been explained, in connection with the interpretation of the preceding verse, that Koheles did not believe in a God Who mixes into the affairs of men capriciously or miraculously. He is a God of Law and Order, Who has established rules of life for mankind to follow. Those individuals or groups, be they the Roman imperium or the Marxist Communists, who do not obey God's rules, were and are doomed to ultimate failure and destruction. In addition to this ideological consideration, the grammatical construction of the Hebrew phrase, translated as "above them both are others even more powerful," does not lend itself to the interpretation that Koheles was alluding, in this phrase, to God.

Koheles says, Chapter Five, Verses Eight and Nine,

"Those things in the world which seem to be superfluous have a definite place in the world plan; even a king needs to make himself the servant of his own field. Those who love money cannot satisfy their appetites by eating it; those whose wealth consists of non-edible goods have a fortune which is absolutely worthless."

Here, again, are two verses which are very difficult to translate. They have been translated and will be interpreted here as Jewish tradition has translated and interpreted them and not as they have been translated and interpreted by most modern Biblical scholars. It is not possible for anyone to state with certainty what these Hebrew verses really mean. However, the Jewish traditional translation seems to make more sense and to be more in keeping with the general spirit of Koheles than most of the more recent translations.

One of the major differences of opinion between the traditional and modern translators is with regard to the division of thought in these two verses. The modernists believe that each verse represents a separate and distinct thought. The Jewish traditionalists believe that 8a conveys a thought which is enlarged upon in 8b-9.

An interesting feature of Koheles 5:8 is that, if one accepts the modernist position, it is possible to interpret this verse in two ways having completely opposite meanings. It may be interpreted to mean: The finest kind of ruler to have is a king who tills the soil; or: The most useless kind of ruler to have is a king who tills the soil. Both interpretations are possible because of the peculiar nature of the Hebrew word "yisron," which occurs in this verse. In Talmudic Hebrew, "yisron" can be translated as "something which is better than average" or, to the contrary, as "something which is superfluous and useless." The word is used a number of times in the Book of Koheles to mean "better than average" but the sages were of the opinion that, in Koheles 5:8, it means "something which is superfluous."

The modern savants who regard Koheles 5:9 as an entity in itself usually translate the verse as "Those who love money never get satisfaction from it; and there is no lasting benefit for those who love wealth; this, too, is vapor." This sentiment would, of course, fit very well into the teachings of Koheles and also can be related easily to the thoughts in the verses that follow. If one can find an appropriate explanation for Verse Eight standing by itself, then Verse Nine may, indeed, be an introductory statement to the observations on wealth in Verses Ten to Thirteen. But if there is no satisfactory explanation for Verse Eight standing by itself, and that seems to be the case, and if there is a satisfactory interpretation for Verses Eight and Nine taken together, and this has been accomplished by Jewish tradition, the second alternative appears to be the more sensible and is the one which has been selected.

Now let us proceed to examine the interpretation of Koheles 5:8-9, as these verses are interpreted in Jewish tradition.

"Those things in the world which seem to be superfluous have a definite place in the world plan."

Midrash Sh'mos Rabba says: There is nothing in the world which is without value, purpose or significance, as it is written, Genesis 1:31, "God saw all that He had made; and it was very good." The sages agree that this is a basic principle of Judaism.

The rabbis said: All things that seem to be unneeded in the world, such as flies, fleas and gnats, are considered necessary or they would not have been created. To each of them God has given a purpose and a mission. This is also true of snakes, bugs and frogs. It is stated at the end of the first chapter of Seder Eliahu Rabba, Midrashic work written in the fifth century, that many of the animals, birds and creeping things in the world were created in order that they might provide man with elements needed to manufacture medicines for healing. Yafe Toar says that the unpleasant creatures of the world were brought into being either to heal the sick or to humble the proud.

Rabbi Judah the Prince taught: Nothing is superfluous. Everything in the world helps to maintain the stability of the world plan. For example, the wood fibers of the palm tree are used in the making of rope; the twigs of the palm tree are useful for garden hedges; these seemingly useless materials contribute to the world plan.

Rabbi Acha ben Chanina, Palestinian amora who taught from 280 to 310, said: Even such creatures as serpents and scorpions have a purpose in the world. God said to the prophets, "Do you think that, if you had not been sent as My representatives, I would have no other representatives to send? Indeed, 'those things in the world which seem superfluous have a useful purpose in the world plan.' If I so desire, I can have My will performed on earth by a serpent or a scorpion or a frog or a hornet. With the frog, Exodus 8:1-10, I punished the Egyptians and with the hornet, Exodus 23:28, I punished the Canaanites."

There are many fanciful tales in the Midrashim on Koheles 5:8 to prove that God uses seemingly insignificant creatures to accomplish important ends. Typical of these stories and probably the most famous is the Midrashic tale of the gnat which caused the death of the wicked Titus Flavius Vespasianus, conqueror of Jerusalem, son of the emperor Vespasian and head of the Roman Empire from 79 until his death in 81:

When Titus the wicked one conquered Jerusalem and destroyed the Temple, he cut down the curtain which hung before the Holy of Holies and entered that most sacred of places with his unsheathed sword in his hand. When he came out, he boasted blasphemously, saying, "I am not as one who

has waged battle with the King in the wilderness and has conquered Him. I am one who has given battle to the King in
His own palace and has conquered Him!" To show his contempt for God and His sanctuary, he opened a Scroll of the
Law, put it upon the Temple altar, ordered two prostitutes to
place their naked bodies upon the pages of the Scroll, and dese-
crated both the Scroll and the altar by stripping off his clothes
and having sexual relations publicly with the prostitutes. Then
he had all the precious cups and dishes, utensils and furniture
of the Temple gathered together and placed on his ship.

While he was on the Mediterranean Sea, en route back
to Rome, a mighty gale struck the ship. Titus said, "It seems
that the God of the Hebrews only has strength when He uses
water. He had to use water to destroy the Generation of the
Flood; He had to use water to destroy Pharoah. When I was
in His house, He was unable to harm me. It is only now, when
He has caught me on the water, that He is able to make trouble
for me." God said, "You wicked son of a wicked father, I
shall take vengeance upon you on land and with the most insignificant creature I have ever made." God signalled to the
sea to cease its raging immediately. The ship arrived in Rome
safely.

When the conqueror of Judea arrived in Rome, vast throngs
of Romans greeted him, shouting, "Hail, mighty conqueror of
barbarians!" . . . The Hebrew word used for conqueror in
this passage, a word taken from the Greek, is "Nekita!!" May
it be "l'havdil!!" . . . Soon after his arrival, Titus went to
a bathhouse and took a bath. When he came out of the bath,
he was given a bowl of spiced wine to drink. He noticed a
tiny gnat in the bowl but he was so thirsty that he lifted the
bowl to his lips without bothering to kill the insignificant creature and without even trying to wave it away. The gnat flew
into the nostril of Titus and penetrated to his brain. It bored

away at the brain of Titus for seven years. In great pain and realizing that he was being punished by the God of the Jews, Titus commanded his doctors to find out what was wrong with him. They opened up his skull and found the gnat. Rabbi Eleazar been Jose said: I was in Rome at that time and can testify that the gnat had become as big as the chick of a dove and weighed twenty-four ounces. The giant gnat rose up, flew away and with it departed the soul of Titus, to dwell eternally in the bottomless pit. . . . There is a difference of opinion in the Talmud as to whether the gnat was gotten out of the brain of Titus while he was still living or after he was dead. . . . Thus was fulfilled the saying of Koheles: "Those things in the world which seem to be superfluous have a useful place in the world plan."

"Even a king needs to make himself the servant of his own field. Those who love money cannot satisfy their appetites by eating it; those whose wealth consists of non-edible goods have a fortune which is absolutely worthless."

Rabbi Judah the Prince taught: Even if a king is master of the whole world, he still needs to cultivate his own farm land. If you inquire, you will discover that the kind of king who loves money and all manner of material things except those which are produced from the ground is the kind of king who knows and cares nothing about farming. Anyone, even a king, who has an insatiable lust for material wealth and material possessions and who does not own and till arable land can never get the fullest pleasure from all that he possesses. . . . (Is this why most commercial kings dream of spending their years of retirement on a farm?)

Rabbi Jonathan bar Joseph and Rabbi Chanan interpreted Ezekiel 27:29, "All that handle the oar, the deck crews and the pilots of the sea shall come down from their ships, they shall stand upon the land," as follows: Does not everyone who gets off a ship stand upon the land? The verse has a deeper significance than appears on the surface. It means that if one owns land and also owns a ship, if his ship sinks, "he stands upon the land," i.e., he is able to survive the financial blow; but, if a shipowner does not own land and loses his ship, he is ruined.

Yafe Toar comments: Rabbi Judah says that there is no advantage in merely having money. The advantage lies in being able to use the money to buy whatever one wants or needs. What advantage is there in having money if, with it, one is unable to buy the products of the ground? Better than the possession of money is the possession of arable land. If one owns arable land, he has little need for large sums of money. Rabbi Jonathan and Rabbi Chanan say that the way of the world is such that one may easily lose his money but, if one owns land, he owns that which is substantial and inde-structible.

Ibn Ezra says: Farming is the best of all possible occupa-tions. It is an employment even for a king, for there is no labor more important than working in the field, from which come those products that sustain the life of the human race.

Sforno agrees with ibn Ezra: The most important kind of physical labor, even for the righteous, i.e., the scholars, is to till the soil, for from it come our food and our clothing. Koheles does not mean that the king should actually work in the fields but rather that he should oversee the labors of those who do. Such work must be done under the direction of the king because, were it not for the law and order which the king imposes on society, men would cease to till the soil and to raise cattle. Instead, they would eat each other.

Koheles says, Chapter Five, Verse Ten,

"Where there is much good food to eat, there are also

many eaters; and what advantage has he who owns it except the pleasure of looking at it?"

Before any one asks, let it be said that there is no indication in any of the classical sources that this verse is making cryptic reference to the subject of payment of taxes, federal, state or local. The section from Verse Ten through Verse Thirteen does, however, deal with a somewhat related subject, i.e., the difficulties of being rich. Verse Ten refers to the many "free loaders" who invite themselves to the soirees of the wealthy. One would think that Koheles means that this makes the host of the evening very unhappy but Sforno thinks otherwise. Sforno says: One who is host at a feast gets much inner pleasure when he sees many people being made happy by the good food he has provided for them.

Koheles says, Chapter Five, Verse Eleven,

"Pleasant is the sleep of the laborer, whether he has eaten little or much; but the superabundance of the rich man does not afford him a restful slumber."

The medieval exegetes interpret this verse quite literally but the Midrashists found in it a consoling thought upon which to meditate when an outstanding young person dies.

Rashi: A farm hand sleeps well whether he has eaten much or little for he is accustomed to do so; but the rich man is so worried about his many business affairs that it is difficult for him to sleep.

Ibn Ezra: The rich man is always worried at night that someone may rob him of his money or he has eaten so much that he is afraid of getting sick. The poor laborer does not have these kinds of worries.

Sforno: The rich man is not only worried about being robbed. He also worries about how he is going to find sufficient sustenance to care for his large household.

Rabbi Tanchuma bar Abba, a Palestinian amora who taught from about 335 to 370, expounded Koheles 5:11 in this manner: How can one possibly say that he who has eaten little will sleep soundly? It is well-known that one who goes to bed hungry cannot sleep well. The Scripture here is not speaking of the physically hungry. It is speaking of the righteous, of those who labor in the Torah. How? Let us examine the verse carefully.

"Pleasant is the sleep of the laborer, whether he has eaten little or much." If a person begins to labor in the Torah and the commandments when he is very young and he dies at age thirty, and another man does the same thing and lives to be eighty years of age, do you think that God gives a greater reward to the one than to the other? Of course not. Both are equally good in His sight.

To what may the matter be compared? To a king who engages many laborers to do his work. Among them is one who is very diligent, more so than any of the others. The king singles out this worker, draws him apart from the rest and walks with him to and fro all the day, conversing with him. In the evening, when the laborers come to get their pay, the king pays his walking-companion as much as he gives the others. Do you think the king should say to him, "You worked for only two hours and you will get paid for only two hours?" Would not the worker reply, "It is because of you that I worked only two hours?" . . . The king is God and the workers are those who labor in the Torah. Those who die young can say to God, "I would have labored in the Torah as long as the others if You had not caused me to die so young." If they do, God will say to them what Koheles said, "Pleasant is the sleep of the laborer, whether he has eaten little or much."

"But the superabundance of the rich man does not afford him a restful slumber." What does this mean? It means that the very great thinkers and scholars, even after they are dead, go on living. From the grave they continue to speak. Every time an opinion is quoted in their name, every time a thought which they produced is reproduced, their lips move. They have not died. Theirs is the only worthy and the only true immortality.

Koheles says, Chapter Five, Verse Twelve and Thirteen,

> "I have seen a deadly evil under the sun: Wealth which brings ruin to him to whom it has been entrusted. The wealth is lost in a corrupt business deal and the man is left penniless, unable to support his family."

This does not require elaborate explanation. The picture is quite clear. We read of such people in the headlines every day.

Two of the sages' comments on this verse are worthy of mention.

Rabbi Chaggai said in the name of Rabbi Isaac: Some rich men lose their wealth because of their attitude toward the poor. If a poor man meets such a rich man on the road and says, "I am hungry; help me;" the rich man refuses and says to the poor man, "Why don't you get yourself a job? Look at your legs; look at your knees; look at your fat belly; look at all that flesh on you." God says to the rich man, "Is it not enough that you have not given him anything? In addition, you are jealous of that which I have given him! Go home and read Koheles 5:13, you cold-blooded fish, and you will find out what is going to happen to you."

Sforno says: Sometimes a rich man loses his money through no fault of his own. Sometimes wicked men bring false charges against the rich man to rob him of his money; and sometimes they not only take his money but they wound or kill him as well.

Sforno's comment reflects the unhappy situation which began to develop for the Jews of Italy in the sixteenth century as the poison of the Spanish Inquisition spread over all Europe and beyond. Sforno, an Italian Jew who died in 1550, was spared living through the reign of the evil Pope Paul IV, 1555-1559, who brought economic ruin to the Jews of the Papal States and instituted a religious Reign of Terror that did not end until Napoleon's army took Pope Pius VI prisoner in 1798 and broke down the gates of the Roman ghetto.

Koheles says, Chapter Five, Verse Fourteen,

> "Just as one comes naked from the womb of his mother, in like condition does he set forth on the return journey; he carries nothing with him which he has acquired through his earthly labors."

Again Koheles returns to the theme with which his book began: "Vapor of vapors, everything is vapor." Life is a mystery beyond man's comprehension. Ambition is worthless. Be content with your portion. This is all that man knows and, presumably, all that he needs to know.

It was taught in the name of Rabbi Meir: When a infant comes into the world, it comes with its little fists clenched, as though to say, "All the world belongs to me." When a man departs from the world his hands are relaxed and unclenched, as though to say, "I am taking with me nothing that belongs to the world."

The sage Geniva said: Human beings may be compared to the fox who discovered a vineyard full of luscious grapes.

He wanted to get in to eat the grapes but he could not do so because the vineyard was inclosed by a very high fence. Finally, the fox found a hole in the fence. When he tried to get through the hole, he was too big and it was too small. So he fasted for three days until he was thin enough to crawl through the hole. After he got into the vineyard, he ate so many grapes that he was soon as fat as before. When he decided that he had had enough and he wanted to leave the vineyard, he was too big to go back through the hole. So again he had to fast for three days in order to get out of the vineyard. When he finally was able to get out, he turned toward the vineyard and said, "Vineyard, vineyard! how good you are and how good are your fruits. Everything about you is pleasant; but there is no permanence to your goodness. When one takes leave of you, he takes with him no more than he brought." The wise Geniva concluded: This is also the way of life and the way of the world.

Koheles says, Chapter Five, Verse Fifteen,

"This, too, is a deadly evil: He leaves with exactly what he had when he arrived; how profitless and fruitless have been his labors."

The only commentator who states in plain and precise language the plain and precise meaning of the verse is ibn Ezra: The deadly evil is that all earth-people come into life naked and go out of life naked; and so what profit have they gained from all their meaningless efforts?

Koheles says, Chapter Five, Verse Sixteen,

"All his life man eats in darkness and is greatly troubled by anxiety and frustration."

Koheles Rabba amends the text to make it read, "All his life man walks in darkness." Whether the Midrashist meant to do this or whether it was a copyist's error is difficult to determine because there is no other passage in Koheles Rabba where the writer suggests a rewording of the Biblical text. However, the emendation is a very good one and makes excellent sense—so maybe the compiler of Koheles Rabba slipped it in to show his independence of judgment.

Ibn Ezra accepts the text as it is and comments: Man does not eat his main meal in the daytime but after dark. The reason is that, during the day, he is so busy working to make a living and to pile up money that he feels he should not spend much time on eating. Because of the way he drives himself, his life is filled with anger, resentment and fear.

Koheles says, Chapter Five, Verse Seventeen,

> "It is my opinion that what is best for a man is to eat and to drink and to get what satisfaction he can out of all his labor that he labors under the sun; for this is his earthly lot, whatever be the number of days of life that God has apportioned to him."

Twice before, in Koheles 2:24 and 3:13, Koheles has expressed this identical opinion. In both previous instances, neither Talmud nor Midrash makes any comment. Now, once again, as Koheles sets forth his hedonistic evaluation of life, Talmud and Midrash remain silent. But ibn Ezra does not maintain silence. He says: This is the third time that Koheles has expressed this same sentiment. In this instance the sentiment is called forth by the previous thought that a man takes no more with him when he goes than he had when he came. So there is absolutely no reason for a man to acquire earthly wealth except in order to sustain himself and to have a good time.

Koheles says, Chapter Five, Verse Eighteen,

> "And, as for him to whom God gives money and property and the ability to be sustained by them and who accepts his lot and is happy in his work, such a one has received a special gift from God."

In Hebrew, the words translated here as "who accepts his lot" mean literally "who carries his lot." Therefore ibn Ezra says that these words refer to the staff of authority which the rich man carries in his hand. In ibn Ezra's opinion, the translation "who accepts his lot" is inappropriate because it has the connotation that a rich man is just as badly off as everyone else. He feels that this is not so, that the situation of a rich man is a good one and that he deserves no pity or sympathy. This conviction was undoubtedly heightened by the fact that ibn Ezra lived in extreme poverty most of his life. However, in the light of the statements about the difficulties of the rich made by Koheles earlier in this chapter, there is little doubt that Koheles means to say here that a wealthy man who has every possible material advantage must still be content with his situation and must derive satisfaction from what he does if he is to be happy.

Koheles says, Chapter Five, Verse Nineteen,

> "He does not give much thought to the brevity of life, because God keeps him busy doing those things which bring him pleasure and satisfaction."

Ibn Ezra translates the first part of the verse differently. His translation of the verse is: "He remembers that the days of his life are few; therefore, God keeps him busy doing those things which bring him pleasure and satisfaction." In order to arrive at this translation, it is necessary for ibn Ezra to rearrange the Hebrew words of the Biblical text.

Whether or not ibn Ezra is correct is a matter of opinion. I prefer my translation to his for two reasons: 1) It does not do violence to the Hebrew text. 2) Considered in conjunction with the thought expressed in the verse which precedes it, it makes better sense than does ibn Ezra's translation.

6

This chapter considers two matters. In Verses One to Nine, Koheles discusses the situation, which he says "one encounters very often," of the man who has been blessed with great material wealth and comfort and yet remains completely dissatisfied. His dissatisfaction is not caused by any desire to improve the quality of his mind or the state of his relationship with God. He exhibits no inclination to enrich himself mentally or spiritually. He is just a lost soul.

The concluding verses of the chapter, Verses Ten to Twelve, deal with a different subject. They teach that man's life is predetermined to such a very large extent that it is quite useless for man to try to achieve a wisdom or a station which lies beyond his given capacity. Koheles almost implies that he believes man to be a mere automaton, with no freedom of action whatsoever. It is clear from other sections in his book that he does not really hold such an extreme position. He intimates here, too, that which he has already stated quite bluntly in Verse Three of Chapter Four, that man would probably be better off if he had never been born. He also states that it is completely impossible for anyone to pierce the veil of the future and to determine the sort of world which will exist after he is dead.

Rabbi Abraham ibn Ezra does not agree that this chapter contains two separate sections. He maintains that Chapter Six is an organic unity, that all twelve verses are concerned with the same subject, i.e., the discontented rich man. Ibn Ezra's comments on this matter will be recorded at the appropriate places in this presentation so that the reader may judge for himself wheher or not ibn Ezra's contention is correct.

Koheles says, Chapter Six, Verses One and Two,

> "There is an evil situation which I see under the sun, an evil situation which one encounters very often. This is the predicament of a man to whom God has given riches and property and honor and whose every material want is satisfied; and God does not permit him to enjoy his good fortune; but a man with whom he has nothing in common will enjoy it; this is vapor and a disastrous affliction."

Sforno offers the following interpretation: This refers to a rich man who gets no pleasure from his riches in his lifetime. After he is dead, his wealth is not inherited by any blood relative but goes to one who is completely unrelated to him. There are many who do not appreciate what they have; it is their attitude which Koheles regards as "vapor." There are some rich people who hate their relatives so much that they leave their wealth to strangers; and it is this which Koheles describes as "a disastrous affliction."

At first reading, Sforno's interpretation may seem to make sense; but, on further examination, it does not hold up. It is true that, if a rich man were to hate his relatives to such an extent that he would bequeath his property to a stranger, this would, indeed, be a grievous and "disastrous affliction" for the relatives, so grievous that they would probably go to court to try to prove that their deceased kinsman was mentally irresponsible when he made this humiliating decision. However, the implication of the words of Koheles is that the "disastrous affliction" is in the mind of the rich man, in his thoughts about what is going to happen to his wealth after he is dead. It is not only his relatives whom this rich man hates. He hates everybody. He is dismayed by the idea that, after he is dead, his property will be in the hands of someone, no matter whom, who will get enjoyment from it, his property which he has gathered together with great effort and yet which gives him no satisfaction. It is quite conceivable that such a miserable misanthrope, if and when he is convinced that the day of death has come, might try to destroy all that he owns, so that no one, neither relative nor non-relative, will ever benefit from it.

Even though Sforno may not have grasped the full significance of the passage, he certainly attempted to interpret it in a way that fitted into the message and mood of Koheles. This is not true of the Talmudic and Midrashic interpretation. The Talmudists found, in Koheles 6:1-2, proof that one who knows Gemarra is far superior to one who knows merely Bible, Mishna and the Tosephta. They said it indicates that proficiency in the legal portions of the Talmud is preferable to mastery of the homiletical, theological and philosophic portions, a not uncommon attitude among the religious atavists of our own generation. But, even as today, there were scholars in Talmudic times who disagreed with this point of view.

Rabbi Levi was a lecturer in the academy at Tiberias, the academy headed by famed Rabbi Jochanan bar Nappacha. Rabbi Levi was well-known as an Aggadist, i.e., an authority on ethical and philosophic problems. No Halachos or laws are quoted in his name, which would seem to indicate that he was not considered an expert in legal matters. This gives added import to the following story, told in Tractate Horayos of Talmud Yerushalmi and repeated in Koheles Rabba:

Rabbi Abba bar Kahana made a long journey in order to visit the academy at Tiberias. While he was there, he attended a lecture by Rabbi Levi and heard him explain the meaning of Koheles 6:2. Rabbi Levi explained it as follows: "This is the predicament of a man to whom God has given riches"—

knowledge of Bible—"and property"—knowledge of Mishna
—"and honor"—knowledge of Tosephta—"and whose every
material want is satisfied"—knowledge of the decisions of the
great sages, like Rabbi Akiba and Rabbi Chiya bar Abba and
Rabbi Hoshaiah and Bar Kappara (these are tannaim who
taught in various academies in Palestine from about 100 to 220
CE)—"and yet God does not permit him to enjoy his good fortune"—he does not have the power and ability to teach law and
to make legal decisions—"but a man with whom he has nothing
in common will enjoy it"—i.e., one who, in addition to having
mastered all the scholarly material already mentioned, also
knows Gemarra. He who is learned in the Gemarra is a Baal
Talmud, a Master of the Talmud. He and he alone has the
ability and authority to teach law and to make decisions on
matters of religious law. . . . After the lecture, Rabbi Abba
bar Kahana kissed Rabbi Levi upon the head and said, "If
I had gained nothing more from my long journey than the
knowledge you have just given to me, it would be enough."

So Rabbi Levi, the Master of Aggada, taught that one who
is a Master of Halacha is more important than he. This conclusion was contested vigorously by Rabbi Ishmael, an amora,
in his interpretation of Proverbs 28:11: "The rich man is wise
in his own eyes"—this refers to a Master of Halacha—"but
the poor who has understanding gets to the root of the matter"
—this is a Master of Aggada. Rabbi Ishmael shows by this
statement that, in his time, the legalist was held in higher esteem than the theologian and philosopher. Yet he decries the
egotism and intellectual superficiality of the Halachist and
praises the Aggadist as the real Master who emphasizes the
spirit rather than the letter of Jewish tradition.

Redal seeks to soothe the wounded spirits on both sides
of the question by declaring that the Baal Talmud, in his own
way, is as deep a thinker as the Baal Aggada, but the average

person prefers the Baal Aggada because he understands the words and meanings of the Baal Aggada more easily and quickly.

Koheles says, Chapter Six, Verse Three,

"If a man begets a hundred children and lives many years and yet is never satisfied with what he has and, in addition, does not have a decent burial, I declare that an aborted fetus is better off than he."

The phrase "and lives many years" appears twice in the Hebrew text, in phrases written one right after the other but using different Hebrew words. In all likelihood, the second was a marginal comment which, by error, was incorporated into the text by a later copyist. It is not reasonable nor necessary to force both phrases into the English translation, as so many translators have done.

It is the custom of the Bible, states ibn Ezra, to use round numbers, such as ten and one hundred and one thousand, when it wishes to speak in broad terms. That is the significance of the phrase "begets a hundred children." The text does not literally mean a hundred children. It simply means "many children."

The force of the phrase "does not have a decent burial" would seem to be that the discontented rich man who dislikes everybody is, in return, so disliked by everybody that nobody comes to his funeral.

As Rashi points out, Verses Four and Five explain why the fate of an aborted fetus is to be preferred to that of a discontented and despised rich man. The fetus is better off because, before it is considered a living creature, it appears and disappears and, therefore, never experiences worry, pain or misfortune.

Koheles says, Chapter Six, Verse Four,

> "For it comes with the mist and departs with the darkness and in the darkness its remembrance is swallowed up."

The fetus comes in the morning and goes with the evening and is forgotten, a poetic way of portraying the brevity of its earthly appearance. Koheles Rabba says: No candle is lighted over it and it is not bathed, i.e., no funeral customs of any kind are observed for an aborted fetus.

Koheles says, Chapter Six, Verse Five,

> "It never really comes to life. Is not the lot of the fetus better than that of the discontented rich man?"

The literal translation of the Hebrew text is: "It never sees or knows the sun. This one has more peace than that one." The translation as given conveys Koheles' thought more clearly than the literal translation.

Ibn Ezra comments: The fetus, which does not see the light and knows nothing, is at rest because it does not have to concern itself with the matters of the world; but the rich man, who sees the light and has knowledge and yet does not have peace of mind, labors without satisfaction and without pleasure in the worlds of life and death, i.e., he has no happiness now and none to look forward to in the future.

The Midrash says: Rabbi Pinchas taught the meaning of "Is not the lot of the fetus better than that of the discontented rich man?" by means of the following parable:

Two men took a voyage on a ship. When they reached the harbor at their destination, one remained on the boat and the other visited the city and saw there many kinds of food and drink and other good things. When he returned to the ship, he said to his companion, "Why did you not visit the city?"

The other replied, "You visited it. What did you see?" "Oh, he said, "I saw all manner of food and drink and good things." "Did you personally partake of and personally enjoy these delights?" "No," he said. "Then," said his companion, "I, who did not visit the city, am better off than you for I did not see and I did not enjoy or refuse to enjoy and so I have nothing to regret."

Koheles says, Chapter Six, Verse Six,

"If one live a thousand years twice over—and does not enjoy living?!! . . . Does not everyone and everything eventually reach the same destination?"

How does one put into a translation a shrug of the shoulders and a helpless lifting of the hands? This has been attempted here through the use of a string of dots. The string of dots in the middle of the sentence symbolizes a shrug of the shoulders and a helpless lifting of the hands.

Koheles says, Chapter Six, Verse Seven,

"All the discontented rich man's labors are for his mouth; and yet his appetite is never satisfied."

In attempting to explain this verse, Talmud, Midrash and exegetes deliver dissertations on how man's mouth gets him into so much trouble that he has to store up good deeds during all his earthly life in order to win eternal life.

The only one who interprets the verse rationally is ibn Ezra: Koheles is amazed that one can be so foolish that he does not see any good in anything and that he spends all his time working to keep himself alive and would remain unsatisfied if he owned all the wealth and all the food there is in the world.

Koheles says, Chapter Six, Verse Eight,

> "What advantage does a discontented rich man, even
> though he be worldly wise, have over a rich fool or over a
> poor man who has learned how to cope with his lot?"

Koheles Rabba asks: Who is "the poor man who has learned
to cope with his lot?" And answers: He is the poor man who
becomes a street pedlar or goes into a modest business or becomes a professional beggar and, with the help of God, makes
a living.

Ibn Ezra comments: Rich wise men, like fools, are usually
only interested in making as much money as they can. The
poor man soon learns that the only way he may get along is
by avoiding those who are both rich and worldly wise and by
playing along with the rich fools, i.e., by outsmarting those who
are both richly stupid and stupidly rich. . . . Quite possibly,
ibn Ezra was giving this advice on the basis of his lifelong
battle with poverty and his efforts to get support from the rich
for himself and his writings.

Koheles says, Chapter Six, Verse Nine,

> "It is better to be satisfied with what one has than to
> strive to satiate one's appetite, which is a vapor and a grasping
> at the wind."

Ibn Ezra links the preceding portion of the chapter to the
part which follows by interpreting this verse to mean: One may
be worldly wise and yet not really wise. The really wise are
those who are satisfied with what they have and who do not
strive to attain the impossible.

The Talmud arrives at other interpretations by translating
the verse in somewhat different ways. Rish Lakish said: Looking
at a beautiful woman is more pleasurable than making love to

her, as Koheles 6:9 says, "It is better just to look than to strive to satiate one's appetite." Rish Lakish was a giant of a man and had extraordinary physical strength. His singular statement leads one to ponder upon the circumstances that gave rise to such a sentiment in such a man. Perhaps he said this when he was quite young and inexperienced and, as the saying goes, did not know his own strength. Many pretty girls are scared of rough, young, big men whose emotions are not sufficiently well controlled. Or perhaps he said this when he was quite old and experienced but, as the saying goes, time had changed many things. Men do ultimately reach a stage where memory takes over but, as the saying goes, one is never too old to look.

Another translation and interpretation came into being as a result of a rabbinic discussion of Deuteronomy 8:3 and 8:16. In these passages, the Torah says twice that God fed the Israelites manna in the wilderness in order to afflict them. Manna was a miraculous food. It had the property of tasting like anything the eater wanted it to taste like. So how is it possible for the Bible to say that the Israelites were afflicted by having to eat manna?

Ammi and Assi, famed amoraim who were on the Tiberias faculty in the time of Rabbi Jochanan bar Nappacha, had a discussion. Rabbi Ammi said that the affliction was that, except on the day preceding the Sabbath, the people were given only one day's supply of manna at a time. They could never be sure that they would be fed again on the next day. Ammi said that a person who has a reserve supply of food has more peace of mind than a person who does not have a reserve supply of food. Rabbi Assi, a Babylonian who had migrated to Palestine, said that the affliction was that, since the manna did not look like what it tasted like, eating it was a not altogether satisfactory experience, for, as Koheles 6:9 says, "It is good to see what one eats when one strives to satisfy one's appetite." The blind do not get the pleasure from eating that sighted people get because the blind do not see their food.

Abbaya, c.280-338, head of the academy at Pumbedita, continued the train of thought of his fellow Babylonian, Rabbi Assi: Since sight helps one to enjoy his food, one should eat only in the daytime. . . . The majority decided that one might eat at night, provided that one ate by candlelight and not in the darkness. It was explained that the reason why Jews are bidden to have lighted candles in their homes on the Sabbath is because, if one were not able to see the Sabbath food he is eating, the Sabbath would not be a pleasure. The affliction with regard to the manna was part of the disciplining and testing the Jews had to undergo in order to make them worthy to receive the Torah. But now that the Torah has been received, it is quite in order for the Jews to enjoy themselves and very much in order for them to see what they are eating on the Sabbath. Therefore, Jewish homes are well illuminated on the Sabbath.

Koheles says, Chapter Six, Verse Ten,

"The nature and fate of man were determined long ago; and man lacks the power to contend with the One Who is mightier than he."

The Midrash explains that this verse refers to Adam. At the time God created Adam, the ministering angels around God's throne were confused because God made Adam in His own image and Adam looked like God and so the angels thought that Adam was another God. They began to sing hymns of praise to the new god. What did God do? He caused Adam to fall into a deep sleep. This made the angels realize that Adam was not like God because, Psalm 121:4, "He Who guards Israel does neither slumber nor sleep."

Rabbi Hoshaiah said: To what may the matter be compared? To a king and his aide who were travelling through the country in the king's coach. The people of a city through which they were passing wanted to serenade the king; but they did not know which of the gentlemen in the coach was he. What did the king do? He pushed his aide out of the coach. Then everyone knew who was the king and who was the aide. So it was with God and Adam. When the angels started to worship Adam, God quickly demonstrated Who was Boss.

Yafe Toar says: It is not possible to believe that the angels, who were created before man and who were consulted regarding man's creation, could have confused man with God. They saw that man has a form and a body and how could they possibly compare him to One Who has neither form nor body? The Midrashic passage does not mean to ascribe such ignorance to the angels. It means, rather, that the other creatures of Earth thought that man was a god and so they started to worship him. When God caused Adam to fall into a deep sleep, the other creatures recognized that he was not a god but one who, like themselves, came from mud and would return to mud.

The exegetes translate Koheles 6:10 in a number of ways. Rashi translates it: "At the end of life, the importance and greatness and power which an individual has acquired is pushed aside and he is treated as a mere man like all other men and he dies like all other men and he is not able to contend with the Angel of Death who is stronger than he."

Ibn Ezra, who believes that the whole chapter is a unity, translates: "A man is what he is, no more and no less; so why should he try to be like somebody else whom he thinks is more important than he is and whose station in life he will never be able to reach? A really wise man will not enter into contention with a situation which is so much bigger and stronger than he is and he will not try to become something he is not meant to become."

Sforno's translation is: "Whether a man is to be rich or poor is predetermined; it is known that man is but a creature of the dust; he will not be able to prevent whatever has been decreed concerning him by One Who is stronger than he."

Koheles says, Chapter Six, Verse Eleven,

> "The many attempts to prove that this is not so has produced only worthless confusion. What possible advantage can man obtain from refusing to face the truth?"

Since there is no feeling among the traditional interpreters that Verses Ten to Twelve form an organic unit, their comments do not reflect the relationship of these verses to each other. Ibn Ezra continues to relate the verses to the preceding section. The others give Verse Eleven an indpendent explanation.

Ibn Ezra says: This verse continues the thought of Verse Eight that "the discontented rich man, even though he be worldly wise" has no advantage over "a poor man who has learned to cope with his lot." The poor man has learned that it is well for him not to strive for those goals which he cannot hope to achieve. In this he is smarter than the rich ones who are so full of material lust that they try to get as much money and power as they can and who want every desire fulfilled. They do not realize how insignificant all this is. It is just so much vapor being pursued by creatures who themselves are nothing but vapor.

The others mistranslate Verse Eleven as: "There are many things being done which are useless. Of what possible benefit are they to mankind?" They misinterpret the verse accordingly.

Some of the Midrashists, presumably those who were not animal lovers, declared that the raising of certain animals was among the "many things being done which are useless." Rav Huna expressed opposition to the raising of monkeys, cats and pigs. Koheles Rabba, with like intent, proscribed the existence of monkeys, cats, porcupines, wild dogs and "mountain men..' These "mountain men" were fierce mythical creatures whom some said were animals that looked like men and others said were a unique kind of human beings who grew up right out of the earth by spontaneous generation without the intermediation of father or mother. Their flesh is not to be used by mankind because of the fear that such use might be cannibalistic. These creatures are very dangerous. They wound, kill and eat the human victims of their fury. One notes the close resemblance between this "mountain man'" myth and that of the Himalayan "abominable snow man." Rashi adds this comment: There are many creatures in which kings delight and which they collect in abundance, such as monkeys, elephants and lions, which have no lasting benefit. . . . Koheles would have disagreed vigorously with the ideas expressed in this paragraph. He could not possibly have said what these translators and interpreters try to make him say. Koheles states his own opinion about all created things clearly in Chapter Five, Verse Eight, "Those things in the world which seem to be superfluous have a definite place in the world plan."

Rabbi Jochanan bar Nappacha said that this verse refers to those who cannot speak without exaggerating the truth and, because of this, cause trouble for mankind and bring rebuke and punishment upon themselves. People exaggerate, he said, for various reasons—they are trying to gain a position of greater importance or they want to get someone else into trouble or they seek to avoid the penalty of wrongdoing—and their exaggerations usually bring about a result which is exactly the opposite of what they desire to accomplish.

Koheles Rabba also says that this verse applies to individuals who lack a social conscience and consideration for the feelings of their fellow men. For example, there is the property owner who clears the rocks from his field and throws them out onto the public highway. Those who pass by cut their feet by stepping on the rocks or bruise themselves by stumbling against the rocks. Of what possible benefit to mankind are individuals who display such little regard for others? There is a story about a farmer who was throwing the stones from his field onto the public road. A God fearing man, who was passing by, said to him: "Why are you taking stones that are not on your property and throwing them onto your property?" The wrongdoer laughed. He thought the God fearing man was joking. Some time later, the stone-thrower was badly in need of money and had to sell his field. As he walked along the public road, he stubbed his toe against a rock and hurt his toe badly. He said to himself, "Now I know that the God fearing man was not joking." . . . This is a good story to meditate upon as you drive your car. The next time you are behind the wheel and are tempted to beat the traffic light, try to imagine how you would feel and react if you were the pedestrian.

Koheles says, Chapter Six, Verse Twelve,

"No mortal really knows whether man receives any benefit from the experience of living through the days of his fleeting life, days which are as insubstantial as a shadow; no one can tell anyone what will happen under the sun after he is gone."

Ibn Ezra brings to a close his argument that Chapter Six is a unity: This verse is also connected with the thought in Verse Eight that the worldly wise rich man has no advantage over the poor man who has learned how to cope with his lot. No one knows whether it is better in life to be rich or to be poor, since life itself seems to be so meaningless and insubstantial. It does seem that one is not able to perfect himself in spiritual matters until he gives up the quest for material wealth. Yet one who concentrates on spiritual matters can no more be absolutely sure that he is acting properly than a rich man can be sure that, after he is gone, his heirs will use his wealth properly. The whole point of the matter is that all that man really is given to use on earth is time. Most men are very much concerned about how they shall spend their allotted time, as wise man or fool, as rich man or as poor man. But time itself is a very shadowy substance and disappears quickly after it has been spent, no matter how it has been spent. So, in the final analysis and in the long run, it would seem to make very little difference how a particular individual expends his limited share of earthly time.

Other commentators do not share ibn Ezra's somber pessimism. Rabbi Pinchas says, in Koheles Rabba: Since man's days are limited and inconsequential, what can be more important for man in this transient life than studying the words of the Torah, which represents Life Eternal? For so it is written, Proverbs 3:18, "Divine Wisdom is a Tree of Life to all who lay hold of her and those who cling to her are happy."

The sages ask: Is it true that "no one can tell anyone what will happen under the sun after he is gone?" It is not entirely true, for Koheles himself says, in the very next sentence, Koheles 7:1, that "a good name," a good reputation, a good remembrance, is "of more worth than precious oil." The most substantial treasure that a father can leave to his children is a good name.

7

In order to convey to the reader a reasonably accurate reproduction of the thoughts and ideas that were in the mind of the original writer, an acceptable translation must meet exacting intellectual as well as linguistic standards. The ability to translate literally from one language to another is not enough. The meanings of many words are fraught with implications and nuances which are difficult to reproduce in translation. Unless the translator is able to capture, in some measure at least, these implications and nuances the reader will get an imperfect reproduction of the message which the original writer was trying to deliver.

This challenge to the translator is quite marked in the Book of Koheles. The book is written in a cryptic Hebrew which is typical of the Mishna rather than of the Bible. It was intended for the intelligent and well informed Jewish Palestinian of the second pre-Christian century who did not need to have every contemporary thought spelled out. Therefore, much is implied rather than stated, presumably because the writer was confident that his audience would comprehend fully. Koheles, a wise but humble man, had not the slightest intimation that his book would still be read with admiration and respect more than two thousand years after he wrote it and would number among its readers many Jews and non-Jews, living amid varying cultural and historical circumstances in many parts of the world. Since he could not know this, he did not write his book with such a larger audience in mind. He wrote only for his own time and his own countrymen. Consequently, those translators who have tried to reproduce the thoughts of Koheles for readers far removed from the time and place of Koheles by translating his words literally have fallen far short of providing an acceptable translation.

The translation of Koheles which is being presented here is not a literal translation of the Hebrew text and is not meant to be. It is an attempt to mirror the thoughts of Koheles without doing unnecessary violence to his words. Undoubtedly, there are a number of passages in this translation where the translator has failed to say exactly what Koheles wanted said. It is quite likely that the old professor might have disapproved strongly of the way in which some of his teachings are being interpreted in this translation and commentary. On the other hand, there is also a good possibility that he would have been very pleased with a translation and commentary which attempts to get to the heart of his doctrines and to present his point of view in a form which seeks to avoid absurdities and to reconcile seeming contradictions. He probably would have dismissed with a scornful grin the ways in which narrow-minded dogmatists have twisted and distorted many of his thoughts and his words. He might not have been quite so unconcerned about the products of more liberal and objective scholars who, translating his words literally, have given him the appearance of being a disorganized, irrational, sensual old fuddy-duddy who made some interesting observations about the state of humanity and fashioned some quotable bons mots but whose philosophy is so confused and contradictory that it does not merit serious consideration.

Chapter Seven may be divided into three sections: Verses One through Six, Verses Seven through Twenty-two and Verses Twenty-three through Twenty-nine.

Verses One through Six deal with the life-goal of the individual. The life-goal of the individual should be to establish a good reputation. This is accomplished by seeking the company of the wise rather than of those whose only interest is in having fun.

Verses Seven through Twenty-two offer some very practical advice to the scholarly: Avoid fraudulent dealings and bribes. Be patient. Maintain your self-control. Do not pine for the "good old days." Accept the present as it is, with whatever satisfactions it may have to offer. If you are wealthy, recognize how lucky you are and enjoy your good fortune while it lasts. Do not think you are rich because you deserve to be rich. The wicked often prosper; the good often suffer. Why? Only God knows. Do not be excessively pious or cunning or too worldly or too much of a clown. Exercise moderation in all things. Wisdom is man's best friend. But even the most wise are not always smart and not always right. There is no one living who never makes a mistake. Do not take to heart the spiteful words people say about you. Just as sometimes you make unkind statements about others, so, too, others will, from time to time, say unkind things about you.

Verses Twenty-three to Twenty-nine discuss the rarity of sound thinking. Koheles has tried very hard to think clearly, although he is not at all satisfied with the results. The past and the future are as much of a mystery to him now as they were when first he began his investigations. He has tried without success to "understand the logic back of providential rewards and punishments and to comprehend the basic nature of human wickedness, human stupidity and insane folly." One discovery he has made: Women were put on earth to breed and to keep house and to give comfort to man in his leisure hours but not to think. Thinking is for men only. Even among men, the ability to think straight is very rare. Not more than one man in a thousand can think straight. "The other nine hundred ninety-nine go rummaging for the truth in the most fantastic ways."

Koheles says, Chapter Seven, Verse One,

> "A good name is more valuable than precious oil; the day of death is better than the day when one was born."

"A good name is more valuable than precious oil."

Koheles Rabba asks: Why is a good name more valuable than precious oil? And answers: Because precious oil can only flow downward and for a very limited distance, perhaps as far as from the top of the head to the bottom of the beard; a good name can flow upward and there is no limit to the heights it may reach. Precious oil travels only from the dressing room to the banquet table or the dance floor; a good name travels from one end of the earth to the other. Precious oil lasts but for an hour; a good name lasts forever. Precious oil costs money; a good name cannot be bought. Precious oil is only for the rich; a good name is within the reach of everyone. Precious oil is used only by the living; a good name is of worth to both the living and the dead. . . . . To this list Sforno adds: Precious oil is only material and only skin-deep; a good name, acquired through study and good deeds, is both material and spiritual and permeates all that one is and does.

Rabbi Simon ben Yochai taught: There are three crowns, the crown of the Torah, the crown of the priesthood and the crown of rulership; but the crown of a good name excels them all. Koheles Rabba points out that one of the proofs for this statement is that, for long periods in Jewish history, there has been neither a Jewish State nor a Holy Temple and sometimes there has been little or no knowledge of the Torah, but at no time in Jewish history has a good name ceased to be held in high esteem.

Rabbi Meir said: Every person is called by three names: One is given to him at birth by his father and mother; the second is the nickname that is given to him by his friends; and the third is the name that he acquires for himself through his deeds, good or bad. Most important of all three is the name that he acquires for himself, as it says, "A good name is more valuable than precious oil."

When Rabbi Meir finished studying the Book of Job, he told his students that the book had taught him these truths: Both men and animals are destined to die. Each has Divinely predetermined tasks to fulfill during its lifetime and after its death. The animal puts on a physical yoke and is used as a beast of burden and for ploughing; the man puts on a spiritual yoke and serves humanity through study of the Torah and good deeds. After the animal has completed its schedule of work, it rounds out its usefulness by being slaughtered so that its body may be used as material food. After a man has finished the earthly course designed by his Creator and has given satisfaction to his Creator, he dies and leaves as his memorial a good name which gives spiritual nourishment to the righteous who live after him.

Ha-rif, Isaac Alfasi, commenting on this statement by Rabbi Meir, says: Rabbi Meir did not mean literally that a man who lives a good life gives satisfaction to God. From the point of view of the philosopher, how can it possibly be within the power of puny man to please or displease Almighty God? The Talmudic text needs to be emended. It should not say that a good man gives satisfaction "l'Yotsro," to his Creator. It should say that the good man gives satisfaction "l'yitsro," to his own inner nature, to himself. When we speak of being accountable to God, we are speaking figuratively. What we really mean is that we are accountable to ourselves to do the very best we can with what we are and what we have. God's Will and

God's Law will take care of our accountability to Him; our love of God and our obedience to His Will and His Law will take care of our accountability to ourselves.

The Talmudic report of the words of Rabbi Meir includes the following sentence: "Happy is the man who creates a good name for himself and leaves behind this good name when he departs from the world." A medieval writer interprets this sentence in this way: Rabbi Meir talks of one who has created a good name for himself rather than of one who enjoys the privilege of having a good name. There are those who obtain wealth, honor and greatness early in life and, thereafter, have a good name. For such a one his good name is no proof that his conduct is blameless; many attain the status of princes who are full of all manner of evil and who even blaspheme God because of the false sense of power given them by their wealth, their position and the flattery they receive. Yet they have a good name among men, even though they do not deserve it. But one whose greatness comes to him because of his good name and nothing else is different. It has nothing to do with the amount of money he has or his power but only the steadfast righteousness of his conduct. He is beloved by God and by his fellow men. Only such as he possess the genuine good name. There are some who are good when they are young and who grow up with a good name, but, because of the great respect accorded them by society, acquire vanity and pride, and sully and sometimes even destroy their good name. To preserve one's good name, one must act righteously all his life. That is why Rabbi Meir says that the good man is not only he who has created a good name for himself but also he who "leaves behind this good name when he departs from the world." His goodness must be an unbroken goodness from the beginning to the end.

"The day of death is better than the day when one was born."

Koheles Rabba says: When one is born, everyone is happy. When one dies, everyone weeps. It should not be so. It should be just the opposite. When one is born, there should be no rejoicing because it cannot be known what kind of life-record the newborn infant will make for himself. But, when one who has a good name dies, all should rejoice, because he has gone forth triumphantly and has left the world better for his having been here. Two seagoing ships once passed each other in the bay of a Mediterranean port. One was leaving the harbor and the other was entering the harbor. On the ship which was leaving the harbor everyone was rejoicing and on the boat which was entering the harbor everyone was sad. A wise man who was present said, "It should be just the reverse. Those aboard the ship leaving the harbor should not rejoice; they do not know if there is sufficient food aboard or how many severe storms they will encounter. On the ship returning to the harbor, all should rejoice because the voyage has been completed safely and peacefully." So it is with life and with death.

When a person is born, they begin to count the number of days likely to pass by before he dies. When a person dies, they count the number of days of his life during which he accomplished some good. To finish life with nothing more to one's credit than so many years, months and days is to have served a boring and meaningless prison sentence. To finish life with many good deeds to one's credit is really to have lived.

When a righteous person is born, no one knows it and no one feels it. When a righteous person dies, everyone knows it and everyone feels it.

The philosopher Joseph Albo wrote: Koheles said that "the day of death is better than the day on which one was born" because, on the day of death, man completes the learning process which began on the day of his birth. On the day of death, that which at birth was only potential becomes wholly actual. At birth the physical properties of man are already quite perfect but his intellectual qualities are not. At the moment of death, his physical qualities have become weak but the summit of his intellectual capabilities has been reached.

Koheles says, Chapter Seven, Verse Two,

> "It is better to go to a house of mourning than to a banquet, since death is the final destination of all and the living should keep this always in mind."

Koheles Rabba says: "It is better to go to a house of mourning than to a banquet" because the pursuit of true wisdom is to be found in the house of mourning. One who mourns has removed himself from the frivolous pursuits of this world and is thinking about his own ultimate destiny, about the day of his own death. In consequence, his love of Torah and of God and his devotion to good deeds are strengthened, temporarily at least. Oftentimes, in periods of mourning, past quarrels between the dead and the living and even between the living and the living are settled peacefully, whereas a banquet is likely to be an occasion for starting a new quarrel rather than for putting an end to an old one. Visiting those who mourn is more spiritually satisfying than attending a banquet for a number of reasons: The first is a benevolent deed; the second is not. The first concerns the living and the dead; the second concerns only the living. The first affects both the rich and the poor; the second affects only the rich. The first is an act which brings comfort and consolation; the second is an act of a less noble sort.

Maharshaw says: Koheles is, of course, referring to the kind of banquet in which only pleasure is involved and in which the performance of a Mitsva is not involved. It is a Mitsva, for example, to go to a marriage feast. As a matter of fact, the Talmud states, Kesubos 17a, that a funeral procession must make way on the street for a marriage procession and both of them must make way for the king.

Jacob Reicher, chief rabbi of Metz, France, from 1716 to 1733, in his Talmudic commentary, *Iyun Yaakov,* written after he was cured of blindness in 1730, says: The implication in the comment of Maharshaw is that a wedding takes precedence over a funeral. This is not so. The opposite opinion is stated many times in classical Jewish literature. Maimonides declares, in his treatise on mourning customs, that "he who has the obligation of preparing for both a wedding and a funeral must give the matter of taking care of the dead precedence over taking care of the needs of the bride." Other traditional sources state that, when a funeral procession and a wedding procession meet, the wedding procession must give way to the funeral procession.

A saying of Rabbi Simon bar Abba, quoted in Midrash Tanchuma, supports Rabbi Reicher. Simon bar Abba says: If one is required to show honor to a bride and to the dead at one and the same time, which takes precedence? Koheles 7:2 settled that question. It is better to go to the house of mourning than to the house of feasting. One shows honor to the dead before showing honor to a bride.

The words of Rashi in his Biblical commentary on this verse also support this position: If one is faced with the choice of going to a wedding or a funeral, he should go to the funeral. He will have other opportunities to show his respect for the persons who are getting married; but this will be his last opportunity to show his respect for the person who is being buried.

"Death is the final destination of all and the living should keep this always in mind."

Mishna is the term for the law code compiled about 200 CE under the direction of Rabbi Judah the Prince. Many tannaitic opinions which were not included in the Mishna have been preserved. Such opinions are known technically as *Baraisa,* which means "excluded." Here is an opinion of Rabbi Meir which has been preserved as a Baraisa: What is the meaning of the phrase "The living should keep this always in mind"? The living should keep the inevitability of death always in mind. In matters connected with death, one must show others the kindnesses which he expects others to show him. Attend the funeral of others as others will attend your funeral. Act as a pallbearer for others as others will carry you. Wail at the passing of others as others will wail for you. Accompany the dead to their last resting place as others will accompany you. Help fill in the grave for others as others will fill in your grave for you. . . . Rashi adds: Do not say, "I will not go to his funeral because he is no relative of mine," but say, "I shall go and I shall mourn for him as I hope that many not related to me will come to my funeral and mourn for me."

Rabbi Mana, a Palestinian amora, said: The text, literally translated, means "The living should put this thought next to his heart." It means that the righteous carry the thought of death right next to their hearts. This explains why those who pray beat their breasts over the heart when they recite the Viddui or confessional prayer.

Koheles says, Chapter Seven, Verses Three to Five,

"Righteous indignation is better than meaningless laughter; when the face is sad, the heart is good. The mind of the wise is in the house of mourning; the mind of the fool is in the house of mirth. He who listens to the rebuke of the wise will be better off than he who listens to the singing of fools."

One of the earliest references to the professional rivalry between the rabbi and the cantor, a rivalry which has been a marked feature of synagogal life for many centuries, is found in the comment of Koheles Rabba on Verse Five. Koheles Rabba asserts that listening to "the rebuke of the wise" refers to the Darshanim, the lecturers, the rabbis who interpret the Torah in the synagogue, while listening to "the singing of fools" is an unkind allusion to the Chazanim, the singers, the cantors who chant the Aramaic and Greek translations of the Torah readings in the religious services. Redal says that one of the reasons cantors are criticized is because they lengthen the services by adding piutim, medieval religious songs, to the fixed order of the prayers. Ibn Ezra also complains about the insertion of piutim into the service. He seems to have been especially irked by the poems of Eleazar Kalir, famed medieval liturgist of unknown time and place, whose songs, ibn Ezra felt, were ungrammatical and irrational.

Rashi remarks that the thoughts of the wise are tempered by their constant awareness of the coming of death. Fools give no thought to the day of death and have no fear of it. Psalm 73:4 says of the fools, "They are not concerned about death because their bodies are sound," i.e., they only begin to think and to worry when they get sick.

Koheles says, Chapter Seven, Verse Six,

> "As the crackling of burning twigs under a boiling pot is the meaningless laughter of a fool."

Sforno comments: The simile is a very good one. Twigs which burn under a copper pot in which meat is being cooked achieve the following results: In the course of the burning, they destroy themselves, they blacken the pot and they cook the meat. Likewise, the meaningless laughter of a fool ends in:

The destruction of the fool, the wasting of the time of the listener and, for a brief time, a pleasurable reaction for the listener. Just as the sun spoils the meat unless the meat is eaten soon after it is cooked, so the enjoyment created by foolish laughter is of short duration and contains nothing of lasting value.

Koheles says, Chapter Seven, Verse Seven,

"Fraudulent dealings make fools of the wise; and a bribe corrupts the mind."

The obvious meaning of the verse is that one who engages in questionable business practices or whose vote or opinion is for sale cannot be regarded as an honest, just or wise man.

The traditional Jewish interpretation is that Koheles is speaking of the complete objectivity which a student of the Law must possess in order to be a genuine scholar. The standards which are set are very high. Who is the genuine scholar? Koheles Rabba states: The majority voted that a genuine scholar is one who has mastered a subject so thoroughly that he can answer any question about it. Rabbi Abbahu said in the name of Rabbi Jochanan: A genuine scholar is one who neglects all worldly matters in order to study. There were those who translated the first part of the verse as follows: "If a scholar busies himself with too great a variety of scholarly matters, he loses his scholarly ability." Others translated this passage: "A scholar who busies himself in community matters loses his sense of scholarship," i.e., he does not have sufficient time to study. Rashi comments: This is true of a scholar who takes part in community affairs which are in the nature of the fulfillment of Mitsvos; how much the more is it true of a scholar who takes part in community affairs which have nothing to do with the fulfillment of Mitsvos.

Koheles Rabba adds: Another circumstance which sometimes causes a scholar to lose his sense of objectivity and to forfeit his claim to genuine scholarship is to have a quarrel with another scholar.

Koheles says, Chapter Seven, Verse Eight,

"The end of a matter is better than its beginning; better is patience of spirit than haughtiness of spirit."

"The end of a matter is better than its beginning."

Jewish tradition associates this saying with the story of Elisha ben Abuyah.

Elisha ben Abuyah is one of the most enigmatic characters in Jewish history. He lived in the second century CE, during the period of the Bar Cochba rebellion and the Hadrianic persecutions, was an associate of Rabbi Akiba and the much beloved teacher of Rabbi Meir. At some point in his career, as a result of his study of non-Pharisaic literature, he abandoned the Pharisaic ways of observing the ceremonial law and, thereafter, he was labelled a heretic by his former colleagues and was given the opprobrious nickname of "Acher," meaning "that other one." The Pharisees, enraged by the defection of such a great scholar, filled their literature with all kinds of charges against him: He spied for the Romans against the Jews, he forced yeshiva students to abandon the study of the Torah, he was mentally unbalanced by excessive preoccupation with mysticism, et cetera, et cetera. Surprisingly, Rabbi Meir's deep and unshakeable admiration for his old teacher was also allowed to stay in the record. It is impossible to believe that such a loyal Jew as was Rabbi Meir would have remained so devoted to Elisha if all the charges listed against him in the Talmud had been true.

In their attempts to explain Elisha's abandonment of Pharisaism, later scholars have labelled Elisha variously: Sadducee, Gnostic, Neo-Platonist, Judeo-Christian. The latter label is, by all odds, the most plausible. The great Talmudic scholar, Jacob Z. Lauterbach, has pointed out that Elisha lived during the time when the final split took place between the Judeo-Christians and the synagogue. Until the Bar Cochba revolt, many Judeo-Christians were still affiliated with the synagogue. But, after 132, when Akiba and many others declared that Bar Cochba was the long awaited Messiah, the Judeo-Christians abandoned the Jewish people because of the Judeo-Christian belief that Jesus the Galilean was the Messiah.

In all likelihood Elisha ben Abuyah became a Judeo-Christian prior to the Bar Cochba rebellion, when Judeo-Christians were still to be found among the Jewish people and in the synagogue. Elisha ben Abuyah was not his real name. As Dr. Lauterbach has stated, in the Hebrew this name may be read as "El Yesha ben Abu Yah," meaning "the God Jesus, son of God the Father," a pseudonym given Elisha by his Pharisaic detractors to conceal his real name. Since the only references to Elisha are in Pharisaic writings, there is no way to find out what his real name was. Elisha's disdain for the great emphasis placed by the Pharisees on the ceremonial law was typical of the attitude and teachings of the Judeo-Christians.

Why was the story of Elisha ben Abuyah and Rabbi Meir included in Koheles Rabba at this particular point? There are at least two reasons: The mention of Koheles 7:8 in the story; and Rabbi Meir's belief that Elisha, before he died, became a Baal Teshuva, a penitent, abandoned Christianity and returned to Judaism. There may also be a third reason: A hint from the compiler of Koheles Rabba to those who study Koheles that a spirit of skepticism and free inquiry has always been part of historical and normative Judaism from the time of the prophets to the present, and that Judaism, unlike its so-called daughter-religions, Christianity and Islam, has no long, black record of mistreating, robbing, stabbing, burning and beheading those who refuse to conform to the superimposed norm.

The explanatory remarks are concluded. And now to the story:

One Sabbath day, Rabbi Meir was teaching in the academy in Tiberias. He was told that his former teacher, Elisha ben Abuyah, out for a ride on his horse, was about to pass by the academy. Rabbi Meir went out and greeted his old teacher. As Elisha continued to ride through the city and into the country, Meir walked by his side. Elisha said to Meir, "What Biblical passage were you expounding just now?" Meir said, "Job 42:12, 'The Lord blessed the end of Job more than his beginning.'" "And how did you interpret it?" "I told my students that it meant that Job became twice as wealthy as he had been before misfortune struck." Elisha responded, "Your teacher, Rabbi Akiba, would not have said that. He would have said that God blessed the end of Job more than his beginning as a recognition of the spirit of humility and good deeds that marked Job's life from the very beginning." Meir then asked, "How would you explain Koheles 7:8, 'The end of a matter is better than its beginning?'" Elisha replied, "Tell me how you explain it." Meir answered, "The meaning of the verse is: There are men who go into business when they are young and fail but, as old men, they prosper in business. There are men who, when they are young, have children and the children die and then, as old men, they have more children and the children live. There are men who do evil when they are young men and in their old age do good. There are men who study Torah in their youth then forget it, but who return to the study of Torah in their old age." "Your teacher, Rabbi Akiba, would not have said that," commented Elisha. "He would have said that a matter which has a good beginning will have an even better ending."

Elisha continued, "This axiom applies in my case. I face an unpleasant end because I had a bad beginning. My father, Abuyah, who was among the great men of his generation, invited all the outstanding citizens of Jerusalem, including Rabbi Eleazar and Rabbi Joshua, to attend the feast celebrating my circumcision. When the group present had eaten and drunk much wine, some of them sang frivolous songs and others recited alphabetic acrostics. Rabbi Eleazar said to Rabbi Joshua, 'This may be some people's idea of how to have a good time but it is not our idea.' Then they began a Biblical discussion which was so animated that sparks flashed on all sides, as when the Torah was given at Sinai. My father was so impressed by the brilliance of their presentation that he said, 'I vow that if this son of mine, who is being circumcised this day, is spared to me, I will dedicate him to the Torah.' Because my father's vow was not without selfish motivation and was not completely pure, my efforts have not served to strengthen the Torah."

And so Elisha and Meir continued to discuss the meaning of Biblical verses, as together they went out of the city and into the country, Elisha on horseback and Meir trudging alongside. After they had proceeded for a short distance into the country, Elisha suddenly said, "Go back. This is as far as you can go. We have reached the Sabbath limit." (The Pharisees had set a 2000-cubit limit to the distance which one might journey beyond the edge of the city on the Sabbath. A cubit was a measure which varied between eighteen and twenty-two inches. Therefore, the maximum distance afforded by the 2000-cubit limit would have been about three-fourths of a mile. However, Rabbi Meir interpreted the location of "the edge of the city" somewhat more liberally than did the majority of his scholarly colleagues. According to Rabbi Meir, as his opinion is cited in Eruvin 5:2, the edge of the city begins 2000 cubits beyond the last city building, whether inhabited or uninhabited. According to the majority, it begins with the last inhabited dwelling.) "How do you know that we have reached the limit?" Meir asked. Elisha replied, "I have been counting the steps of my horse and we have already gone two thousand cubits." Meir stopped and said, "Why not respect the Sabbath limit and return with me to the city? How can a person as keen-witted as you not want to be part of the mainstream of Jewish tradition?" Elisha replied, "Even if I should want to do so, I could not." "Why?" asked Meir. Elisha answered, "During last Yom Kippur, which happened to fall on the Sabbath, I was riding my horse past the ruins of the Temple on Mount Zion. I heard a Bas Kol, a voice from the sky, say: "The Biblical verse, Malachi 3:7, 'Return to Me and I will return to you, says the Lord of hosts' applies to every Jew except Elisha ben Abuyah, for he knows My power and yet he has rebelled against Me.'

What caused Elisha to rebel against God? One story is that, on the Sabbath, while Elisha was sitting and studying in the valley of Kinneres in Galilee, he watched a man climb to the top of a palm tree, take a mother bird from her nest of little chicks, an act forbidden in Deuteronomy 22:6-7, and come down from the tree and go away safely. After the Sabbath was over, he saw another man climb a palm tree, remove the chicks from a nest but leave the mother bird, a procedure approved by Deuteronomy 22:6-7. As this second man climbed down from the tree, he was bitten by a snake and died immediately. Elisha said to himself, "The Torah says, in Deuteronomy, that the first man committed a sinful act and will be destroyed, and the second man, who acted properly, will become prosperous and live many years. Where are the prosperity and long life which were promised? Where is the justice of God and the truth supposed to be contained in the Torah?" ... There are others who say that Elisha rebelled against God when he saw Roman soldiers kill the great sage, Rabbi Judah the Baker (it is presumed that this was Rabbi Judah ben Baba), cut out his tongue and feed it to a dog. Elisha said, "If such can be the end of a tongue which spent all its life teaching Torah, it is ridiculous to believe that the righteous are rewarded either in this life or any other." ... There are still others who say that Elisha's fate was sealed before his birth. While his mother was carrying him in her womb, she passed by a Christian church while a service was in progress, smelled the incense that was being burned, went in and took holy communion and, as a result, her whole system was poisoned as though she had been bitten by a venomous snake. (This last bit of ridiculous and malicious folklore is included here to show that in the time Koheles Rabba was written, perhaps as early as the Eighth Century, the prevailing theory was that Elisha ben Abuyah had been a Judeo-Christian.)

Some time later, Elisha became very ill. Meir came to visit him. Meir said to him, "Come back to us." Elisha replied, "How can anyone whose heresy is as extensive as mine be taken back?" Meir said, "Is it not written, Psalm 90:3, 'God accepts the repentance of man until the end,' until life is completely extinct?" When he said this, Elisha started to weep and, as he wept, he died. Meir rejoiced and said, "I believe that my teacher fully repented before he died." After the funeral of Elisha, a fire came down from heaven and set fire to his grave. Meir was told, "The grave of your teacher is burning." Meir went and spread his Tallis, his prayer shawl, over the grave. He stood beside the grave and prayed: "Dear God, it is my earnest hope that, in the world to come, You will give Elisha a place among the righteous; but, whether

You do this or not, I shall always number Elisha among the righteous and shall give him the honor due a righteous man." As Meir prayed, the fire over the grave died away.

His disciples asked him, "Rabbi, in the world to come, if they ask you: 'Whom do you seek, your father or your teacher?' what will you reply?" Meir said, "I will ask first for my father and then for my teacher." Again they asked, "And will your request be granted?" Meir replied, "Is it not written that we preserve a box because of the manuscript which it contains, that we keep the Tefillin bag because of the Tefillin it holds? In like manner, Elisha will be preserved because of the Torah he taught."

Rabbi Meir prayed that the soul of Elisha be sent to Gehinnom and then, after twelve months of purification, be admitted to Gan Eden. He asked that, if his request were granted, this be made known to him by a pillar of smoke rising from the grave of Elisha. Shortly thereafter, a column of smoke was seen above the grave. Rabbi Meir was filled with gratitude. "Koheles spoke the truth when he declared that 'the end of a matter is better than its beginning,'" Meir said.

"Better is patience of spirit than haughtiness of spirit."

This saying furnishes Koheles Rabba with an excuse for telling another story: A Parsee once came to Rav, 175-247, head of the yeshiva at Sura in Babylonia. (Parsee is another term for Zoroastrian. Zoroastrian beliefs concerning life after death strongly influenced the development of similar beliefs among the Pharisees. In 226, the Sassanian Persians conquered the Parthians and established Zoroastrianism as the state religion of Babylonia. The Parthians, an illiterate and crude people, had treated the Jews very well. The Persians, well educated, artistic, religious fanatics, were very cruel toward the Jews, who were regarded as religious rivals. The Persian dynasty in Babylon was overthrown by the Muslim Arabs in 640.) The Parsee said to Rav, "Teach me the Torah." Rav said, "Say Aleph." The Parsee began to argue, "How do you know that this is an Aleph? Perhaps it is not an Aleph." Rav said, "Say Bes." The Parsee again wanted to know, "What makes you certain that this is a Bes?" Rav became very angry and sent the Parsee away. The Parsee then went to Mar Samuel, 180-257, head of the yeshiva at Nehardea. He said to Samuel, "Teach me the Torah." Samuel said to him, "Say Aleph." The Parsee began to argue, "How do you know that this is an Aleph?" Samuel said, "Say Bes." The Parsee asked, "What makes you certain that it is a Bes?" Samuel grabbed the Parsee's ear and pinched it. The Parsee yelled, "Ouch! My ear! My ear!" Samuel said, "How do you know that that is your ear?" The Parsee replied, "The whole world knows that this is my ear." "And likewise," said Samuel calmly, "the whole world knows that this is an Aleph and this is a Bes." The Parsee immediately ceased acting like a child and received the proferred instruction in the proper spirit. Some time later, he converted to Judaism. As Koheles said, "Better patience of spirit than haughtiness of spirit." Had Samuel not been forbearing, the Parsee would have retained his erroneous religious beliefs and practices.

Sforno comments: Even if one who is slow to anger is also slow to forgive, such a person is to be preferred to one who gets angry quickly and who forgives quickly.

Koheles says, Chapter Seven, Verse Nine,

> "Do not allow yourself to get so angry that you lose your self-control, for that kind of anger is the mark of the fool."

Rabbi Yudan said: There are two proverbs which describe this situation very well. The first proverb: When a kettle boils over, the boiling liquid pours over the kettle's own exterior.

So it is with a person who, in anger, loses his self-control. He hurts himself more than he hurts anyone else. The second proverb: He who is so foolish as to spit straight up should not be amazed when the spit falls back on his own face. He who gets angry without cause should not be surprised if he is the one whose reputation is damaged.

Koheles says, Chapter Seven, Verse Ten,

"Do not say: How is it that the olden times were better than the present? A wise person will never make such a remark."

This same subject has already been discussed in the commentary on Chapter One, Verse Four. A few additional comments by the exegetes are worth recording.

Rashi says: Each generation gets the kind of leadership and the kind of peace and prosperity that it deserves.

Ibn Ezra says: This verse is a warning to the wise man to be satisfied with his lot, even if he is poor, as Koheles has already indicated in Chapter Six, Verse Eight. (Koheles 6:8 seems to have been ibn Ezra's favorite verse in Koheles.) It warns the wise not to strive to acquire more money than he actually needs and not to fret because there are fools who have more money than he has. He should live in the here-and-now and should never long for "the good old days," as do fools whose importance has diminished or who have lost their money and whose world has gone topsy-turvy because they do not have sufficient intellectual and spiritual strength to bear up under all conditions and circumstances. The intelligent person knows that all times are essentially alike and the people and the conditions under which people live are, in all generations, essentially the same. The exact circumstances under which any particular individual lives in any particular generation are entirely a matter of chance.

Koheles says, Chapter Seven, Verse Eleven,

> "The wise man who lives on inherited wealth is better off than any other earthly being."

Koheles Rabba translates and interprets this verse in two ways.

First translation: "It is good to be wise and, at the same time, to have inherited a business." Interpretation: Wisdom which is accompanied by an inherited business is a fine combination. As Rabban Gamliel, the son of Rabbi Judah the Prince, said in Pirke Avos: Excellent is the study of the Law when combined with a worldly occupation, for working in both the realm of the spiritual and the realm of the worldly keeps sin from entering one's mind. To engage in the study of the Law without also engaging in worldly labor is without lasting benefit and brings sin in its wake.

Second translation: "Wisdom is good when it is accompanied by the protecting influence of one's ancestors." Interpretation: Wisdom which breaks too radically with tradition is no good. Tradition serves as a steadying influence. Happy is he who is strengthened by the meritorious influence of his fathers and who is enlightened by it.

The comment of ibn Ezra strikes a very practical note: The wise man who lives on inherited wealth is fortunate because those of his generation who do not respect him because of his wisdom will respect him because of his wealth.

Koheles says, Chapter Seven, Verse Twelve,

> "One is protected by both his wisdom and his wealth. The advantage of having great wisdom is that it continually invigorates those who possess it."

Talmud Pesachim 53b states that "One is protected by

both his wisdom and his wealth" means that one who uses his money to support scholars and charitable enterprises has earned for himself as much merit as the scholars and institutions that he supports. Rabbi Jochanan said: Everyone who uses profits from his business to help scholars has won for himself the right to enroll as a student in the Academy on High. Rashi, in commenting on this passage, says: One who makes it possible for a Talmid Chacham, a scholar, to earn a livelihood and also to study will be greatly honored. The benefactor, even though he devotes his time solely to business, may receive a spiritual reward as great as the reward of those who apply themselves both to business and to scholarship.

Talmud Sabbath 63a reports that Rabbi Simon ben Lakish said: He who loans another person money is more worthy than he who gives charity. He who makes it possible for another to earn a livelihood by taking him into his business as a partner is even more worthy. Most worthy of all is he who takes a scholar into his business as a partner and who spends his time taking care of the business while the scholarly partner devotes his time to study.

Rashi says, in his Bible commentary: Anyone who lives under the shadow of wisdom also lives in the shadow of wealth, i.e., anyone who decides to use his wisdom to acquire wealth can do so. But wisdom, in and of itself, will accomplish more than wisdom with wealth. Wealth deadens wisdom. Without wealth, wisdom invigorates and inspires.

Ibn Ezra translates the concluding part of the verse as "Great wisdom gives life to those who possess it" and then comments: The basic difference between wealth and wisdom is that wealth is material and transitory, while wisdom is the form of the highest spiritual essence and does not die when the body dies.

Koheles says, Chapter Seven, Verse Thirteen,

> "Consider the way of God: Who is able to straighten out that which He has made crooked?"

A similar statement by Koheles in Chapter One, Verse Fifteen, has already been explained. Ibn Ezra offers this further comment: Let the wise man who has neither inheritance nor money rejoice in his wisdom and not be angry because he is poor. His lot was decreed from the very moment of Creation. One must accept his lot as he accepts the will of God. If it has been decreed that one is to be lacking in money or anything else, there is no use complaining. This is the way it was meant to be and this is the way it is going to be.

Koheles says, Chapter Seven, Verse Fourteen,

> "Enjoy a period of prosperity while it lasts and, in the time of adversity, consider the way of God; God causes these inexplicable opposites to exist in order that man may realize his ignorance of ultimate verities."

Rabbi Tanchum bar Chiyya was an amora who taught in Palestine from about 250 to 280 and Rabbi Tanchum bar Chanilai was a Palestinian amora who taught a generation later. Rabbi Tanchum bar Chiyya (and some say it was Rabbi Tanchum bar Chanilai) translated the first part of Koheles 7:14 as follows: "In time of prosperity, do that which is right and consider the possibility that a time of adversity may come." Rabbi Tanchum's philosophy was that the rich should help the poor so that, if the rich should ever become poor, others who will then be rich will come to their aid. In keeping with this point of view, Rabbi Tanchum, whenever he went to the market to buy meat or vegetables or any other kind of food, would buy twice as much as he needed and give half to the poor. He is said to have learned this practice from his mother. His mother taught him that Exodus 22:24 "The poor are with you" means that poverty is an ever present threat to everyone. Therefore, in all circumstances, the rich and the poor should be helpful to each other.

Rashi says that the phrase "in order that man may realize his ignorance of ultimate verities" means that man should never seek to determine the ultimate intention of the Holy One, blessed be He.

Ibn Ezra teaches: Why should the rich man gloat over something which will not endure? He should get what pleasure he may out of his wealth but he must always remember that a day of adversity is likely to come. Koheles teaches this same lesson later in Chapter Eleven, Verse Nine, with a different emphasis but with the same ring of truth: "Rejoice, young man, in your youth"; have fun while you can, because you may not always have it so good. The intent of Koheles 7:14 is that everything belongs to God and everything eventually returns to God; so why should man complain, no matter what be his lot, and why should man seek to comprehend life situations which he will never be able to understand?

Koheles says, Chapter Seven, Verse Fifteen,

"It seems fruitless to me to discuss why a completely righteous person dies young, while a completely evil person lives beyond the normal span of years."

Neither Talmud nor Midrash have any comment to make on this verse beyond repeating the rationalization of the "old time religion" that all good people go to Heaven, regardless of how long they have lived on earth, and that really bad people sometimes live long on earth in order that they may receive, here and now, all the rewards coming to them for whatever good deeds they have to their credit in order that, when at last they die, God can really let them have it for all the wicked things they have done. Ibn Ezra is more astute. He makes no attempt "to unscrew the inscrutable" except to offer his explanation as to why some righteous people die young: Some righteous young people bring on their early demise by excessive asceticism; while some very wicked people live on and on, eating, drinking, having a good time and enjoying every sort of sensual delight.

Koheles says, Chapter Seven, Verse Sixteen,

"Be not overly righteous nor overly cunning, unless you want others to avoid associating with you."

In discussing the phrase "Be not overly righteous," Koheles Rabba gets to the heart of the matter quickly and simply: Do not be more righteous than God. Do not pass judgment where God has not passed judgment.

Ibn Ezra comments: If one prays from morning to night and afflicts himself and the like, as do the Christian and Muslim monks, he departs from the accepted social pattern. This is also true of those who are always trying to outsmart their fellow men. Both of these patterns of conduct will be avoided by persons possessing a normal mentality and a normal ethical sense.

Koheles says, Chapter Seven, Verse Seventeen,

"Do not concern yourself too much with worldly affairs; do not play the fool; why should you die before your time?"

The literal translation of the first part of this verse is "Do not be overly wicked." Such a translation does not make sense, Would Koheles have been willing for people to be deliberately but moderately wicked? Of course not. The Midrash says that Koheles meant that, if a person has committed a wrong once, he should not do so a second time. This is a rather weak interpretation. The translation and explanation of ibn Ezra are more acceptable.

Ibn Ezra says: The wickedness referred to in this verse is that of busying oneself too much with worldly affairs. Koheles says, Don't be a fool. Spend only as much time on worldly affairs as is necessary to make a living. Spend the rest of your time in study and meditation. "Why should you die before your time?" The folly of attaching too much importance to petty worldly matters causes a man to die before his time. The tension and the ulcers and the high blood pressure acquired by those who lack the ability to distinguish between the important and the unimportant cause them to die before their time.

Sforno translates and interprets the Hebrew text altogether differently: "Do not be excessively cruel"—Do not be unduly harsh on the wicked. If a criminal has been condemned to receive forty lashes, see that he gets forty lashes and no more. "Do not play the fool"—Do not turn aside completely from worldly affairs, even to busy yourself in Torah and Mitsvos. "Why should you die before your time?"—If you do not give due place to the supplying of material wants, you will not succeed materially or spiritually.

Koheles says, Chapter Seven, Verse Eighteen,

> "The best way to live is to interest oneself in spiritual concerns but also to give a proper place to material concerns; he who truly fears God will not allow either the one concern or the other to become his master."

Ibn Ezra: All that is expected of the righteous man is that he follow the laws and commandments set forth in the Torah.

Sforno: It is God's intention that man shall give a proper place in his life to both spiritual and material considerations.

Koheles says, Chapter Seven, Verse Nineteen,

> "Wisdom gives more protection to a wise man than ten city magistrates."

The Midrash relates this verse to the sin of Adam. It says that the proper exercise of his intelligence would have prevented Adam from incurring Divine displeasure. Instead he relied upon the mechanical actions of ten of his bodily organs and they got him into trouble. There are two lists of these ten organs in the Midrash and another in the Talmud. I have not attempted to figure out the exact relationship of each organ to the Adam and Eve story nor have I consulted any medical authorities to discover whether or not there is scientific warrant for any of the statements of the Midrashists. From Biblical times to the present, classical Jewish literature has displayed a keen interest in psychosomatism. There has always been a firm belief that certain emotions and actions are controlled by bodily organs fashioned to produce specific stimuli or responses. For the edification of all and the use of that reader who may desire to do further research in the "science" of Midrashic psychophysics, here are the Midrashic lists of the bodily organs, together with the supposed capabilities and effects of each.

Koheles Rabba 7:19:1 states that the ten bodily organs which were responsible for Adam eating the fruit from the Tree of Knowledge were: 1. The throat (used for receiving food); 2. The windpipe (for producing sound); 3. The liver (for producing anger); 4. The gall bladder (for producing jealousy); 5. The lungs (for producing good feeling); 6. The first stomach (for "grinding" or dissolving food); 7. The spleen (for producing laughter); 8. The kidneys (for producing deep thought); 9. The heart (the seat of intelligence); and 10. The tongue (which brings together the work of all the other organs).

A somewhat different list is given in Vayikra Rabba 4:4 and Midrash Tehillim 103:1: 1. Throat (sustenance); 2. Windpipe (sound); 3. Liver (anger); 4. Lungs (for drinking); 5. First stomach (dissolving food); 6. Spleen (laughter); 7. Second stomach (for producing sleep); 8. Gall bladder (jealousy); 9. Kidneys (deep thought); and 10. Heart (which brings together the work of all the other organs).

A much more simplified list is given in the Talmud in Nedarim 32b. Here it states that the ten "magistrates" are the two hands, the two feet, the two eyes, the two ears, the head of the penis and the mouth. Rashi, in his Biblical commentary, expands on the Talmudic statement. He says: "The ten 'magistrates' that get man into trouble are his two eyes, which show him sinful things, his two ears, which cause him to listen to unimportant matters, his two hands, that rob and do violence, his two feet, that lead him into evil places, his mouth and his heart." Significantly, Rashi omits the penis from his list and substitutes the heart. In the writing of Koheles, the heart is synonymous with the mind but, in most of Jewish classical religious literature, the heart is considered to be the seat of the emotions. In drawing up his list, Rashi certainly intended to give the influence of the heart an emotional rather than a rational role.

It is noteworthy that the reproductive organs are not mentioned in the Midrashic lists and that Rashi excluded such a mention from his list. The Midrashists believed that the sin committed by Adam and Eve was that of disobedience to God's command and was not connected, in any way, with the sexual act. Sexual relations between male and female are regarded by the Midrash, as well as by Bible and Talmud, as being normal and natural, pleasurable and good. There is no taint of evil in the sex act per se. Properly motivated and used, it is beneficial to the individual and to society. Uncontrolled and abused, it is harmful to both the individual and society. Rashi may not have included the sexual organs in his list because of a belief that these bodily mechanisms are not really masters of their own destinies or responsible for their actions. They obey mechanically the desires and demands of the eyes, the ears, the hands, the mouth and the heart.

The comments of ibn Ezra and Sforno reflect accurately what Koheles had in mind when he wrote this verse. Ibn Ezra says: Koheles again emphasizes the importance of wisdom, which is greater than any other earthly quality, possession or power. Sforno says: Wisdom gives the intellect the power necessary to control the emotions.

Koheles says, Chapter Seven, Verse Twenty,

"There is no one on earth so perfect that he always does the right thing and never does anything wrong."

Ibn Ezra comments: This is an amplification of the assertion of Koheles in Verse Sixteen, "Do not be overly righteous." No one is perfect. Everyone makes mistakes either in deed, in speech or in thought, as Proverbs 6:16-19 says: "There are six things that the Lord hates, yes, seven which are repugnant to Him: Haughty eyes, a lying tongue, and hands that shed innocent blood; a heart that devises wicked thoughts, feet that are swift in running toward evil; a false witness who breathes out lies and he who sows discord among brethren."

An important statement in connection with this verse appears in Albo's *Sefer Ha-Ikkarim*, Book Four, Chapter Seven: In many places in Jewish tradition, the prophets and the scholars complain about the prosperity of the wicked and the affliction of the righteous. Despite all that has been written, these two situations are not comparable. The complaint about the prosperity of the wicked is justified and is very difficult to explain away. Everyone can see with his own eyes that there are wicked people who are idolatrous and immoral and murderous and violent and openly defiant of God; and yet, despite all this, they prosper. This causes mankind to doubt the justice of Divine Providence. However, the matter of the righteous who suffer does not present this same difficulty, because all sins are not revealed to the eyes of man. Everyone knows that, as Koheles says, "There is no one on earth who is so perfect that he always does the right thing and never does anything wrong," whether his wrongdoing be occasional or habitual. If a seemingly righteous man gets into serious trouble, none should be surprised. It can be said that he has sinned secretly in a way known to none but God. He is being punished openly for that which he did in secret; or perhaps his thoughts have been sinful. It is clear that none can really judge who is sinful and who is not. Man knows only what his eyes see and, on this basis, he decides that a certain person is righteous; while God, Who can look into the heart, may know that this person is not righteous but evil. . . .

If Albo had followed his train of thought to its logical conclusion, he would not have taken it for granted that the wicked are wicked because, in the eyes of men, they appear to be wicked. He would have taken "the leap of faith" in fullest measure and would have concluded that there is a possibility that, in the sight of God, "sub specie aeternitatis," many whom man considers wicked are not wicked at all but are quite righteous. Reason by itself can supply no credible solution to this riddle. Reason linked with faith gives a satisfactory and satisfying answer.

Koheles says, Chapter Seven, Verse Twenty-one,
"Do not take to heart everything people say about you, or else you will hear your own servant curse you."

Ibn Ezra says: The advice of Koheles to the wise is: If you wish to have peace of mind, do not pay atttention to every remark people make. If you do, you will get angry and lose your sense of objectivity. You will make false accusations and mistreat those around you; and your own servant will curse you.

Sforno translates the verse as follows: "Do not take to heart everything people say about you, even when you hear your own servant curse you." You should not get excited even when your own servant curses you. He is cursing you because of his inferior mentality, his low social status and his tedious tasks. He is reacting emotionally rather than rationally.

Koheles says, Chapter Seven, Verse Twenty-two,

> "You know that there have been many times when you have cursed others."

Ibn Ezra: Even if you have not cursed others out loud, such phrases have risen to your lips or been in your thoughts.

Sforno: This happens whenever one allows his emotions to get control over his intelligence. Recognize that, whenever this occurs, you sink to the intellectual level of your servants.

Koheles says, Chapter Seven, Verse Twenty-three,

> "I have attempted to approach all this with wisdom; I said to myself, 'I must think clearly'; and yet I feel that I am as far away as ever from the ultimate truth."

Koheles Rabba: The only way to approach any matter is with wisdom. There is a proverb: He who lacks wisdom owns nothing; he who owns wisdom lacks nothing. Explanation: A sharper can relieve a fool of everything that he possesses; a wise man, by using his knowledge, can get almost anything he wants.

Ibn Ezra: Koheles is saying: Everything which I have said, I have tried to say wisely. I have endeavored to become ever more wise but I find this very difficult. It is of little use to try to become overly wise, for it is impossible for man to comprehend or to understand more than God wants him to comprehend and understand.

Sforno: No matter how hard man may try, it is not within the capabilities of his limited mind to decipher the way or the mind of God.

Koheles says, Chapter Seven, Verse Twenty-four,

"That which happened long ago is completely gone and which will be is buried in mystery. Who can hope to uncover either the past or the future?"

Ibn Ezra comments: There are those who think they can unearth the secrets of the past. It is of no use to attempt to discover that which no longer exists. Koheles says that what lies ahead is equally unknowable. It is as useless to try to penetrate the nonexistent future as it is to try to dig into the nonexistent past.

Koheles says, Chapter Seven, Verse Twenty-five,

"My mind has sought in every possible way to understand the logic back of providential rewards and punishments and to comprehend the basic nature of human wickedness, human stupidity and insane folly."

Rashi gives his interpretation of Verses Twenty-three through Twenty-five: "I have attempted to approach all this through wisdom"—through study of the Torah. "That which happened long ago is completely gone"—The secrets of Creation are completely incomprehensible. "That which will be is buried in mystery."—No human mind can understand what is above or below or what has happened in ages long past or what will happen in future ages. Even such a comparatively simple matter as the determination of the exact time of the coming of the Messianic Age is beyond the ability of man. "My mind has sought . . . to comprehend the basic nature of human wickedness, human stupidity and insane folly"—I have tried to understand the teaching of the freethinkers and the heretics and the confused and destructive doctrines which are found therein.

Ibn Ezra, as usual, has the simple and rational explanation: I have turned my thoughts in every possible direction to find some sort of connection between human intelligence and human wickedness, stupidity and folly.

Sforno makes a gallant stab at the meaning of the verse: I have tried through study of supernatural phenomena, logic and history to discover what God had in mind when He created the world and why man is unable to exercise any control whatsoever over Nature and why, from the very beginning, Adam, Eve and the Serpent acted without fear of Divine punishment, without allowing their minds to control their emotions and without regard to the evils that would come upon them if they were influenced by heretical thoughts.

Koheles says, Chapter Seven, Verse Twenty-six,

"I have discovered that a man's relationship with a woman can be more bitter than the pangs of death, when the woman makes up her mind to ensnare the male and to get him in her clutches; one who is favored by God will escape from her but he who makes the wrong move will be entrapped."

This is one verse in Koheles about which both Talmud and Midrash have much to say. Presumably the outcry of Koheles against the wiles of the crafty female produced a sympathetic response in even the rabbinic mind. A not-so-crafty female once told me that rabbis and policemen are sexless. It is not so, ladies, it is not so.

Talmud Berachos 8a asks: What is the significance of Psalm 32:6, "For this let every one that is pious pray unto Thee: for a time of 'm'tso?' " Rabbi Chananiah said, "The word 'm'tso' is a term used for living with a wife, i.e., marriage. For so Scripture says, Proverbs 18:22, 'Matsa isha matsa tov,' 'He who has found a good wife has found a treasure.' " In Palestine, when a man got married, they asked him: "Have you found a 'matsa,' a good wife, or a 'motsey,' a bad wife?" This refers to what Scripture says, in Proverbs 18:22, where the term "matsa" is used for a good wife, and Koheles 7:26, where the term "motsey" is used for a bad wife. The Hebrew in Koheles 7:26 reads: "U-motsey ani mar mimaves es ha-isha," "I have found that a man's relationship with a wife can be more bitter than the pangs of death."

The commentary *Ahavas Eson,* written by Rabbi Abraham of Minsk, Russia, explains: Why was this question asked in Palestine and not in Babylon? Because in Palestine a man got married before he settled down to a life of study of the Torah and in Babylon he did not get married until after he had settled down to a life of study of the Torah. Study of the Torah protects one from the danger of selecting a bad wife. Therefore it was necessary to ask the question in Palestine but not in Babylon.

The Rif says: The question which the Palestinians asked the groom was a very difficult one, because it was a question which he would not be able to answer until some time after he was married. What is the sense in asking such a question of a man when he gets married? If one has married a good woman, she will remain a good woman; and, if he has married a bad woman, what can he possibly do to change her nature? In the latter case, all one can do is express one's sympathy to the husband for his misfortune. The real intent of the question is to put the groom on guard with regard to his marital obligations. The questioner is saying, in a roundabout manner, "In marriage, you may follow one or the other of two paths. One will result in a happy marriage and the other in an unhappy marriage. If you follow the precepts of religion in your marriage and live a life of goodness, you will find favor in the sight of God and your marriage will be blessed; but, if you act like a fool or like an indecent human being, your marriage will not be favored by God, your wife will turn against you and your married life will be unhappy; for no one can be more cruel than a woman who hates her husband; she can inflict tortures more terrible than the pains of death."

Talmud Yebamos 63a says: Raba bar Joseph taught: It is a Mitsva to divorce a bad wife. A bad wife is as hard to bear as a stormy day. How precious is a good wife and how evil is a bad wife! A good wife is as priceless a possession as the Torah. A bad wife is the first step on the road to Gehinnom.

The Rif asks: Why did Raba say that a bad wife is as hard to bear as a stormy day? A stormy day is a day of thunder, wind and lightning. A man who gets caught in such a storm becomes so confused that he does not know which way to turn. If he is at home when such a storm breaks out, he is like one trapped for he is unable to get out. Woe unto the man who has such a wife! If he stays at home, he gets into one argument after another with her and, if he goes out, everywhere he goes he carries with him the thought of what will be waiting for him when he returns home.

Maharshaw says: It is better to live alone in a corner on the roof than in a beautiful mansion with a spiteful woman.

Yebamos 63a continues: How does one know when he has a bad wife? Abbaya said: At the time that she has his meal ready for him, she also has her mouth ready for him. She cannot wait until he is through eating to reprove him or to give him bad news. Raba said: She gives him his meal and turns her back on him. She refuses to eat with him in order to make him miserable. She is deliberately offensive at mealtime because of an unconscious desire to make him sick and get rid of him.

Enoch ben Joseph Zundel, in his commentary *Anaf Yosef,* says: As evil as is the bad wife described by Abbaya and Raba, twice as evil is the wife who pretends to love her husband and who serves him a good meal and then undoes all the good she has done by the bitterness and the wickedness of her words.

The Midrash also has some unkind words for the bad wife.

Koheles Rabba 7:26: Part One: The rabbis say: The wife described in Koheles 7:26 is the wife who demands from her husband things which he is unable to give her. In the end she causes him to die a miserable death. The following story is told: There was a man who had a neighbor who was a thief. During the day he had a respectable job and at night he would go out and rob. His neighbor's wife said to her husband: "How did I ever have the hard luck to get married to you? What fine clothes the wife and children of the thief have! What good food they have to eat! What a fine house they have!" The man replied, "Do you want me to do what he does, to go out at night and rob people?" "So what is so bad about that?" she asked. He said to her, "O.K. Go to the thief. Be nice to him. Be so nice that, when you ask him to take me along with him tonight, he will consent." She went and she was so nice that the thief readily consented. That night, after the two men had already successfully and easily robbed some very elderly and very rich persons, other robbers came and robbed them of the money which they had just stolen. The robbers robbing the robbers created such a commotion that the police were summoned. The experienced robbers, being well versed in the tricks of the trade, fled and saved their lives. The one who was robbing for the first time in his life and who was not well versed in the business of thievery was captured and hanged. There is an appropriate proverb: He who is last among the robbers is first to be hanged.

Koheles Rabba 7:26: Part Two: Rabbi Judah the Prince said: There are fourteen things, each of which is tougher than the other and each of which lords it over the other. The Great Deep is tough but the Earth lords it over the Great Deep and conquers it. The Earth is tough but the mountains lord it over the Earth. The mountains are tough but iron is tougher and breaks the mountains. Iron is tough but fire crumbles it. Fire is tough but water is its master and quenches it. Water is tough but the clouds can contain it. Clouds are tough but the wind scatters them. The wind is tough but the wall lords it over the wind and stands up against it. The wall is tough but man lords it over the wall and tears it down. Man is tough but trouble hollows him out. Trouble is tough but wine lords it over trouble and makes one forget it. Wine is tough but sleep counteracts its effects. Sleep is tough but sickness lords it over sleep and causes it to vanish. Sickness is tough but the angel of death lord it over sickness and takes away man's life. And a bad wife is tougher than the angel of death.

Ibn Ezra says: Sexual desire blinds the eyes of the wise, distorts their thoughts and destroys their wisdom. A woman always has her heart and her mind concentrated on spreading nets to ensnare the unwary. Her arms are a prison-house for those who fall therein. For the wise man, death is sometimes preferable to yielding to sexual desire.

Sforno comments: It is as the sages say in Pirke Avos: "He who talks too much to women brings evil upon himself, neglects the study of the Torah and in the end will go to Gehinnom." When a man has been seduced by a woman, he falls into her clutches and is compelled to do her will. "One who is favored by God" will never allow himself to be enticed by a woman. "He who makes the wrong move" and allows himself to be entrapped is on the road that leads to Gehinnom.

Koheles says, Chapter Seven, Verses Twenty-seven and Twenty-eight,

"I have tried very hard to find consistency of thought or conduct in the various individuals whom I have known. Despite all my efforts, I have been unable to find more than one man in a thousand whose thoughts and actions are consistent; and among women consistency in thought and action is completely nonexistent."

Ibn Ezra comments: Koheles is still trying to emphasize that a wise man should have as little to do with women as possible. With regard to consistency, he seems to be trying to say that we may only understand something by studying its relationship to its opposite. We only understand bigness as we come to know littleness; we only know wisdom when we comprehend the nature of folly, et cetera. Nothing in and of itself is consistent and nothing in and of itself is complete. When we put together the knowledge we obtain from the study of opposites, we begin to grasp something of the nature of that which we are studying and the whole thing begins to take on a definite pattern. There is, perhaps, one man in a thousand who has the necessary intelligence, wisdom and respect for truth and knowledge to achieve this kind of intellectual synthesis in his personal philosophy and to deserve, thereby, the title of straight-thinker. This quality is found only in man. The nature of woman is such that she is unable to attain the status of straight-thinker.

Koheles says, Chapter Seven, Verse Twenty-nine,

> "I discerned that God has made this one man in a thousand a straight-thinking person, while the other nine hundred ninety-nine go rummaging for the truth in the most fantastic ways."

Ibn Ezra comments: God has given every man the opportunity to think straight but very few succeed in doing so. The overwhelming majority choose to follow the tortuous paths of fantasy rather than the straight path of truth.

8

With the first verse of Chapter Eight, Koheles concludes the discussion of true wisdom which he began in Chapter Seven, Verse Twenty-three. The truly wise man is a gracious and an humble man. Then, abruptly, Koheles starts to comment upon the wise man's relation to the king and the state. One who is a loyal subject and good citizen must obey the wishes of his king and the laws of the state. Because the king's power is absolute, the wise man will never deliberately incur the sovereign's displeasure. The law is more elastic and objective than the regal mind. Therefore, by carrying through well calculated actions at the appropriate time, the wise man can take certain liberties with the law which he cannot take with the king. This is a procedure to be essayed only by the very astute. The average person lacks the mental ability and agility necessary to circumvent the law legally.

Beginning with Verse Eight, the thoughts of Koheles take a somewhat different turn. Man does not have the power to control the forces of nature or his own ultimate destiny. But some men do have the power to rule over other men and to ruin them. Human nature is unpredictable and fickle. The public enthrones and acclaims the wicked and often ignores and forgets the righteous. Justice is not measured out quickly or fairly. Good people who have done no wrong are punished and bad people get to the very top of the social and political heaps. The dominant mood of the masses is: To cheat, rob or swindle is no crime; getting caught is the crime. He who does not get caught is a wise man; he who gets caught is a fool. And what of the idealist who wants to improve the na-

ture of man and the state of society? Koheles infers that he
is the biggest fool of all. "The best attitude to take is to regard
the world with amusement." Does God play a direct role in
what is going on down here? Koheles concludes the chapter
by saying that this is a question that the wisest of the wise
cannot answer.

Koheles says, Chapter Eight, Verse One,

> "Who beside the wise can determine the real meaning of
> a matter? Wisdom brightens the face and softens the inflexi-
> bility of the arrogant."

"Who beside the wise can determine the real nature of
a matter?"

Sforno says that this phrase is linked to the one man in
a thousand who is mentioned in Koheles 7:28. Only that one
man in a thousand is able to determine the real meaning of a
matter, because only that one man in a thousand has an intellect strong enough to control his emotions completely.

"Wisdom brightens the face."

Talmud Nedarim 49b tells that a Roman countess noticed
that the face of Rabbi Judah bar Illai was shining brightly.
Judah bar Illai was a tanna and a contemporary of Rabbi Meir.
She said to him: "Is it possible that one who teaches others
to behave properly would appear in public in an intoxicated
condition?" "My dear lady," replied Judah, "I am not intoxicated. As a matter of fact, the only times that I drink wine
are for the Sabbath blessings and on Passover. And those four
cups of wine I am compelled to drink at the Seder give me
such a headache that I have to keep a cloth wrapped around
my head every year from Passover until Shevuos. No, I am
not drunk, but, as Koheles says, 'Wisdom brightens the face.' "

Ha-rif comments: It is not proper to boast of one's wisdom and Rabbi Judah was far too wise to speak in a boastful manner. The rest of the passage in Nedarim explains why Rabbi Judah's face was shining. It is clear that Rabbi Judah did not answer the lady as he did because he wanted to boast but rather because he was trying to avoid telling her the truth. Rabbi Judah's face was normally very bright. This he attributed to the fact that he moved his bowels regularly and often. On this particular day, his face was especially bright because, as he explained to Rabbi Tarphon, he had eaten a certain variety of beets. He did not want to mention the matter of the beets to the noble lady because he did not think she would believe him and he did not want to discuss the movements of his bowels with the lady because this is not the sort of matter which a rabbi normally discusses with a countess. In addition, there is a commonly held notion that going to the toilet frequently weakens a person rather than improves him and Rabbi Judah did not want to get into an argument with the lady with regard to the relationship between euphoria and dejection.

"Wisdom softens the inflexibility of the arrogant."

Talmud Taanis 7b states: Rabbi Nachman bar Isaac said, "Despite what is written in Leviticus 19:18, 'You shall love your neighbor as much as you love yourself,' it is permitted to hate an arrogant man. This principle is stated in Koheles 8:1. This verse should not be translated 'Wisdom softens the inflexibility of the arrogant.' It should be translated 'Wisdom hates the inflexibility of the arrogant.' "

Rabbi Nachman arrived at his change in translation by emending a word in the Hebrew text from "yeshunneh," to change, to mitigate, to soften, to "yesunneh," to hate. Some scholars believe that this emendation is correct and that Rabbi Nachman restored the original text and meaning of this phrase.

Koheles says, Chapter Eight, Verse Two,

> "I say: Obey the laws of the ruler because of your sworn oath of allegiance."

Ibn Ezra comments: Having finished his warning to the wise against falling into a trap set by a wily woman, Koheles now warns the wise man against another external danger: He is not to trust in his wisdom to the extent of despising the command of his king. If he does, the king will look upon him as a fool and the king will not hesitate to get rid of him, in one way or another.

Talmud Kesubos 17a has already been mentioned in connection with the commentary on Koheles 7:2. It is fitting to quote this Talmudic passage more fully at this point because it expresses clearly the traditional Jewish principle that the ruler of one's country must be held in the highest respect: The rabbis taught: A funeral procession takes precedence over a marriage procession and the procession of a Jewish king takes precedence over both. King Herod Agrippa I, ruler of Judea from 41 to 44, once ordered a wedding procession that was about to cross his path to halt until his own procession had passed by. The sages praised him for this. They said that this is the proper way for a king to act. Rabbi Ashi said: If a prince desires to forego the honor due him, this may be done; but, if a king desires to forego the honor due him, this may not be done. For Scripture says, Deuteronomy 17:15, "You shall surely set over yourselves a king" whom you shall respect.

Bamidbar Rabba 14:6 says: If the king commands you to respect him and to obey him, do as he says, in accordance with Deuteronomy 17:15 and also Joshua 1:18, "Whosoever he be that will rebel against your command and will not obey your orders shall be put to death." Does this mean that one must obey the king even if he gives an order to transgress the word of God? No. Koheles 8:2 says, "Obey the laws of the ruler and also your oath to God." (The Midrashic interpretation indicates that the compiler of Bamidbar Rabba translated the latter half of Koheles 8:2 as referring to one's allegiance to God rather than to one's ruler.) The Scripture tells you here that your obligation to God takes precedence over the command of mortal man and that you must thwart the will of mortal man in order to carry out the will of God. You must put your loyalty to the Torah above your loyalty to the king.

After quoting Koheles 8:2, Tanchuma Noach 10 says: God has said to Israel, "If a secular authority shall impose upon you severe decrees, do not rebel against the secular authority because of the severe decrees. Only when such an authority orders you to disregard the Torah and its commandments should you refuse to obey. Say to the authority: 'I shall keep the king's laws as long as they do not contravene the laws of God.' So long as the Jewish people exists, it will never be free from the obligation of giving My commandments top priority."

Tanchuma Noach continues: The story in the third chapter of the Book of Daniel illustrates this principle. When Nebuchadnezzar ordered Shadrach, Meshach and Abednego to bow down before the idol which he had erected, they refused. When the king wanted to know why they were disobeying his order, the trio replied, Daniel 3:16, "O Nebuchadnezzar, we have no need to answer you in this matter." The rabbis point out that they do not address him as king but as Nebuchadnezzar, a mere mortal man. The implication of their reply is: "We shall obey any legitimate order which you give us in your role as our earthly ruler. Any taxes you impose upon us we shall pay. But when you ask us to deny our God and to bow down to an idol, we shall not obey. When you command us to violate a cardinal principle of our religion, we cease to be accountable to you for our actions and must make answer only to God."

Koheles says, Chapter Eight, Verses Three to Seven,

"Do not depart from the presence of the king in a disrespectful manner; do not disagree with him persistently; for whatever he wants to do, he can do. The will of the ruler must prevail. Who dares say to him: 'What are you doing?' He who obeys the law will not get into difficulty; the actions of the wise man are based on his knowledgeable calculation of the appropriate time and the appropriate law. There is an appropriate time and an appropriate law for every matter; but the average man is too empty headed to comprehend this. He is intellectually incapable of calculating when a predictable event will take place. Even after it has occurred, he cannot understand how and why it happened."

In interpreting this passage, the classical exegetes missed the boat completely. With the exception of ibn Ezra, they took it for granted that the ruler in question is God. Ibn Ezra took a somewhat more logical position. He stated that the passage is discussing both the Heavenly Ruler and earthly rulers. The advice which Koheles gives to the wise in these verses is so practical and has in it so little of the theological that it would seem to be self-evident that he had only earthly potentates in mind and was not discussing man's relationship with God. The meaning of the passage has already been indicated in the introduction to this chapter. The essence of Koheles' thinking about rulers and laws is: Because human nature is as it is, the wise man will never express publicly any vigorous disagreement with the policies of his boss. He will, on occasion and discreetly, interpret these policies in ways that suit his own opinions and his own convenience.

A comment of Koheles Rabba on Verse Three contains a

large sized grain of wisdom: When one is under the necessity of discussing an unpleasant matter with either his employer or one of his employees, or, for that matter, with anyone, he should begin and end the conversation with a "d'var tov," a compliment, a smile, a pleasant remark.

Koheles says, Chapter Eight, Verse Eight,

"Man does not have the power to imprison the wind or to control the day of death or to choose not to fight."

The concluding phrase in the Hebrew text, which means "and wickedness will not deliver the wicked in time of danger," has been omitted from the translation. It must be regarded as the interpolation of a pious editor who could not resist the temptation to slip in the thought that the wicked will get their just deserts either here or hereafter. This is so completely contrary to the opinion expressed in the remainder of this chapter as well as in the rest of the book that it could not possibly be part of the original text. An added indication that this is a later addition is that, in the Hebrew, the phrase does not fit in, stylistically and grammatically, to the rest of the sentence. The original part of the verse is written in the present tense and the added portion is in the future tense. Koheles is talking about the here and now. The pious editor seems more concerned about what is going to happen to people after they die.

With reference to the phrase, "to choose not to fight": In the Hebrew text, the literal translation of this phrase is "to be discharged from the army while the war is in progress." The inference is that the individual has no choice but to fight. He cannot go home, no matter how little his heart may be in the cause for which he is fighting, no matter how much he may be opposed to this war or any war. The average individual has no control over the making or the ending of wars.

Koheles Rabba states: The rabbis translate this verse as follows: "Man does not have the power to hold on to his breath or to control the day of death or to send a substitute in his place nor will the wickedness of the wicked save him when he faces the Heavenly Tribunal." It means that man does not have the strength to keep the Angel of Death from fulfilling his assigned mission. He cannot say to the Angel, "Wait until I have straightened out my affairs; wait until I have said 'farewell' to my family; and then I will go with you." He cannot say to the Angel, "Take my servant or my son or grandson instead of me." The wicked cannot bribe the Heavenly Judge in the same way that they have been able to bribe earthly judges.

In Devarim Rabba, it is reported that Rabbi Simon ben Chalafta made the following additional observations on this verse: When one finally meets the Angel of Death face to face, it is useless to try to rebuff his embrace with any kind of man-made weapon. The Angel of Death never says, "Because you are a king, I will wait for you an extra day or two." The Angel of Death is no respecter of persons or titles or wealth or earthly power or wisdom or anything terrestrial whatsoever.

Koheles says, Chapter Eight, Verse Nine,

"I considered all this and pondered over everything which happens under the sun: how, at times, one man has the ability to exercise harmful control over another."

Ibn Ezra states that, in this verse, Koheles continues to give counsel to the wise with regard to earthly rulers, the topic which he began to discuss in Verse Two. I do not think that this is so. It is not necessary to go back that far to discover the meaning of Verse Nine. Verse Nine is an integral part of the chain of thought that begins with Verse Eight and continues without interruption to the end of the chapter: Man, as an individual and in the aggregate, is a powerless, insecure, unpredictable, conniving, ignorant creature. Verse Nine affirms that the only semblance of power which man really possesses is that some human beings either seize or are given the temporary authority to make life uncomfortable, and at times even unbearable, for some other human beings.

Koheles says, Chapter Eight, Verse Ten,

> "Indeed, I have seen the wicked buried with honor and their families have continued to thrive while, at the same time, the righteous have died without issue and have been forgotten by the city for whose good they labored; this, too, is vapor."

This is an extremely difficult verse to translate. In all likelihood, it has not been preserved in its original form. In formulating the translation of the verse, the format suggested by ibn Ezra has been followed. In addition to suggesting a very acceptable translation of the text, ibn Ezra makes this comment: The translations and explanations of this verse offered by earlier Bible interpreters are incorrect. The correct interpretation of this verse is: Koheles saw that the wicked who rule over mankind and do evil to their fellow men die without suffering any punishment. They are buried with honor and their children govern in their stead and keep alive their memory. But the righteous often die without issue and are forgotten by the community in which they lived. Koheles questions the justice of a process which destroys the memory of the righteous and the record of the good they have done, while the wicked die happily and leave behind them children who continue in the successful and evil ways of their fathers. This is, indeed, vapor.

A different translation and interpretation is offered by the Midrash, in Koheles Rabba and Tanchuma Yisro. The Midrashic translation is quite esoteric: "I have seen wrong-doers buried and continue to live, after they have come forth from the holy place. Their former wrongdoings are forgotten because of the good lives they now live. That many others do not follow their example is vapor." What does this mean? How is it to be interpreted? The verse refers to converts to Judaism. In their former states of wrong belief, disbelief or unbelief, they were buried in wrongdoing. After receiving instruction in "the holy place," i.e., the synagogues and the Jewish schools, their lives have been revitalized by their acceptance of Jewish beliefs and their acceptance by the Jewish people. They lead fine Jewish lives and are a welcome part of the Jewish community. The reactions of other non-Jews to this phenomenon cannot be explained rationally. They see that these former Gentiles are living fuller and more meaningful lives as Jews than they ever did as Gentiles and yet, seeing this, the other Gentiles do not clamor to be admitted into the Jewish religious fellowship.

Koheles says, Chapter Eight, Verse Eleven,

"Because the penalty for committing a crime is not exacted speedily, the minds of men are filled with many schemes for circumventing the law."

Koheles Rabba comments: This refers to those who break the law and get away with it. This is what they say about some of the Romans. They know Roman law so well that they sneak just outside the law and then sneak back again and their feet do not slip.

Sforno comments: Not only do those who break the law get away with it but they also brag about their misdeeds and about not being caught and punished. This encourages others to behave in like manner.

Koheles says, Chapter Eight, Verse Twelve A,

"A wrongdoer can commit a hundred crimes and still live to a very old age."

Verses Twelve B and Thirteen are omitted from this translation because they are completely out of tune with the message expounded in this book. Once again, the omitted portion must be considered the work of some later pietistic editor. Koheles makes it quite clear in this chapter and elsewhere that he does not believe that the righteous are rewarded on earth or the wicked punished. He also makes it quite clear a number of times that he does not believe that the individual human being continues to exist after death. The pietistic editor, determined to get in a good word for "the old time religion," inserted the following immediately after Koheles 8:12a: "But I also know that it will be well with those who have feared God and led righteous lives, and it will not be well with the wicked who will not live to a very old age and will pass away like a shadow, because they have not feared God." These sentiments are directly contrary to what Koheles says in the verse which precedes and the verse which follows and, indeed, throughout the entire book. The inserted passage represents a transparent, clumsy effort to tone down the rationalism of the author.

Koheles Rabba has something to say about practically every word in the Book of Koheles, but he passes by Koheles 8:12b-13 without a word of comment. This indicates that he must have had a strong feeling that this portion does not represent the thinking of Koheles and does not belong in the text. It is significant, too, that none of the commentators on Koheles Rabba (Matnos Kehuna, Yafe Toar, Redal, Maharzu, Y'de Moshe) makes mention of the omission or makes any comment on Koheles 8:12b-13. All seem to share the presumed feeling of Koheles Rabba that this little section was not written by Koheles. Why did not Koheles Rabba or any of the commentators state this opinion plainly? Probably because they feared that less sensitive and more hidebound rabbis would accuse them of heresy. It has been noted once before in this commentary that the silence of the wise sometimes produces a longer lasting noise than the shouting of fools.

Koheles says, Chapter Eight, Verse Fourteen,

"There is a cloudy situation upon the earth: There are righteous people who are treated as though they are wicked and there are wicked people who are treated as though they are righteous; I say that this, too, is vapor."

Rashi comments: In Talmud Horayos 10b, the rabbis explain that this verse means that the righteous suffer in this world in order to get their reward later and the wicked prosper here in order that they may be punished later. . . . This is, quite obviously, not the meaning of the verse. If it were, Koheles would not have concluded the verse by saying, "This, too, is vapor."

Ibn Ezra comments: From Koheles 8:14 through 9:12, the author is discussing the seemingly unjust way in which the righteous and the wicked are treated upon earth. He seems to have been so shaken by his inability to find a satisfactory explanation for this condition that he was on the verge of going out of his mind.

Sforno comments: There are righteous people who have a bad public reputation because people think they are pious fools. There are clever wicked people who acquire for themselves a good public reputation by acting in a hypocritical manner. Often the good public reputation which one enjoys has the value of "vapor" because the majority of human beings are dolts.

Koheles says, Chapter Eight, Verse Fifteen,

> "So I think that the best attitude to take is to regard the world with amusement, and that there is nothing better for man under the sun than to eat and to drink and to amuse himself; this attitude will lighten his labor for whatever number of years God has given him under the sun."

Rashi comments: Koheles is saying that one should be satisfied with the portion which God has allotted to him. He who lives righteously and concerns himself with matters appropriate to his position finds happiness. Those who are not satisfied with their lot are the world's trouble makers. It is they who sin and rob and oppress their fellow men.

Koheles says, Chapter Eight, Verses Sixteen and Seventeen,

> "When I made up my mind to find wisdom and to understand what is going on in the world—and I devoted myself to this task day and night—and to determine whether God's providence is concerned with all this, I concluded that man is able to understand nothing of what goes on under the sun; even though he study and search with all his strength, he will find out nothing; even if the wisest of the wise makes the attempt, he will not succeed."

"I devoted myself to this task day and night."
The literal translation of this Hebrew text is: "He is un-

able to sleep either during the day or at night." In connection with the rest of the verse, this does not make much sense. Therefore, ibn Ezra changed it to "I was unable to sleep either during the day or at night." I have translated it as "I devoted myself to this task day and night" because it is my belief that this is the meaning Koheles is trying to convey.

Koheles Rabba interprets this phrase: I devoted myself to this task when death seemed far off and when death seemed near, i.e., both in youth and old age.

Ibn Ezra decides: Koheles does not mean that all knowledge is false or that all study is vain. He is speaking specifically of the problem of good and evil. He is saying that the way in which God handles the problem of good and evil and the ways in which righteousness is rewarded and wickedness is punished are matters which are completely beyond human comprehension.

9

In Chapters One to Four, Koheles speaks to humanity in general about a variety of matters. After tearing down many of the cherished illusions of his time and, for that matter, of our time as well, he gives his readers some practical advice. He says to them: Since life and the world are as they are, the only sensible course for a sensitive person to follow is to find himself a good companion, live well but not ostentatiously, and get as much satisfaction as he possibly can out of what he is doing. Then, in the next four chapters, he addresses himself rather specifically to the scholarly and the rich. He speaks with bitterness of the fickleness and stupidity of the mass mind, of its utter inability to grasp the realities of the situation in which God has placed man. The wisest attitude for a thinking person to assume is to accept his lot gracefully and to regard with a composed grin the meaningless ambitions and frustrations and delusions of mankind.

In the first twelve verses of Chapter Nine, Koheles turns away from the wise and the wealthy and speaks to "the average man." He tells "the average man" that the righteous and the intelligent and those who have money are really no better off than he is. Practically everything they are and do was foreordained by God, "whether for their benefit or their hurt, no one knows." They are going to die just as he is going to die. Everyone, no matter what his station in life, hopes that he will escape death because the will to live is basic in human nature. But, even though the living do not want to die, they are sensible enough to know that they are going to die. In this, they are superior to the dead, who know nothing and have nothing and are nothing.

So, Mr. Average Man, you who will never be among the wise or the wealthy, how does Koheles tell you to live? He says to you, in Chapter Nine: Eat well; drink well; dress well; get yourself a woman to love; enjoy your work; do it efficiently; for "this is your lot in life and the sum total of what you will be able to achieve."

Beginning with Verse Thirteen, Koheles tells a little story in which he again extols wisdom and bemoans the insensate behavior of the general public. A wise man delivers a beleaguered city from danger but his deed is soon forgotten by those whom he has saved. The confused multitudes are attracted more by the shouting of a fool than by the quiet words of the wise; but, in the end, implies Koheles, the shouting of the fool will result in the destruction of his followers, while those who have listened intently to the quiet words of wisdom may be able to save something of what is left after the fool has had his day. Koheles concludes the chapter with a statement which, in the light of the present world situation, seems almost prophetic:

"Wisdom can accomplish more lasting good than weapons of war; but one very powerful fool can destroy the work of many less powerful wise men."

Koheles says, Chapter Nine, Verse One,

"After examining carefully all the available evidence, I decided that the righteous and the wise and everything they do are controlled by God; whether for their benefit or for their hurt, no one knows, for a heavy mist beclouds this matter."

The Septuagint is the first Greek translation of the Bible,

a translation completed in Alexandria, Egypt, about 100 BCE. Since the Book of Koheles was written about 200 BCE, the Septuagint translation of Koheles must certainly be based on the original Hebrew text. The translation of Chapter Nine, Verse One, as given here, reflects the influence of the Septuagint. The Septuagint translation indicates that the word "ha-kol," which is the first Hebrew word in Verse Two, should really be "hevel" and should be the last Hebrew word in Verse One. When the original Hebrew text was recopied, two scribal errors seem to have been committed. A scribe changed the Hebrew letter Bes in "hevel" to a Kaf; and this same scribe or some other scribe put the period ending the sentence in the wrong place. The Septuagint rendering makes much better sense than the Hebrew text as it now stands and, therefore, there is little doubt that this emendation is correct.

On this verse, ibn Ezra makes the following comment: The righteous and the wise understand that they do not control their own destinies. Sometimes they get the feeling that it is useless for them to do anything, because whatever is going to happen has already been decided.

Koheles says, Chapter Nine, Verse Two,

> "The same fate awaits everyone: the righteous, the wicked; the pure, the impure; he who offers sacrifice and he who does not offer sacrifice; it makes no difference whether one is saint or sinner, whether he swears falsely or truly."

In this verse, too, a copyist's error appears to have been made in the original Hebrew text. The sixth Hebrew word, "la-tov," meaning "the good," is completely superfluous and disturbs the smooth flowing poetic structure of the rest of the verse. Therefore this word has been omitted from the translation.

Ibn Ezra says: The reason that Koheles mentions these various categories of individuals is as follows: "The righteous, the wicked" refers to human deeds; "the pure, the impure" refers to bodily cleanliness; "he who offers sacrifice and he who does not offer sacrifice" refers to the way in which one uses his money; "saint or sinner" refers to the thoughts of the heart; "whether he swears falsely or truly" refers to the manner in which one keeps his word.

Koheles says, Chapter Nine, Verse Three,

> "Nothing that happens under the sun is more pernicious than that the same fate awaits everyone; this thought fills mankind with the corrupting notion that life is merely a frenzied madness, ending in death."

Even ibn Ezra makes no noteworthy comment on this hard hitting verse. As for the Talmud and Midrash, they have very little to say about the first three verses of Chapter Nine and what little they do say indicates a complete unwillingness to concede that Koheles states in these verses: 1) That righteousness and wickedness may be a matter of predestination rather than of human choice; 2) That whether it pays to be good is highly questionable; and 3) That, whatever be the truth behind the first two propositions, it is the opinion of Koheles that the good receive no eternal reward and the evil no eternal punishment but both share a common fate, i.e., the total and everlasting annihilation of death.

Koheles says, Chapter Nine, Verse Four,

> "However, while there is life, there is hope; a live dog is better off than a dead lion."

Ibn Ezra comments: The hope to which Koheles refers is

the nonsensical belief of the supremely egotistical individual that, through some miraculous Divine dispensation, he differs from the rest of mankind and will be saved from the fate of the rest of mankind.

The Midrash contains some very interesting interpretations of this verse.

Koheles Rabba 9:1:2 says: "While there is life, there is hope." Even for those wicked ones who stretch forth their hands against the Holy Temple itself, who do everything in their power to destroy the Jewish people and the Jewish religion, there is hope that, if they truly repent, their sins will be forgiven. As indicated in the story of Elisha ben Abuya, included in the discussion of Koheles 7:8, Judaism does not regard anyone as being hopelessly wicked. The gates of repentance and forgiveness stand open for everyone, no matter how impious, no matter how bad, no matter how depraved. Man is not born through sin or in sin. Man is born naturally and in a state of innocent goodness. God gives man the right to choose between the good and the evil. If man chooses the evil, the opportunity to abandon the evil and to return to the good is his as long as he lives.

"While there is life, there is hope."

The Talmud and Midrash contribute another interpretation: When a fetus is created in the womb, three partners share in its creation: its father, its mother and the Holy One, blessed be He. Its father contributes the fertilizing semen from which are created the white substances in the embryonic body, the brain, the fingernails, the toenails, the white in the eyes, the bones and the veins. Its mother contributes the fertilized egg from which are formed the red substances in the embryonic body, the blood, the skin, the flesh, the hair and the dark part of the eyes. The Holy One, blessed be He, contributes ten things: the soul, breath, the facial expression, sight, hearing, speech, the ability to lift the arms, the ability to walk, strength and wisdom-understanding-knowledge.

When the time comes for a person to die, God takes back what He has given and leaves intact the items supplied by the father and mother. The father and mother weep. God says to them, "Why are you weeping? I am taking nothing which you gave. I take back only what I gave." They say before Him, "Master of the universe, all the time that Your part was mixed with our part, our part was safe from the worms; but now that You have taken back Your part, our part is no good and will be eaten by the worms."

Rabbi Judah the Prince supplied the following analogy: To what may this be compared? To a king who had a vineyard and sublet it to a tenant. At harvest time, the king said to his servants, "Go, harvest my portion of the vineyard but do not touch the part which belongs to the tenant." When the servants obeyed the king's command, the tenant began to protest and to weep. The king said, "I have taken nothing of yours. I have taken only what belongs to me." "That is true," replied the tenant, "but all the time that my portion was with your portion, my portion was safe from theft. Now that you have removed your portion, my portion is no longer safe."

"A live dog is better off than a dead lion."

Rabbi Simon ben Eleazar said: A baby one day old does not have to be guarded from the weasel, the mouse and the snake. They look at the baby and flee. But when a person dies, even if he looks as imposing as Og king of Bashan, his body has to be guarded against the weasel, the mouse and the snake. As long as a man is alive, his fear is upon all beasts and creeping things. When he dies, he is no longer feared.

David, king of Israel, died on the Sabbath. After he was dead, the sages allowed the Sabbath to be profaned for his dogs but not for him. This is why Koheles says, "A live dog is better off than a dead lion." What is the story back of this statement?

Rabbi Judah said in the name of Rav: What is the significance of Psalm 39:5, "Lord, make known to me my end and what will be the measure of my days?" David said to God, "Master of the universe, tell me when I am going to die." God answered, "I have decreed that no human being may know when he is to die." Then David said, "At least let me know how many years I am going to live." God answered, "I have decreed that no human being may know how many years he is going to live." "Then," said David, "at least let me know on what day of the week I am going to die." God replied, "On the Sabbath." "I do not want to die on the Sabbath;" said David, "let me live until Sunday." "No," said God, "I cannot permit that. The reign of your son Solomon will have already begun and I cannot permit you to remain on earth an instant after your reign is over." "Then," said David, "let me die before the Sabbath begins." "No," said God, "I want you to study Torah until the very last moment. One day that you sit and study Torah means more to Me than a thousand sacrifices offered on the altar of the Temple that your son Solomon is going to build."

Every Sabbath David sat and studied all night and all day. On the Sabbath that he was scheduled to die, he was sitting in his house and audibly reciting the Torah from memory. When the Angel of Death arrived, he was not allowed to disturb David while words of Torah were on his lips. The Angel waited and waited but David's lips never stopped moving. Finally, the Angel became impatient. He went into the garden behind the house and began to shake one of the fruit trees vigorously. David's attention was attracted by the noise. Still reciting the verses of the Torah, he walked into the garden and up to the tree. He could not figure out why the tree was shaking. He decided to get a ladder, climb into the tree and investigate. As he was going up the ladder, with his lips still moving, the Angel pushed the ladder out from under him. David fell to the ground and, for an instant, he had to stop reciting Torah in order to catch his breath. In that instant, the Angel planted upon the lips of David the kiss of death.

Solomon was informed that his father was dead. When he reached David's house, he saw his father's body lying on the ground and he heard his father's dogs inside the house clamoring for food. The Sabbath was not yet over. What should he do? Was he permitted to feed the dogs? Was he permitted to remove his father's body? He sent a messenger to the house of study to ask the sages for the answers to these questions. The reply came: "You may feed the hungry dogs. You may not move your father's body by itself; but, if the body, as it is being moved, is used to perform a useful service, you may move it. Place upon the body a loaf of bread, which you will feed to the dogs. You may then move the body because, as a means of conveyance for the bread, the body will be serving a useful purpose." This decision caused Solomon to utter the Scriptural saying, "A live dog is better off than a dead lion."

What are the religious principles which this story teaches? We are permitted to violate the Sabbath to relieve the suffering of a living being. Especially are we permitted to help a suffering living human being, because, through our violation of one Sabbath, we may be making it possible for this human being to live to observe many Sabbaths. But since a dead person is free from the obligation of observing the commandments of the Torah and will, therefore, observe no more earthly

Sabbaths, we may not violate the Sabbath for him, even if he be David, king of Israel, "lion of Judah," for, in death, there is neither king nor commoner. All are equal.

Koheles says, Chapter Nine, Verse Five,

> "The living know that they are going to die; the dead know nothing at all; they no longer hope for a Heavenly reward; they are gone and forgotten."

As might be expected, the majority of the Talmudists did not accept the literal meaning of this strong statement. Berachos 18ab declares that the phrase "The living know" refers to the righteous who, even after death, are still characterized as "living." The phrase "the dead know nothing" refers to the wicked who, even while living, are characterized as "dead." This is a soothing application of hermeneutical principles; but it is not an acceptable explanation of the plain sense of the text. On the next page of the Talmud, Berachos 19a, Rabbi Isaac, probably Rabbi Isaac Nappacha, indicates that he knew what was in the mind of Koheles: "He who speaks about the dead is as if he were speaking about a stone." Just as the stone does not hear or know, so the dead does not hear or know. There are some who agree with Rabbi Isaac. There are other sages who say that the dead hears and knows but does not care. Unlike the living, the dead does not react emotionally to what others say about him.

In a comment on Berachos 19a, Rashi says that Rabbi Isaac's opinion holds true only when one speaks disrespectfully or critically of the dead. The implication is that, when one praises the dead, the dead listens; but, when one condemns the dead, the dead pays no attention. However, Rashi's reaction to Koheles 9:5 in his Biblical commentary is somewhat more rationalistic: After the righteous are dead, they know nothing and they have no further opportunities to earn any more rewards; but he who toils before the Sabbath will surely eat on the Sabbath. . . . In the latter comment, Rashi seems to be torn between what his reason tells him is so and what his faith urges him to believe.

As usual, ibn Ezra does not shrink from saying what Koheles thinks: The living, even if they are fools, know that they are going to die. The dead, even if they were wise, know nothing; they hope for nothing; their name and their memory are eventually forgotten.

Koheles says, Chapter Nine, Verse Six,

> "Their loves, their hates, their jealousies are ended; never again will they share in anything that happens under the sun."

Again ibn Ezra: For the dead, the loves, the hates, the jealousies of earthly life are over. . . . They are at peace with themselves and with the universe. They have found eternal rest.

Koheles says, Chapter Nine, Verse Seven,

> "Go, banquet well and often; drink to your heart's content; for this is the way, it appears, that God wants you to live."

Suddenly the mood changes. After assuring "the average man" that "the same fate awaits everyone," Koheles tells him to enjoy his days on earth just as much as he possibly can. Three times before, in 2:24, 3:13 and 5:17, Koheles has advised mankind to enjoy eating and drinking. Ibn Ezra has accepted all three verses without protest, probably because, in all three instances, Koheles seems to be giving this counsel to those of above average intelligence. But, this time, when

Koheles is addressing himself to "the average man" and emphasizing the hedonistic approach more strongly than in any of the previous verses, ibn Ezra refuses to believe that Koheles means what he says: This is not the way that Koheles thinks and this is not the way that Koheles lives. He is merely setting forth the foolish thoughts that are in the minds of most men. Most men think, "Since death is the end of everything, I shall spend my time, while I am alive, merrily eating and drinking, because this is the way God wants me to live."

Koheles says, Chapter Nine, Verse Eight,

"Let your clothes be festive at all times; never appear in public without perfumed oil in your hair."

Translated literally, the first part of this verse means: "Let your clothes be white at all times." White was the color worn on festive occasions. This accounts for the translation "Let your clothes be festive at all times." But white was also the color one wore at his funeral, i.e., he was clothed and buried in a white shroud. And so the Talmudic sages interpreted this verse to mean: Always live as though you will soon be attending your own funeral.

Rabbi Eliezer ben Hyrcanus, a tanna who lived after the destruction of the Temple, a pupil of Rabbi Jochanan ben Zakkai and the teacher of Rabbi Akiba, is quoted in Mishna Avos 2:10 as having said, "Repent one day before your death." His disciples asked, "How does one know on what day he is going to die?" Rabbi Eliezer replied, "He does not know. Therefore, one should be in a repentant mood and ready for death every day of his life, as it is said, 'Let your clothes be white at all times.' "

In Talmud and Midrash, the following passage appears: "Let your clothes be white at all times." Let your conduct always be such that you can depart from the world at any time without regret.

Rabbi Judah the Prince said: To what may the matter be compared? To a king who invited a number of townspeople to come to a banquet at his palace. He said to them, "Go home; wash and iron your clothes; take a bath; rub oil on your skin; be ready for the feast." He did not tell them exactly when the banquet would begin. The wise ones among those who were invited got ready immediately and stood around the doors of the palace, waiting for the festivities to commence. Some of the invitees were fools. They did not take the king's words seriously. They said, "Why should we be overly anxious because we have been invited to a royal banquet? After we are told just when to appear at the palace, we shall have sufficient time to prepare. Even a king cannot manage to have a banquet without a number of meetings with the caterers, without buying and washing and soaking the meat and the vegetables, without planning the seating arrangements." And so the town plasterer continued to plaster, the town potter to make pots, the town blacksmith to work at his smithy, the town launderer to operate his laundry. Suddenly came the announcement: "Let all the guests come at once to the king's banquet." The guests assembled hastily. The wise ones came into the king's presence dressed immaculately and scented elegantly. The fools arrived in filthy and smelly garments, each accompanied by the distinctive odor of his particular occupation. The king was proud of the wise citizens who had taken his words seriously and whose appearance showed proper respect for him and for the palace. He was very angry at the fools, whose attitude and habiliments were disgraceful. He said, "Let those who are appropriately attired come and eat at the king's table. Let those not appropriately attired refrain from eating at the king's table." One might think that he allowed the latter group to depart. Not so. He continued: "Let those who are appropriately attired sit down and eat and drink in good spirit. Let those not appropriately attired remain standing and let them meditate upon their sorry appearances, their pale faces and their troubled looks."

Zivay, the son-in-law of Rabbi Meir, reported that Rabbi Meir had told a story very much like this one but had ended it differently: The unsightly fools were not told to remain standing. They were told to sit down. The wise ones sat and ate and drank; the fools sat and did not eat and did not drink. This was even worse than standing and not eating and not drinking. When one stands and does not eat, he may be thought to be a servant, a bus boy, a waiter. But when he sits and does not eat, his embarrassment is doubled and tripled. His face changes color like the crocus-flower because of the sights and smells that pass him by. At times, he is orange; at times, purple; at times, yellow. He will never forget the one time he was invited to banquet with a king.

. . . A parable of somewhat similar import, usually referred to as "the parable of the wise and foolish virgins," is found in the New Testament in Matthew 25:1-13. This New Testament book is believed to have been written between the years 80 and 90 CE. Modern scholars think that the word "virgin," as used in the King James translation of this passage in Matthew, really means "bridesmaid."

In commenting on Verse Seven, ibn Ezra declined to go along with the literal meaning of the verse. Now, in commenting on Verse Eight, he rejects, in even stronger language, the Talmudic and Midrashic interpretations of Verses Eight through Ten: The early commentators say that Verse Eight is concerned with the idea of doing good and being repentant and getting ready for death and Verse Nine commands one to get

married and not look at strange women and Verse Ten tells
us to do all the good we can in this world so that we shall
be rewarded in the next world. These verses do not contain
any of these meanings. Koheles is simply musing to himself.
All his references to eating and drinking and dressing and
anointing and having a woman are merely a recounting of the
different ways in which human beings enjoy the delights of
the body. They have nothing whatsoever to do with anything
else.

Koheles says, Chapter Nine, Verse Nine,

> "Enjoy life with the woman you love during all your days
> of hollow existence, which He has granted you under the sun.
> This is your lot in life and the sum total of what you will
> be able to achieve under the sun."

In the Hebrew text the words "during all your days of
hollow existence" are repeated, probably through a copyist's
error. Since the repetition of these words is superfluous, the
unneeded words have been omitted from the translation.

Those readers of the gentler sex who may have been a little
annoyed by some of the unkind remarks about bad wives,
found in Talmudic and Midrashic reactions to Koheles 7:26-
28, are urged to read with care what these same classical works
have to say about the good wife, meaning, of course, the
angelic female spirit conjured up by the opening words of
Koheles 9:9, "Enjoy life with the woman you love":

Rabbi Tanchum said in the name of his father, Rabbi
Chanilai, a Palestinian amora: He who is not married lives
without good, for so the Bible says, Genesis 2:18, "It is not
good for man to be alone."

Rabbi Tanchum also said his father said: He who is not

married lives without a helper, for so the Bible says, Genesis 2:18, "I will make for him a helper." Rabbi Eleazar ben Pedas said: What kind of helper is woman to man? She helps to bring out in him the sort of person he is. If he turns out to be a good husband, she works with him; if he turns out to be a bad husband, she works against him.

Rabbi Tanchum also said his father said: He who is not married lives without joy, for so the Bible says, Deuteronomy 14:26, "You and your family shall rejoice." Wherever the word "family" is used in Scripture, it refers primarily to one's wife. To live without joy means to be without the comforting understanding that only a wife can give. It is as Rabbi Joshua ben Korcha, a tannaitic contemporary of Rabbi Meir, said to the eunuch, in Sabbath 152a, "One who lives alone has no joy because man's nature is such that, if he has none with whom to share his secrets, his heart fills with anxiety." And this is why Midrash Tehillim says, "He who has no companion will find death preferable." Jacob ben Asher, the famous "Baal Haturim," who was born in Germany about 1269 and died in Spain about 1340, says in his *Tur Even Ha-ezer*: He who has reached the age of marriage and is not married is without joy because he really has no home to call his own.

Rabbi Tanchum also said his father said: He who is not married lives without blessing, as the Bible says, Ezekiel 44:30, "To cause a blessing to rest on your family." When there is happiness in the home, God's very Presence abides in the home and the house and family are blessed. . . . Yafe Toar, a Midrashic commentator, says that Rabbi Chanilai also meant that he who has a wife who watches carefully over the finances of the household is blessed.

Rabbi Jacob said: He who is not married lives without redemption, as the Bible says, Leviticus 16:11, "To atone for himself and his family." Woman is man's redeemer. When a man gets married, he puts away the wildness of youth, stops wasting his time and sets his mind on building a home and a family and becoming successful in his profession.

Rava bar Ulla said: He who is not married lives without peace. A woman brings peace into a man's life. She stops the quarrels in the home. She mitigates her husband's harsh judgments. She calms her man down when he gets excited. She makes home life so attractive for him that he has no urge to go out and "walk in an evil way."

In Palestine, there was a saying: He who is not married lives without Torah. The Talmud contains a law that a man should first marry and, after that, he should study Torah. Rabbi Jochanan bar Napacha once said: The man who obeys this law is tying a millstone around his neck. . . . The Tosephos explains that there was no genuine difference of opinion between Rabbi Jochanan and this law. Rabbi Jochanan was speaking to a group of his students who were from Babylon, who had travelled a long way in order to study at his academy in Tiberias, Palestine. He said to these foreign students that, if they were to get married, they would be tying a millstone about their necks, because it would be almost impossible for them to support their wives and continue their studies at one and the same time. But the law was meant to apply only to Palestinian students who could live in the homes of their in-laws while they went on with their studies. So the Talmud says clearly that the saying applies only to those "in Palestine," i.e., native Palestinians. It does not apply to foreign students who come to Palestine to study. Such foreign students should complete their academic studies before they get married.

There was another saying in Palestine: He who is not married lives without a wall. What does this mean? It means that he who has no wife is without a wall of moral protection, i.e., in order to ease his sexual hunger he is likely to get himself into unpleasant social situations, a likelihood that marriage lessens considerably.

Yafe Toar asks: Why are all these marital advantages expressed negatively rather than positively? Why do the rabbis not say: He who is married lives with good, a helper, joy, blessing, etc., etc.? The reason is that marriages are not always successful. All marriages do not bring all these advantages. There are bad wives as well as good wives. The difference between a married and an unmarried man is that the married man may or may not have good, joy, blessing, etc. The unmarried man has not even the possibility of obtaining these advantages unless and until he takes the marital gamble.

Rabbi Joshua ben Levi said: A bachelor is not really living, as the Bible says, Koheles 9:9, "Enjoy life with the woman you love." One might think that it is just the reverse, that he who goes to bed with a different woman every night is living more pleasantly than he who has the same bed companion every night. It is not so, said Rabbi Joshua ben Levi. In order that the Biblical ideal may be achieved which is expressed in Job 5:24, "You shall know that there is peace in your tent," you cannot have too many women in that tent. For most tents, one woman is enough. And, said Rabbi Joshua sternly: Anyone who knows that he has a virtuous wife and does not make love to her regularly is a sinner. One is under an especial obligation to make love to his wife just before leaving her behind on a long business trip. The sages asked: How may one make sure that there will be peace in his tent? And they answered: Let him who wishes to have peace in his tent love his wife as much as he loves himself; let him honor his wife more than he honors himself; let him bring up his children properly and marry them off at the proper time. Rashi asked: Why should a man honor his wife more than he honors himself? And he answered: Because a woman's pride is more easily hurt than a man's. And Maharshaw asked: How does a man honor his wife more than he honors himself? And he answered: By buying her better clothes than he buys for himself.

Rabbi Chiyya bar Gamda said: A bachelor is not a complete man, as the Bible says, Genesis 5:2, "And God blessed male and female and called them 'Man.' " Only when a man and woman are wrapped in warm marital embrace does "Man" reach his most complete fulfillment.

Sforno interprets Koheles 9:9 entirely differently: "Enjoy life"—Have a good time while you are young. "With the woman you love"—Drink to the full all the sweetness that the cup of life has to offer. "During all your days of hollow existence"—This means the years of youth, which constitute the only period of existence when one is really living, in contrast to the years of old age, which are referred to often as "the bad days." The rest of the verse means that, after the fling of youth has passed, one should turn to the ways of the Torah and should seek to win the eternal reward which comes from following the ways of the Torah.

Koheles says, Chapter Nine, Verse Ten,

> "Whatever you are required to do, do effectively; for neither physical labor nor mathematical skill nor common sense nor learning will be required in the hole toward which you are travelling."

Koheles Rabba states: Rabbi Menachama in the name of Rabbi Abin interchanged the two parts of the verse and translated it as follows: "If you believe that there is neither physical labor nor mathematical skill nor common sense nor learning in the hole toward which you are travelling, then, whatever you want to do, do it as much and as often as you want." In other words, if you are one of those who do not believe in reward or punishment after death, romp to your heart's content, because, according to your belief, this is all the life you will ever have. . . . Ibn Ezra, in his comment, agrees with Rabbi Abin's translation.

Koheles says, Chapter Nine, Verse Eleven,

"I meditated upon the fact that, under the sun, the race is not always won by the swift nor wars by the brave nor do the wise always have enough to eat nor are the intelligent always wealthy nor are those who have knowledge always treated well; time and chance determine the fate of all mankind."

Ibn Ezra comments: Koheles regrets that he has praised having fun and saying that it is good for man to seek pleasure, for man is not really able to have fun in this world, because there is really no fun in it. The fleet stumble and are left without strength to continue running. Greatness of courage does not win the battle for the brave. The wise should be rich and should be ruling over the poor and, ofttimes, it is just the reverse. Ofttimes the intelligent do not find favor in the sight of those in power. The lives of all men, the wise, the fools, the strong, the weak, are governed by luck. Man has no power whatsoever over himself. The wise and those who work the hardest often have the least to eat. Those who say "Whatever you are required to do, do effectively" speak nonsense; how you do your work means little; whatever has been determined from the very beginning of Creation will shape your particular fate.

Koheles says, Chapter Nine, Verse Twelve,

"No man knows the date of his death; like fish entangled in an escape-proof net and like birds caught in a trap, mankind

is hemmed in, as each mortal awaits the hapless day that will
come surely and without warning."

Ibn Ezra comments: Koheles says time and chance compel
man to act as he does. Death comes to him suddenly. Man
is compared to fish and birds who do not know until they are
trapped that they will not be able to escape.

Koheles says, Chapter Nine, Verses Thirteen to Sixteen,

"I witnessed an incident under the sun in which, it seemed
to me, wisdom was employed in a very significant manner.
There was a little city with a small population. A great king
came and besieged it. He built huge siege towers before its
walls. And there was found in that city a poor wise man and,
by his wisdom, he saved it. And what that poor man did for
the city is now forgotten. As a result of this incident, I noted:
Wisdom triumphed over brute strength; and yet the wisdom
of the poor man is despised and his deeds are not extolled."

In Talmud Nedarim 32b, Rabbi Ammi bar Abba wove
the following parable out of Koheles 9:14-15: "A little city"
is the body. The "small population" are the organs and limbs
of the body. "A great king came and besieged it" is the Evil Inclination. The "siege towers" are sins caused by the Evil Inclination. "A poor wise man" is the Good Inclination. "And he saved
the city by his wisdom" refers to repentance and good deeds.
"And what that poor wise man did for the city is now forgotten" means that, when men once again turn to the Evil
Inclination, the Good Inclination is forgotten.

Ha-rif makes the following comment: This parable is fine
up to the very last sentence, and then it breaks down. If, after
the Good Inclination has saved the body by repentance and
good deeds, the body returns to the influence of the Evil Inclination, then the influence of the Good Inclination does not

amount to very much. The parable should have been completed differently. It should have been completed as follows: The Good Inclination here is called "poor" and it is also called "wise." When the Good Inclination is used "poorly," it is not listened to. When it used "wisely," it is listened to. After it has been used wisely, people are inclined to forget the days when they were under the influence of the Evil Inclination, the days in which the Good Inclination was used poorly. That is what Koheles 9:15 says. It says that the Good Inclination saved the person "by his wisdom" and that, after that, no one remembered "the poor man."

Another medieval commentator states: From this parable, it is clear that the Good Inclination is in the body before the Evil Inclination, since, when the Evil Inclination arrives, the Good Inclination is already there. And yet, as we have been told in Koheles Rabba 4:13, a person is completely under the control of the Evil Inclination for the first thirteen years of his life. One statement seems to contradict the other. But this is not so. During those first thirteen years, the Good Inclination is present but powerless. The Evil Inclination is inside the body like a hub inside a wheel. The spokes of its influence go out to all parts of the body and there is no way to fight it. But, when the person gets to be thirteen years of age and has acquired a certain degree of knowledge, the Evil Inclination may be resisted. One can then build defenses against it and wall it in. From within its enclosure, the Evil Inclination will continue to shoot out arrows and to try to hit a vital spot whenever it can. But now the Good Inclination is able to fight valiantly and it does so. The Evil Inclination, in this struggle, has an initial advantage, in that it has had more experience and is, therefore, more skilled. So there is a long, bitterly fought battle inside every individual before his Good Inclination is able to obtain mastery over his Evil Inclination.

Ibn Ezra denies emphatically that the foregoing interpretation is correct: Jewish tradition says that this passage is a parable about the Good Inclination and the Evil Inclination. It is nothing of the sort. It is an account of a wise man who was lightly esteemed and who seldom had enough to eat. (Again, a somewhat autobiographical reference is discernible.) As Koheles 6:8 says, "The poor man who has learned to cope with his lot" knows that, even though his wisdom will never make him rich, there will be times when it will stand him in better stead than if he were king and had not wisdom. Koheles tells that there was a little city that became involved in a war. A great king came and surrounded it with a mighty army. The city was defended by a small number of men. The city was in a valley and the enemy was able to build siege towers on the hills around it and thus shoot their deadly missiles directly into the city. There seemed to be little doubt that the city would be destroyed or captured. There seemed to be no way to save it. But in that city was a poor wise man who, by his wisdom, saved the city. Before he performed this great deed, he was not known at all by the people of the city. After the war was won, he slipped back into the obscurity from whence he had come. Yet, even though his wisdom had been and, seemingly, would continue to be despised and even though he was not rewarded suitably for what he had done, for the rest of his life the poor wise man would have the satisfaction of knowing that, in the hour of need, his wisdom had accomplished what the city's soldiers alone had been unable to accomplish.

Koheles Rabba contains a quaint exposition of this section which indicates that congregational traits have not changed very much during the last one thousand years: "There was a little city"—This is a synagogue. "With a small population"

—This is its congregation. "A great king came"—This is the King of kings, the Holy One, blessed be He. "And besieged it"—He challenges it to be worthy of being the repository of the Torah. "He built huge siege towers before its walls." —He makes it very difficult to be a good Jew; He says that to be a good Jew one must not only be honest and kind but he must also know the Bible, the Midrash, the Mishna, the Gemarra. "And there was found in that city a poor wise man" —This is the Chacham or the Chazan, the underpaid Jewish community professional who manages the synagogue program. "By his wisdom, he saved it"—When God hears the Chacham expounding the laws of the Torah to the little congregation or the chant of the Chazan, with the congregation responding, "Amen, may God's great name be blessed," He says to Himself that, even though their sins are so weighty that they deserve a hundred years' punishment, He must forgive them. "And what that poor man did for the city is now forgotten"—That Chacham or that Chazan is soon forgotten by the congregation, but God does not forget him.

. . . As was explained in connection with Koheles 5:5, leading the congregation in prayer was only one of many functions of the Chazan in Talmudic times. The Chacham was a scholarly person who acted as a spiritual advisor to the congregation. He gave instruction to the congregation on religious subjects, taught in the congregational school, answered routine ritual questions and was qualified to serve as a member of a Bes Din or judicial panel in a lawsuit. He was what today would be known as a licensed minister. He was not ordained. He was not a Rabbi. He was inferior in rank to a Rabbi. In Talmudic times, a Rabbi was a person of great learning and prestige. Sometimes the Rabbi was also the political head of the community. Sometimes he taught in a great Yeshiva or Academy, the Talmudic equivalent of a modern university.

Ofttimes he earned his livelihood through a completely secular profession or trade. Rabbi was a title and position of importance but completely honorary; it carried with it no financial rewards; the rabbinate was not, in Talmudic times, a paid profession. The practice of hiring rabbis as congregational employees and paying them a salary only dates back to about the fifteenth century.

Sforno makes the following comment on Verse Sixteen: If a wise man, who is also rich and well-known, performs for a community what seems to be a magic deed, he is praised and honored and given a position of even greater importance in community affairs. But if a similar miracle is done by a wise man who is poor and unknown, the community will accept the benefits of the miracle gladly but will give neither the poor man nor his wisdom the honor due them. "He is really not that smart," the people will say. "It was just luck."

Koheles says, Chapter Nine, Verse Seventeen,

> "The words of the wise are listened to quietly, in contrast to the way in which the ruler shouts among his buffoons."

In the comment of Koheles Rabba on this verse is found another reference to the professional jealousy between Rabbi and Chazan, a rivalry which has already been noted in Koheles Rabba 7:5. Since Koheles Rabba was written either by a rabbi or one who was very favorably disposed toward rabbis, it is not difficult to guess who comes off second best in the remarks of Koheles Rabba: "The words of the wise are listened to quietly"—These are the Darshanim, the lecturers, the rabbis, the interpreters of the Torah. "The ruler" who "shouts among his buffoons"—These are the Meturgemanim, the translators, the Chazanim, the cantors, who translate the Biblical portion read at the services into Aramaic or Greek.

Redal explains what Koheles Rabba has in mind: The Darshan delivers his lecture quietly and concisely, so that only those who are sitting close to him hear him and only those among his hearers who are learned understand him. The Meturgeman speaks or sings in a very loud voice so that the whole congregation can hear him and he adds a lengthy explanation to his translation so that the congregation may comprehend the meaning of the Biblical portion that has been read and translated.

. . . It would seem that Koheles Rabba was irked because most congregants seemed to prefer the singing of the cantor to the preaching of the rabbi. Redal's explanation for this is that the average congregant is Jewishly ignorant and unwilling to be enlightened; but he gets much pleasure from listening to a man with a booming voice make a joyful noise unto the Lord.

Ibn Ezra explains the verse rationally: Because a ruler is rich and powerful, he is listened to immediately, whether his words make sense or not. But the words of the wise make their impact in a different manner. Even though the wise knows that he knows, he will usually speak more quietly and less boldly than the fool, who does not know that he does not know. At first, the words of the wise are not heeded, but, as time goes on, their validity is established. In the end, it is the advice of the wise that will be followed and not the bellowed nonsense of the foolish ruler.

Sforno feels that Verses Seventeen and Eighteen are directly related to the preceding verses about the wise man and the besieged city; and so his comments on this and the following verse are couched in military terms. Sforno was, by profession, a physician, but these comments indicate a more than casual acquaintance with military matters: When a military commander arranges his plans quietly and with wisdom before beginning the actual campaign and shares as much information as possible with his army, the soldiers will listen to his words more respectfully and intently and will carry out his orders more willingly and successfully than if the commander is a ruler, unversed in military matters, who treats his soldiers like puppets and issues his commands in an unmilitary and strident manner.

Koheles says, Chapter Nine, Verse Eighteen,

"Wisdom can accomplish more lasting good than weapons of war; but one very powerful fool can destroy the work of many less powerful wise men."

Koheles Rabba says: The kind of wisdom which is meant here is not the wisdom of the pacifist, the kind of wisdom which is used instead of weapons; the wisdom meant here is the wisdom of the activist, the kind of wisdom used in addition to or in connection with weapons. It is the kind of wisdom employed by Jacob when, as described in Chapter Thirty-two of Genesis, he was preparing to meet his brother Esau. He knew that Esau hated him and he was not sure just how his brother would receive him. So he took no chances. Rabbi Levi said: Jacob and his retinue wore white outer garments but, underneath those garments, they carried stout clubs and sharp knives. Jacob was ready for any one of three possibilities: 1) that God would act as Mediator and would make peace between Esau and himself; 2) that Esau would want peace as much as he wanted peace and would talk and act accordingly; and 3) that Esau would fight. Because Jacob had conditioned himself, mentally and physically, for each of these eventualities, there was no fight. . . . And those who are truly wise will understand.

Ibn Ezra links this verse to Verse Seventeen: The wise man may save his community by the quiet and peaceful manner in which he negotiates the settlement of a dispute, while the bragging and blustering ruler brings only ruin to himself, his buffoons and many wise and innocent people.

Sforno makes another astute military observation: It is good for a country to have a thoroughly developed campaign plan as well as superior weapons before it goes to war with another nation. Superior weapons alone will not win a war. There must be a plan and a purpose to which both nation and army are dedicated. "One fool can destroy the work of many wise men."—One foolhardy, cowardly or traitorous national or military leader can nullify the efforts of many wise, brave and loyal men. Nations must seek, at all times, to select their leaders carefully; but this is especially essential in a period when the nation may find itself at war.

10

Chapter Ten is different from every other chapter in the Book of Koheles. It does not discuss the past or the future of the individual or of the human race. It consists of a series of seemingly unrelated aphorisms, much in the style of the Book of Proverbs. Ibn Ezra and Sforno, in their commentaries, try mightily but rather unsuccessfully to relate the statements in this chapter to what has gone before. The contents and tone of the tenth chapter are so different from the rest of Koheles that some modern scholars have contended that this tenth chapter is not by Koheles but is a later editorial insertion. It is difficult to fathom what purpose such a later writer would have had in mind in interposing these verses at this point in the book. The verses do not combat or even weaken the pessimistic philosophy of Koheles; at the same time, they cannot be said to add much strength to the basic concepts of the book. It is easier to believe that this chapter is the work of Koheles and that he put it in here for the very simple reason that there seemed to be no better place to put it. The episode with which Chapter Nine concludes has to do with a ruler and a wise man and fools. Since most of Chapter Ten also concerns itself with rulers and wise men and fools, this was as logical a place as any to record these particular observations. Like many another writer, Koheles may have collected in his notebooks a number of what seemed to him to be very brilliant epigrams, as some of them truly are, and he just had to get them into his published writings somewhere and somehow.

Let us take a look at this collection of random thoughts of the old professor.

Koheles says, Chapter Ten, Verse One,

"As dead flies make the perfumer's ointment stink, so a little foolish behavior may undo a lifelong reputation for good judgment."

Ibn Ezra says: The thought in this verse is connected to the thought in the last verse of Chapter Nine. Just as the sins of one evil man can undo the work of many righteous men, so one foolish act can sometimes undo a whole lifetime of sensible acts.

Sforno says: This is especially true of a man who holds a position of public trust. The public mind is fickle and will turn against a man in public office for making one bad mistake, even though he may have served faithfully and well for many years.

Koheles says, Chapter Ten, Verse Two,

"The instinctive reactions of the wise are sound; the instinctive reactions of the fool are stupid."

The literal translation of this verse is: "The heart of the wise man is on his right side; the heart of the fool is on his left side." This is as ambiguous rhetorically as it is inaccurate biologically. It is understandable only when one remembers that, in the time of Koheles, going toward the right meant going in the auspicious, the correct, the sensible direction. Witness the modern word "dexterous," which comes from a Latin word meaning "to go to the right." Going toward the left meant going in the unlucky, the evil, the unwise direction. Witness the modern word "sinister," which comes from a Latin word meaning "to go to the left." Ibn Ezra gives a further reason for the analogy. He says that, in most human beings, the right arm is much stronger than the left.

Koheles says, Chapter Ten, Verse Three,

> "In everything that a fool does he displays his ignorance;
> by his deeds he tells the world that he is a fool."

There are some translators, ancient and modern, who have translated the second part of the verse as "He thinks that everyone else is a fool." As Koheles Rabba observes, this is, indeed, the hallmark of a genuine, clean-cut, simple-simon-pure fool. Koheles undoubtedly would have agreed with this sentiment; but this is not what he says in Chapter Ten, Verse Three. The translation as given is an accurate reproduction of the thought conveyed by the Hebrew text. The translation, "He thinks that everyone else is a fool," cannot be substantiated grammatically.

Koheles says, Chapter Ten, Verse Four,

> "If the ruler gets angry at you, do not become panicky;
> a calm demeanor can soften the ruler's reaction to very disas-
> trous mistakes."

This is a very difficult verse to translate. Modern translators are in quite general agreement that the meaning of the Hebrew text is as rendered here. Koheles Rabba translates the first part of the verse as "If you are placed in a position of authority, retain the quality of humility." This is a very meritorious thought. However the technique advocated by Koheles is not based on as noble a concept as that suggested by the translation of Koheles Rabba. It is much more practical and self-protective, especially when used by the congenital dullard, he whom some describe as "the strong, silent type" and others, less gullible, refer to by his Hebrew name, "Golem."

Koheles says, Chapter Ten, Verses Five to Seven,

> "There is an evil I have seen under the sun, a mistake that
> rulers commit unintentionally: Fools are placed in many im-

portant positions, while capable men are given unimportant posts. I have seen knaves riding on horses and princely men trudging along like servants."

Let him who agrees with this statement take a good look at himself. Let him who fails to agree with this statement write his own foolhardy comment.

Koheles says, Chapter Ten, Verses Eight and Nine,

"He who sets a trap may fall therein; he who breaks into another's property may be bitten by a poisonous snake. He who digs out rocks may hurt himself; he who chops up wood may put himself in jeopardy."

The meaning of Verse Eight is quite clear: When you try to make trouble for someone else, beware, lest it be you who ends up at the bottom of the pit. The reference to the poisonous snake biting the trespasser may be based upon the same ancient notion mentioned in Amos 5:19, where a man is pictured as fleeing into a strange house, leaning his hand against the wall and being bitten by a poisonous snake, i.e., poisonous snakes protect vacant houses against intruders.

The meaning of Verse Nine is not so clear. Why should one be cautioned against digging out rocks or chopping up wood? Both would seem to be salutary and useful activities, especially in a society that was predominantly agrarian, as was the Palestinian community in the time of Koheles. The medieval exegetes tried to offer plausible explanations.

Rashi: This means that one who quarries rocks from the side of a mountain has a very fatiguing occupation and may overtax himself. One who chops up wood is in danger of overheating himself and being stricken with heat exhaustion.

Ibn Ezra: All kinds of human labor, including the digging

out of rocks and the chopping up of wood, are accompanied by a certain amount of effort, fatigue and hazard.

Sforno: He who digs out rocks and throws them onto the road, where others may stumble against them, is likely to stumble against them himself and be hurt by his own carelessness. And one who chops up wood too zealously, thinking that he is benefiting himself by his efforts, may become overheated and do himself more harm than good.

Koheles says, Chapter Ten, Verse Ten,

"If an iron tool is blunt because it has not been properly sharpened and, consequently, one must employ greater strength in using it, he who is wisest will have the greatest success."

The plain meaning of this statement is that, if one uses his brains as well as his muscles, he will complete a task involving manual labor more easily and quickly than if he relies solely on his muscles. It also implies that an intelligent man will sharpen a tool before he attempts to use it. Several of the Talmudic sages read into this quite mundane axiom some interesting pedagogical deductions.

Rish Lakish said: "If an iron tool is blunt because it has not been properly sharpened"—If a student is having great difficulty in learning because he has not developed systematic study habits,—what should be done to improve the student? He should increase the amount of time that he spends on study, as it says, "One must employ greater strength." "He who is wisest will have the greatest success" means that the best student is the one who develops the most systematic study habits.

Raba bar Joseph said: Ofttimes a student has difficulty with his studies because his teacher does not encourage him and give him proper guidance, as it says, "The iron tool is blunt because it has not been properly sharpened." How does one improve this situation? He sees to it that such a student prepares his lessons in the company of qualified but congenial fellow students, as it says, "One must use greater strength." And what is the meaning of the final phrase, "He who is wisest will have the greatest success"? The phrase means: How much better a student this one would be if, from the very beginning, he had been handled properly by his teacher.

The statements just quoted are found in the Talmud, Taanis 7b-8a. Koheles Rabba also believes that Koheles 10:10 refers to pedagogical matters but his interpretation differs somewhat from that of the Talmudic sages: "If an iron tool is blunt"—If the teacher's attitude toward the pupil is unyielding and harsh, either because the teacher loses patience quickly or because of the pupil's lack of intelligence or wearisome questions,—"because it has not been properly sharpened" —and, because of the teacher's unfriendly attitude and his unwillingness to give the student appropriate explanations, the knowledge of the student is deficient—what should such a student do? He should "employ greater strength." He should send a delegation of respected citizens to the teacher to placate him. The teacher's anger will abate and his attitude toward the student will improve.

Koheles Rabba has a second interpretation: "If an iron tool be blunt"—If the lesson one is trying to master is unusually difficult—"because it has not been properly sharpened"—and one does not understand what the text is trying to convey— "one must use greater strength"—he should go over it again and again until he understands it fully.

Koheles says, Chapter Ten, Verse Eleven,

"If a snake bites without having been charmed, there is no advantage in being a snake charmer."

The meaning of this verse would seem to be that, if a snake bites when he feels like biting and not when his charmer tells him to bite, there is no advantage in being a snake charmer, because such a snake charmer has no control over such a snake. It is much as if the text said, "If an automobile were able to go wherever it wanted to go, there would be no advantage in being an automobile driver,'" or "If an army were to march when and where it pleased and to shoot at whom it pleased, the general of such an army would find himself in a quite awkward position."

Reacting as has practically every other translator and interpreter, ancient and modern, Rashi refuses to believe that this proverb in Koheles carries with it the implication that a snake charmer would deliberately charm a snake into biting a human being. So Rashi twists the meaning of the verse in order to make it say exactly the opposite of what it actually says: If a snake charmer, who knows how to charm snakes so that they will not bite fails to make use of his talents, and the snake whom he could have charmed continues to bite, there is no advantage to a community in having such a snake charmer in its midst. Similarly, if there is a learned man in a community who takes no interest whatsoever in the community's affairs, there is no advantage to the community in having such a learned man in its midst. . . . It would seem that Rashi gave no thought to the possibility of using the home and possessions of such a person as a tourist attraction.

Koheles says, Chapter Ten, Verses Twelve to Fourteen,

"The words of the wise are received graciously; the lips of the fool destroy him. He begins his speech with nonsense and ends his speech with evil madness. The fool talks big, even though mankind knows nothing of the future nor can anyone even surmise what the future may hold in store for him."

Rashi says: "The words of the wise are received graciously" —They make a good impression upon those who hear them; they are accepted, respected and heeded. "The lips of the fool destroy him"—The fool tries to entice mankind from the right path but, in attempting to do so, brings about his own destruction. The fool says, "Tomorrow I shall do thus-and-so to so-and-so," when he is not at all sure that he will still be alive tomorrow. And, as for what may happen in the distant future, it is not possible for him to know anything at all about that.

Koheles says, Chapter Ten, Verse Fifteen,

> "The fool is always tired because he does everything the hard way."

The literal meaning of this verse is "The effort of the fool tires him out, because he does not know the way to the city." Rashi establishes the connection between what the words say and what they mean: The folly of the fool gets him into trouble because, when he prepares to enter a city, he does not ask where the gates of the city are located. Instead, he tries to squeeze in through openings in the city wall which are too narrow or he walks into the moats and through the water ditches and his sandals become bogged down in mud and filth and he enters the city disgusted and worn out.

Koheles says, Chapter Ten, Verse Sixteen,

> "Woe unto the land whose ruler is a youth and whose governors banquet early in the day."

Rashi: Woe unto the land whose leaders act like children.
Sforno: When the ruler is a child, he surrounds himself with childish advisors. They banquet in the morning, as is

the custom of children, because they lack intelligence, common sense and experience. They depend on the opinions of others, who often make these opinions accord with their own desires and their own advantage and whose counsel may lead to the ruler's downfall and the country's ruin.

Koheles says, Chapter Ten, Verse Seventeen,

> "Fortunate is the land whose ruler is of noble birth and whose governors banquet at the proper time, with dignity and temperately."

Ibn Ezra: The implication of the phrase "whose ruler is of noble birth" is that a ruler blessed with good parents and wise teachers will rule with kindness and with justice.

Sforno: The meaning of "whose ruler is of noble birth" is that such a ruler is a man who controls his passions and does not misuse his power, who is intelligent and whose major concern is to improve the lot of his people.

Talmud Shabbas 10a states that Koheles 10:16-17 refers to those who preside over courts of law. "Woe unto the land whose ruler is a youth"—Woe unto that land whose judges are unlearned and inexperienced. "And whose governors banquet early in the day"—and whose judges adjourn the sessions of the court early for their own convenience and with no concern for the many untried cases still on the docket. Rav Sheshes, a Babylonian amora who taught in the academies of Pumbedita and Shili at the end of the third century, asked, "How long should a judge continue to sit on a day when the court is in session?" and answered, "At least until it is time for the evening meal." "Fortunate is the land whose ruler is of noble birth"—Fortunate is the land whose judges are learned in the law and completely impartial. "And whose governors banquet at the proper time, with dignity and temperately"—and whose

judges are hard working, unselfish, and so imbued with the
dignity and importance of their office that they walk at all
times as if they were carrying the Torah and never, either pri-
vately or publicly, allow their utterances or opinions to be
influenced by the aroma or the taste of intoxicating beverages.

Koheles says, Chapter Ten, Verse Eighteen,

> "Because of human indolence, houses fall down; because
> of human neglect, roofs leak."

Koheles says, Chapter Ten, Verse Nineteen,

> "If you want to have fun, plan a party; if you want it
> to be a lively, happy party, bring along a bottle; if you have
> the money, you can get anything you want."

Koheles says, Chapter Ten, Verse Twenty,

> "Do not rail at the government, even in your thoughts;
> do not curse the rich, even in the privacy of your home; for
> there is a special bird that carries your voice, a special bird
> that reports everything you say."

The comments of the medieval exegetes on these last three
verses do not deepen our comprehension of their meaning.
The verses themselves make their points so clearly that detailed exposition would seem to be unnecessary. Yet some
words of explanation are needed. Are these verses meant to
be cynical, misanthropic, pessimistic? No, not really. Most
likely, they are intended to be quite realistic and practical. In
these proverbs or sayings, Koheles is giving further advice to
"the average man" to whom he addressed himself in the first
part of Chapter Nine. He warns him against using his seemingly purposeless existence as an excuse for laziness. In Verse
Eighteen, he repeats in different language what he has already

said in Chapter Four, Verse Five, "The fool folds his arms together and eats his own flesh." In Verse Nineteen, he again urges the average man "to live it up," to enjoy himself to the full, as he has already done in Chapter Nine, Verses Seven to Nine, "Banquet well and often; drink to your heart's content; . . . enjoy life with the woman you love." He gives another reason why everyone should do a reasonable amount of work: One should work in order to obtain enough money to have a good time. In Verse Twenty, he advises the average man to avoid getting mixed up in politics and not to rebel against the rich. In the twentieth century CE, such an admonition may sound very reactionary but, given the political and economic circumstances of Koheles' time and place, this advice makes very good sense. One of the principal reasons why Koheles and many another wisely written book are widely misinterpreted and misunderstood is that the interpreters often insist on transplanting the thoughts of the writer from their native intellectual and cultural soil to that of the interpreter; whereas, in all fairness, it is incumbent upon the fair-minded and intelligent interpreter to uproot himself from the cultural soil of his own time, insofar as this is humanly possible, and to transplant himself into the same historical soil from which the writer drew his inspiration and sustenance.

In the Midrash, Rabbi Abin interprets the "Do not rail at the Government, even in your thoughts" in a way that would have had Koheles' complete approval. The word "government" is capitalized because, according to Rabbi Abin, it refers to God: The Holy One, blessed be He, says to man, "I have given eyes, ears, mouth, hands and feet to both man and beast. Therefore, one might think that man and beast are completely alike. They are not. I have given man the ability to think and to speak. Neither of these gifts has been offered to the beast. And yet the beasts do not complain. They do My will, they obey My orders faithfully and complacently. But you, man, are completely unappreciative of the favors I have bestowed upon you. You complain. You curse and blaspheme in My presence. You use the powers of thought and of speech, given so that you might live more fully and serve Me more worthily, to dishonor Me and to destroy yourselves."

11 — 12

Were Chapters Eleven and Twelve originally written as one chapter and then cut in two by a later editor? There is reason to believe that this is so. It is true that the subject matter of the closing portion of the book may be subdivided into two sections, 11:1-8 and 11:9 to 12:8. But there are other single chapters in the book which likewise may be subdivided into a number of separate sections. The original concluding chapter may have been split in two by the pietistic editor who added the final six verses of the book as it now stands, 12:9-14, an appendix apparently intended to take some of the sting out of the plain language of the old professor. Perhaps this editor decided, after he had added the extra verses, that the chapter was now too long; and so he divided it into two chapters. Be this as it may, Chapters Eleven and Twelve will be treated in this translation and commentary as though they were one chapter, because the "feel" of Koheles' style that one gets from the rest of the book gives the deep impression that these concluding chapters have been created artificially and unintelligently out of what was originally one chapter.

Chapter Eleven starts out in the same vein with which Chapter Ten has been concluded. Koheles bids his readers realize that while, from the vantage point of God, every event that is going to take place is predetermined and known, man has no such inside information. For man, life is a gamble and must be lived as such. Therefore, a man should not hesitate to engage in the hazards of trade; but he should protect himself to some extent by not investing too much of his assets in any single venture. He should keep busy all the days of his life, for this is the surest way to find happiness and contentment. "No matter how long a man lives, let him try to get satisfaction out of every moment of life."

Then, suddenly, the mood of the old man changes, as back in Chapter Two, it changed just as suddenly while the philosopher was extolling the virtue of wisdom and the wickedness of folly. The old man remembers the glorious days of his youth, days without care, days without sickness and pain. Oh, to be young again! "Rejoice, young man, in your youth," he cries. Make the most of it. "Let your heart be gay; do as you wish; go wherever your eyes bid you go." Have fun, my boy, have fun. If you are smart, my boy, you will realize that the grave waits for all mankind and that, for the elderly, life holds but little pleasure. As one gets older, he loses his health and his strength. He loses his courage and his confidence. "He is afraid to climb a hill; when he walks along the street, he is easily frightened; his hair turns as white as the almond blossom; he drags himself along like a broken down grasshopper." Finally, fear, frustration, weakness, pain terminate in death "and the mud is once again mixed into the earth and the life-spirit returns to the Power Which gave it." Koheles finishes his book with the same grim words with which he began: "Vapor of vapors, everything is vapor."

Koheles says, Chapter Eleven, Verses One and Two,

"Ship your products to other countries; this is an excellent long-term business enterprise. Invest your money in seven or eight different commercial ventures; you cannot foretell which of them may meet with some unanticipated misfortune."

This translation is more in keeping with the practical and realistic thinking of Koheles than the wistful traditional translation, "Cast your bread upon the waters and, after many days, you will find it." It is hard to imagine the hardheaded old professor propounding such a wholly mystical, completely irrational economic doctrine.

The classical interpretations of Verses One and Two are based on the traditional translation. The sages say the text means that, when one gives charity, he should give it without thought of recompense, and that, even though the charity is given in such an unselfish spirit, the reward will come nevertheless. Koheles Rabba, in commenting on these verses, tells many amazing stories of people who performed acts of kindness out of the goodness of their hearts and, later, were saved from certain death by those to whom they had been unselfishly kind.

If one accepts the traditional translation of Verse One, it is possible to translate Verse Two as "Give charity to all who ask; you cannot foresee when you yourself may be in need of charity." Accordingly, Rashi comments: Never reach the point where you say, "I have given enough. I shall give no more." The time may come when you will be not the giver but the recipient and you would not want others to say this to you.

It is more logical to believe that these verses refer to maritime commerce because such a translation fits more easily into the thought pattern of the rest of the book. There is a somewhat analogous verse in the Book of Proverbs, Proverbs 31:14. This verse in Proverbs is part of the familiar passage describing the perfect wife, a passage read in many Jewish homes at the evening meal on the Sabbath. Proverbs 31:14 says, concerning the perfect wife, "She is like the merchant ships, bringing the needs of her household from afar." The Hebrew word, translated in Koheles 11:1 as "products" and in Proverbs 31:14 as "needs of her household," is "lechem," which means literally "bread" or "food." The writers of both these Biblical passages were thinking of maritime commerce when they wrote their respective verses. It was very natural that they should do so. Proverbs 31:10-31 is an alphabetic acrostic, composed about the same time that Koheles was written. These Palestinian Jews were writing at a moment in history when the Jewish community in Alexandria was an important part of the commercial life of that great Egyptian seaport. Cargoes of Egyptian grain were being carried to all parts of the Mediterranean world and beyond by Jewish merchants on Jewish ships. The Palestinian Jews were not as well off as their brethren in Alexandria. They were looking for some means to better their situation. Their many contacts with Alexandrian Jewry probably convinced them that engaging in foreign trade would be an effective way to improve their economic status.

Koheles says, Chapter Eleven, Verse Three,

> "When the clouds are filled with rain, they pour it upon the earth; whether a tree falls in the south or in the north, wherever it falls, there it lies."

Having advised his readers to lead an active life, to engage in business, to try to achieve financial success and having also warned his readers that matters do not always turn out as originally planned, Koheles restates the idea that is basic to his whole philosophy: Everything occurs and reoccurs in a fixed pattern according to a predetermined Divine plan. Nothing man can do will change the pattern or interfere with the plan. When a certain amount of water has been gathered up by the clouds, the water is poured back upon the earth as rain. When a tree has lived out the span of years allotted to it, it dies and falls. It lies upon the ground, helpless and lifeless. Nothing that anyone can do will restore life to the dead tree. Wherever the dead tree is destined to lie, there it lies. The inference is that the individual person and mankind in general have not the slightest control over their ultimate destiny.

The first eight verses of Chapter Eleven contain an answer to a question often asked about Koheles: Is the philosophy he presents one of pure pessimism and pure fatalism? Pure pessimism? If to delude oneself by believing in a God Who watches Personally over every act of every person and Who guarantees eternal survival of the individual ego and Who protects His creatures by means of angels and saints and fairies and other equally childish fantasies is to be an optimist, and to look at God and life and the world realistically and honestly is to be a pessimist, Koheles was a pure pessimist. Pure fatalism? If by pure fatalist is meant one who believes that control of the ultimate fate of the individual and the world is completely beyond the power of the human race, Koheles was a pure fatalist. If by pure fatalist is meant one who ceases to do or to care because of this belief, Koheles was not a pure fatalist. He was not one of the living dead who sit with crossed legs and contemplate the ends of their noses or their navels. He was definitely an activist, not because he expected his activities to cause any appreciable change of any kind in the nature of man or the universe or God but because, in these activities, he found a use for his mind, a release for his energies, a source of happiness and satisfaction. Within the permitted limits, he wanted to spend his time on earth as enjoyably as possible. He found his enjoyment in a well balanced diet of the physical and the intellectual, the practical and the spiritual. No philosophic contradiction will be felt in the verses which have preceded this comment or in the verses which immediately follow it if one understands the tenor of the message of Koheles: Keep busy. Be active as long as you can. The end will come soon enough. Exercise your limited freedom by finding satisfaction in whatever activities make most sense to you. Always remember that, regardless of what you do or do not do, God will carry out His will in the way that makes most sense to Him.

Koheles says, Chapter Eleven, Verse Four,

> "He who watches the wind will not sow; he who gazes
> at the clouds will not reap."

Rashi understands well what Koheles was saying: The
farmer who waits for exactly the right kind of wind to blow
before he sows his seed will wait in vain. The farmer who
waits for a completely cloudless sky before he begins to harvest
his grain will wait in vain. The person who waits for everything
to be just right, the person who refuses to take chances, the
person who does what he does and lives as he lives only because it is the way that "they" do it and the way that "they"
live, such a person is even less important than a statistic. He
is a cipher.

Koheles says, Chapter Eleven, Verse Five,

> "Just as we do not know exactly what life is or how the
> bones of a baby are formed in the impregnated womb, so we
> have no real comprehension of the doings of God, the Creator
> of every existing thing."

Talmud Pesachim 54b states and the Midrash, in Bereshis
Rabba and Koheles Rabba, repeats: Seven important things are
hidden from man:

1. The day of death. Yafe Toar comments: If a man knew
just when he was going to die, he would waste away from
anxiety as the day of death drew near. He would cease to take
an interest in the affairs of the world as the day of death drew
near. He would not begin to atone for his failings until the
day of death drew near.

2. The day that his troubles will end. Rashi and Maharshaw
say that this may mean the day when the people of Israel will
return to the Holy Land. Yafe Toar comments: It is good

that a man does not know when his troubles will end, so that he lives and waits and hopes for a day which may or may not come.

3. The profound truths of Divine judgment. Yafe Toar comments: If people knew the full meaning of life and all the secrets of the universe had been uncovered, the desire and the ability to meditate and to study would disappear.

4. Which of his business ventures will turn out well. Yafe Toar comments: If people knew in advance which of their commercial endeavors would succeed and which would not, the sharpness of thought which experience in business develops would be dulled and the uncommon common sense which may be acquired in the market place would become a boring and valueless commodity.

5. What is in the mind of one's companion. Yafe Toar comments: If everyone knew what was in the mind of his companion, friendship, compassion and love would cease and quarrelsomeness, jealousy and hate would increase.

6. What is in the belly of a pregnant female. Yafe Toar comments: If married couples knew with certainty what was going to emerge from the pregnant wife's womb, many would develop all sorts of emotional tensions during the period of pregnancy because of their frustration and disappointment in not getting what they wanted, i.e., a boy and not a girl or twin sons instead of only one son. Even if they knew from the very beginning that the expectant mother was going to bear a baby boy, this would decrease their happiness, because they would be deprived of the greater joy which comes with such a birth after the suspense of months and months of waiting.

7. Pesachim 54b says, "When the Persian Empire will be destroyed." Bereshis Rabba says, "When the wicked empire will crumble." Koheles Rabba says, "When the kingdom of

Edom will perish." Each passage reflects the Jewish wishful thinking of the time in which it was written. Pesachim 54b was referring to the fanatical Sassanian Parsees who ruled over Babylon from the third to the seventh centuries. Bereshis Rabba was probably referring to the Empire of Rome. Koheles Rabba was probably referring to the Church of Rome. Yafe Toar comments: If the Jews were certain that the downfall of their Gentile masters was to be delayed beyond their lifetimes, many Jews would abandon Judaism.

Yafe Toar makes this final comment: Many other important matters are also hidden from man—What is above; what is below; what has happened; what will happen; and, as mentioned in Koheles 11:5, the nature of the life principle and how the bones of a baby are formed in the womb. It is not that man is too stupid to understand these things. Even the wisest cannot understand them; even the prophets did not understand them. God, in His infinite wisdom, has decreed that these shall remain eternal mysteries, which shall keep both the wise and the foolish eternally ignorant.

Koheles says, Chapter Eleven, Verses Six to Eight,

> "In the morning of life, sow your seed; in the evening of life, let not your hands be idle; no one really knows whether one time of life is more important than the other; no one really knows whether one time of life is as good as the other. The warmth of life is delicious; it is good when the eyes are able to behold the rays of the sun. No matter how long a man lives, let him try to get satisfaction out of every moment of life; let him be continually mindful that the darkness of the grave is endless, that, after life, there is nothing."

The meaning of these verses is crystal clear: As a youth, prepare yourself for your life's work. Then, for the rest of your life, busy yourself with the task for which you have

prepared. In the morning, sow the seed; in the evening, reap
the harvest. He who does not school himself properly in his
early years will not employ his later years profitably. Therefore,
it is difficult to determine which is the more important, the
time of training or the time of doing. It is also difficult to
judge which gives a person more satisfaction, the joy of learning or the joy of achieving. Of this we may be sure—that life
is better than death and that each period of life has its rewards
and its compensations. Our goal should be to live each moment
to the full, to get as much happiness and enjoyment out of
each moment as is possible—for life must end in death and
"after life, there is nothing." Because life is all there is, and
because all there is is now, live and let live, be happy and
make others happy, make the most of every hour of every day.

"Well spoken!" you say? The medieval commentators do
not seem to have thought so. Some of their interpretations of
"In the morning of life, sow your seed; in the evening of life,
let not your hands be idle" are: If you gave alms to a beggar
in the morning and the same beggar approaches you in the
evening, give again. If you were charitable as a young man,
continue to be charitable as an old man. If you have children
as a young man, and your wife dies, remarry and, as an old
man, beget more children. If you studied or taught Torah as
a young man, continue to study and teach Torah as an old man.
The comments on the rest of the passage evince a similar unwillingness to come to grips with the real meaning of these
verses. Here, then, are more words of Koheles which the Pharisaic mind did not understand or did not want to understand
or, what is much more likely, did not want to indicate that
it understood.

Koheles says, Chapter Eleven, Verses Nine and Ten,

"Rejoice, young man, in your youth; let your heart be

gay in life's most carefree days; do as you wish; go wherever your eyes bid you go. May unhappiness be absent from your thoughts; may nothing evil afflict your body; for childhood and youth pass by so quickly."

The concluding phrase of Verse Nine in the Hebrew text "and know that for all this God will hold you accountable" could not possibly have been written by Koheles and must be regarded as the insertion of a later pietist, who was trying to tone down Koheles' counsel to youth to be carefree and gay and to do pretty much as it damned well pleases.

As was mentioned in the introductory comments to this chapter, we find here a change in mood that is as sudden and dramatic as that which Koheles experienced while writing Chapter Two. He has just said, in Verse Six, that both youth and old age serve useful personal and social purposes. He has stated that no one really knows which of the two is the better time of life. Now, after another moment's reflection, he is filled with the realization that old age is, for him, predominantly, a time of misery and pain while youth was, predominantly, a time of carefree exuberance and joy. How can one possibly be compared to the other? How can one possibly think that the period of decline is as happy as the period of growth? Utterly nonsensical to do so, Koheles decides. No matter how hard one may try to rationalize the whole matter, there is really nothing very valuable or good about old age. Youth is the only time of life when one is really happy, when one really lives. Wine, women, and song—that's what real living is. Have fun. Be gay. "Do as you wish. . . . Go where your eyes bid you go. . . . Rejoice in your youth. . . . Youth passes by so quickly."

The last phrase is what is known in the vernacular of the

magician as "the giveaway," the external expression that betrays
the internal secret. It reveals the reason for the sudden change
in mood. As, in Goethe's *Faust,* the hero cries out, in his moment of greatest happiness, "Verweile doch, du bist so schoen,"
"O moment of supreme ecstasy, stay a while; you are so precious!", so also the aging Hebrew philosopher, weary, full of
aches and pains, conscious of the great disparity between youth
and old age and of the brevity of the time and advantages of
youth, cries out, in his "moment of truth": "Rejoice, O young
man, in your youth!" Make the most of it. Enjoy it before it
is too late.

The exegetes were greatly shocked by this display of candor.
They could not believe that King Solomon, wisest of all men
and the supposed author of the book, would have made this
kind of statement. So they came to the conclusion that Solomon
did not really write these words. They were slipped into the text
by the Yetser Hara, the Evil Inclination, and were meant to
imply, "It is more meritorious to sin and then to repent than
never to sin at all. So, go ahead, son, sin now and repent later
and everything will be just fine."

Koheles Rabba states that, when the sages examined Koheles 11:9, the only reason they did not declare its sentiment
to be completely heretical was because of the concluding phrase,
"and know that for all this God will hold you accountable."

Koheles Rabba makes a feeble attempt to explain away the
obvious meaning of the verse: Rabbi Yudan said, "Rejoice,
young man, in your youth"—this refers to the study of Bible
in youth; "let your heart be gay in life's most carefree days"—
this refers to the study of Mishna in youth; "do as you wish;
go wherever your eyes bid you go"—this refers to the study
of Gemarra in youth; "and know that for all this God will

hold you accountable"—this refers to observance of the commandments and to good deeds.

Koheles says, Chapter Twelve, Verse One,

"Bless your Creator in the days of your youth, before the ominous days begin, before the years come when you will be tempted to say that life has lost all zest."

The literal and generally accepted translation of the beginning of this verse is "Remember your Creator in the days of your youth." Many a fervid homily has been delivered at college baccalaureate services with this inaccurate translation as the sermon text. What sense does it make for one with the point of view of Koheles to advise the reader to remember his Creator in the days of his youth? What is there to remember? That the Creator is unknowable and His plan and His purposes are incomprehensible? That He uses the creatures of earth, all of them, man included, as his tools and that, after these instruments have completed the functions for which they were created, He destroys them? Is that what youth is to remember? Would such a recollection increase the joy, the freedom from care in the time of youth? Hardly. It would be much more likely to detract from the enjoyment than add to it.

The correct translation of the first Hebrew word of Koheles 12:1 is to be found in a secondary meaning of the Hebrew root, "zachar," a meaning which may be translated variously as "to memorialize," "to remember for good," "to offer up prayers for," "to praise," "to bless." Normally this meaning is used with reference to the righteous dead. But in Koheles 12:1 it refers to the feeling of thankfulness to God that should be felt by the youth for having been granted the privilege of years of health and happiness before the years of pain and misery begin. It is Koheles' way of saying to mankind, "Since man is but a tool in the hands of God and since the ways of God are inscrutable and since God, if He so willed, could make all our days miserable and painful, let us be grateful to Him for whatever pleasure we get out of life. Let us not question nor complain. Whatever is is because God means it to be so. Therefore, accept life as it is and for what it is."

Nowhere does Koheles refer to the middle years of life. He speaks only of youth and of old age. We must assume, therefore, that, by youth, he meant more than just the years before one grows to normal adulthood. He seems to have meant all the years after childhood and before old age. Just how many years this might be would vary in different epochs, areas, countries, groups and individuals. In the twentieth century United States, for example, one might say that, with the average person, this period of "youth" would last for about thirty-five years, from fifteen to fifty. Among the exceptions would be a handful of inordinately vain and highly imaginative males and females, who are so blind to their own inadequacies that, even after seventy, they continue to try to scrutinize, flirt, squire and woo.

Koheles says, Chapter Twelve, Verse Two,

"Before the light of the sun and the moon and the stars begin to darken and the clouds return after the rain."

Koheles now begins to describe what happens when "the ominous days begin."

When the body starts to age, one of the first signs is a change in facial expression. "The light of the sun and the moon and the stars begins to darken"—the face which has been smooth and colorful and bright begins to get wrinkled, to become pale and dull. "The clouds return after the rain"—one begins to cry more often because of pain, trouble and sorrow. When the rain has ceased, the sun does not begin to shine again but the clouds return to fill the sky. When one is old, crying does not bring one's sorrows and troubles to an end. After one has cried and cried, his troubles and his sorrows are still there.

Koheles says, Chapter Twelve, Verse Three,

> "When the watchmen tremble and the soldiers no longer stand erect and the millstones stop grinding for lack of workers and the lattices of the windows are closed."

"When the house watchmen tremble"—these are the ribs which hold the body together. "And the soldiers no longer stand erect"—these are the legs which can no longer support the full weight of the body. "The millstones stop grinding for lack of workers"—this means that, when one is no longer able to chew his food properly, because of lack of teeth, the stomach is no longer able to digest the food properly, and, as a result, the elderly person is constipated. "The lattices of the windows are closed"—the eyelids of many old people droop so that oftentimes they give the impression of being continually asleep.

Koheles says, Chapter Twelve, Verse Four,

> "The doors to the street are blocked; the noise of the grinding of the millstone is not heard; there are times when one will be startled by the chirp of a bird and other times when one will not be moved by the music of a lovely chorale."

"The doors to the street are blocked"—the organs for urination and defication do not operate effectively. "The noise of the grinding of the millstone is not heard"—when one loses his ability to chew, he eats less and then the stomach has less work to do; as a result, the stomach ceases to send forth the loud and redolent noises which the healthy person sometimes emits, while food is being ground up in the stomach. "There are times when one will be startled by the chirp of a bird"— a hearty meal induces sleep; when one is no longer able to eat well, he does not sleep soundly and he is easily awakened. There are "times when one will not be moved by the music of a lovely chorale"—some old people lose their hearing and are no longer able to enjoy good music; others become so melancholy or so childish that they lose their taste for good music.

Koheles says, Chapter Twelve, Verse Five,

"He is afraid to climb a hill; when he walks along the street, he is easily frightened; his hair turns as white as the almond blossom; he drags himself along like a broken down grasshopper; all sexual desire is gone; his journey to the grave has already begun; the professional weepers are already making plans for his funeral route."

"He is afraid to climb a hill; when he walks along the street, he is easily frightened." Koheles Rabba remarks: When one says to an old man, "Go to a certain place," he asks, "Are there steps there? Does one have to go up and down?" When an old man is invited to a feast, he is afraid to make the trip; it takes him a long time to decide whether or not to go; if he does go, he makes marks on houses or trees as he goes along to make sure that he will find his way back; when he ventures out, he is frightened easily, so he always tries to figure out the shortest route to his destination.

"He drags himself along like a broken down grasshopper." Rashi says: He walks like one who carries a heavy burden.

"The professional weepers are already making plans for his funeral route."—Just as, in our day, professional musicians and singers are hired to perform at weddings, so, in the time of Koheles, professional mourners were engaged to weep at funerals. Koheles refers sarcastically to the "performance" put on by these professional weepers. He indicates that they plan in advance at what points along the route of the funeral procession they will emit their loudest wails, presumably those points where those who will pay them are assembled or where the groups of curious onlookers are thickest.

Koheles says, Chapter Twelve, Verse Six,
> "Before the silver cord is snapped and the golden bowl is crushed; before the pitcher by the well is broken and the wheel over the well is shattered."

This verse is a clever Mashal or parable. The picture the verse intends to convey is as follows: There is a wheel over a well which is used to draw water from the well. Attached to the wheel is one end of a silver cord. A golden bowl is attached to the other end of the silver cord. By means of the wheel, the bowl is lowered into the well and filled with water. After the bowl is raised from the well, the water in the bowl is poured into a pitcher which stands by the side of the well. This lovely rustic scene symbolizes the act of procreation. The wheel over the well is the male brain which sends a message by way of the silver cord, the central nervous system, to the male organ of generation to fill itself with fluid from the well of life and to deposit this fluid in the female organ of reproduction. This verse is Koheles' picturesque and somewhat esoteric way of telling healthy, youthful males and females to make good and proper use of their brains and other bodily contrivances before it is too late.

Koheles says, Chapter Twelve, Verses Seven and Eight,
> "And the mud is once again mixed into the earth and the life-spirit returns to the Power Which gave it. Vapor of vapors, everything is vapor."

Koheles ends with the same pessimistic words with which he began. With these words, the teachings of Koheles are concluded.

Sometime later, someone who admired Koheles greatly but was afraid of the effect that his teachings might have upon the masses, added the following six verses:

"Koheles was a very wise man. He taught his people knowledge; he considered and examined everything; he composed many proverbs. Koheles tried to discover the meaning of everything; he was an able expounder of the truth, as he understood it. The words of the wise are like goads and, when the head of a convocation of sages makes known the findings of the convocation, his words are like driven nails. But be careful, my son; there is no limit to the kinds of things you will find written in books; spending too much time on what is written in books can become downright tiresome. After considering everything that Koheles has to say, one must still conclude that the traditional way is the best way: Fear God; keep His commandments; man has no other choice. Ultimately God may make known the meaning of everything which we do not now understand; whether that will be good or bad, only time will tell."

With these editorial words, the Book of Koheles comes to an end.

SUMMATION

Koheles is a book of Jewish philosophy, Bible style. It is not written systematically nor are all its statements completely consistent one with the other. It is written as one speaks rather than as one thinks and, at a few points, the writer gets so emotionally involved that he becomes self-contradictory. It was composed before the Greek insistence on orderliness and the Roman insistence on logic found such absolute acceptance in the mind-processes of medieval and modern Jewish thinkers that they put aside the heated and somewhat exaggerative literary style of their Oriental forebears in order to clothe their thoughts in the cold, precise language of the Occidental.

This does not mean that the thoughts of Koheles contain neither system nor logic. If we analyze the meaning of each sentence carefully, we find that the Book of Koheles contains a thoroughly consistent, thoroughly logical point of view. The primary purpose of this summation will be to present that point of view in a systematic and logical manner.

Let us first eliminate from consideration those few portions of the book which Koheles did not write. He did not write 1:1, 1:12, 3:17, the concluding phrase of 8:8, 8:12b-13, the concluding phrase of 11:9, and 12:9-14. He may or may not have written 4:13-16.

Koheles 1:1 and 1:12 try to prove that Koheles was King Solomon. Koheles 3:17, the concluding phrase of 8:8, 8:12b-13 and the concluding phrase of 11:9 are attempts by a Pharisaic editor or editors to inject into the book the idea that God systematically punishes the wicked and rewards the righteous, an idea which Koheles rejects completely. Koheles 12:9-14 is an editorial epilogue.

The most obvious inconsistencies in the book are: After having emphasized that one should not put too much stress upon the acquisition of material gain, Koheles bemoans the fact that he is going to have to leave his hard won wealth to those who are not worthy to receive it (2:18-21; 6:1-2). After extolling the benefits of wisdom, Koheles suddenly declares that wisdom has no lasting value (2:14). After stating in 11:6 that the later years, rather than the years of youth, may be the more valuable part of life, he says (11:9-10) that the time of youth is the only time of life when one is genuinely happy. He bids man to enjoy life with the woman he loves (9:9) and yet complains that women are conniving creatures (7:26) and incapable of straight or deep thought (7:28). While he most certainly does not believe in a Personal God, he speaks of God anthropomorphically in a number of places. One is not to "provoke the anger of God" (5:5). One is to fear God (3:14; 5:6; 7:18). These are, in all likelihood, stylistic expressions, meant to be taken seriously but not literally.

So much for the book's editorial insertions and logical imperfections. Now let us set down, in as orderly a form as possible, the message of the Book of Koheles.

Nowhere in his book does Koheles attempt to state what God is. He only tells what God does.

God controls every movement in the universe and every event in the life of man (9:1). Everything is the way God wants it to be; nothing of Earth has the power to change the will or the way of God (1:15; 3:14; 7:13; 8:8). Nothing in the world is devoid of purpose or meaning (5:8). Everything that happens happens at the time and in the manner that God decided, ages ago, that it should happen (3:1,2-8,11,14). Everything that happens occurs and reoccurs according to a fixed, predetermined Divine plan (11:3). The past was no better than the present (7:10) and about the future man knows nothing (3:22; 6:12; 7:24).

"The nature and fate of man were determined long ago (6:10)." Man is just a beast like all other beasts. He has much the same nature as the rest of the beasts. He lives in much the same way as do the beasts and as the beast dies, so he dies (3:18-20). Individual beings come and go; only the world endures (1:4). All of man's efforts to realize his desires and his ambitions are, sub specie aeternitatis, meaningless (1:2; 2:17). Man brings nothing of material worth with him when he is ushered into the world and he carries nothing of material worth with him when he departs (5:14-15). His earthly labors earn for him no lasting reward (1:3).

Earthly success and happiness are largely matters of luck. "Time and chance determine the fate of all mankind (9:11)." The belief that God rewards the good and punishes the wicked is sheer nonsense (2:26; 8:10,12a,14). "If you see that the poor in the land are oppressed and that justice and righteousness have been stealthily removed, do not be surprised at this state of affairs (5:7)." The public mind is fickle; it neither appreciates goodness nor rewards it (9:13-16; 10:1). Justice and righteousness do not exist on earth (3:16). How may one speak of justice and righteousness in a world in which some human beings are given the power to inflict harm on other human beings (8:9), a world in which men callously ignore the plight of those who are oppressed (4:1)?

When the life of the individual is ended, he disappears completely and is forgotten completely (1:11; 9:5). Death is inevitable, inescapable (9:12). "While there is life, there is hope" is the sentiment of a fool, a fool who believes that he may be able to escape death (9:4). God has put the hope of eternal life in the mass-mind in order to confuse it (3:11). There is no eternal life for man (2:14-16; 3:20-21). Death is

the end for both the righteous and the wicked, the wise and
the foolish (2:14; 9:2). "Their loves, their hates, their jealousies are ended; never again will they share in anything that
happens under the sun (9:6)." "The darkness of the grave
is endless; after life, there is nothing (11:8)."

In the person who lacks religious faith, the thought that
death is the end produces "the corrupting notion that life is
merely a frenzied madness" (9:3). But, for the unselfish man,
the incorruptible man, the genuinely wise man, the truly religious man, awareness of the transiency of life and the finality
of death is a spiritual blessing, an ever present thought which
serves him continually as a sobering, an enlightening, a beneficial influence (7:2-5).

One proves that he has attained maturity when he accepts
life as it is, with all its contradictions, paradoxes, limitations
and unpleasantnesses, when he no longer seeks to attain the
impossible or strains for that which is beyond his grasp (6:8-
11; 7:14-15). To attempt to fathom the unfathomable is not
wise; such an effort brings only vexation and pain. True wisdom lies in complete and wholehearted acceptance of the fact
that God controls everything and man controls nothing (2:12-
14; 5:6). This kind of wisdom provides more protection to
him who possesses it than ten city magistrates (7:19). This
kind of wisdom gives its owner the rare ability to live intelligently and consistently. "I have been unable to find more than
one man in a thousand whose thoughts and actions are consistent; and among women consistency in thought and action
is completely nonexistent. I discerned that God has made this
one man in a thousand a straight-thinking person, while the
other nine hundred ninety-nine go rummaging for the truth
in the most fantastic ways (7:28-29)." Yet the very wisest
among men have no knowledge of the Ultimate Truth (7:23;

8:16-17). "We have no real comprehension of the doings of God, the Creator of every existing thing (11:5)."

The dead are better off than the living (4:2). Most fortunate of all are those who have not yet lived (4:3). It is highly questionable whether the experience of living is of any benefit to those who go through the experience (6:12).

"The best attitude to take is to regard the world with amusement (8:15)." The happiest individual is he who enjoys eating and drinking and gets satisfaction from his work (2:24; 3:12-13,22; 5:17; 9:7). Luckiest of all is the wise man who has inherited wealth and, therefore, does not have to worry about making a living and can spend his time doing only that which gives him pleasure and satisfaction (5:18-19; 7:11-12). One should strive to do whatever he does as well as possible (9:10). One should try to get as much satisfaction as possible out of every moment of life (11:8).

"Two are better than one." Unfortunate is he who has no life-companion (4:9-12). "Enjoy life with the woman you love (9:9)."

"Rejoice, young man, in your youth; let your heart be gay in life's most carefree days; do as you wish; go wherever your eyes bid you go (11:9)." "Bless your Creator in the days of your youth, before the ominous days begin, before the years come when you will be tempted to say that life has lost all zest (12:1)." School yourself well in the time of youth for the work which will occupy your time in later years (11:6).

What are useful ways in which one may occupy his adult years? Farming is the most essential occupation of all, because life is not possible without food and because land is the most enduring form of wealth (5:8-9). To engage in foreign trade is an interesting and challenging enterprise (11:1-2). Whenever one has the opportunity, he should go to "the house of

God" and listen to the learned discussions that are carried on there. This is a much more worthy form of religious expression than the offering of sacrifices (4:17). When one is present at such discussions, he should only speak when he has something really worthwhile to say. His words should be brief and carefully chosen (5:1). "Too many words is the mark of the fool (5:2)." The wise man speaks quietly; the fool shouts (9:17). "The words of the wise are received graciously; the lips of the fool destroy him (10:12)."

"The best way to live is to interest oneself in spiritual concerns but also to give a proper place to material concerns; he who truly fears God will not allow either the one concern or the other to become his master (7:18)." It is quite proper to try to achieve a financial position in which one may live comfortably and enjoy himself (10:19). But there are limits to the satisfactions which may be gotten from either the business world or the world of the senses. Devoting oneself overly much to business, to the acquisition of wealth, and even to philanthropic enterprises, are activities which do not bring lasting satisfaction (2:4-8,11). Too much attention to business causes nightmares (5:2) and shortens life (7:17). To be a wealthy man is to bear a heavy responsibility (5:10-13). He who has been successful in his effort to acquire wealth must endure the jealousy of the unsuccessful (4:4). To have wealth and to enjoy it is a blessing; but to have wealth and not enjoy it, to be a discontented rich man, is a curse (6:1-9).

Even more senseless and meaningless than a continual thirst for wealth is the way of the sensualist, devoting one's life completely to the pursuit of physical pleasure (2:1-3,8,11). He who seeks only material success may have some measure of wisdom in him, but he who spends all his time in search of sensual pleasure has the heart and mind of a fool (7:4-6).

"As the crackling of burning twigs under a boiling pot is the meaningless laughter of a fool."

What was the attitude of Koheles toward the government? It must be kept in mind that, in his day, the Jews were helpless subjects of either the Egyptians or the Syrians. Koheles advised: Do not criticize the government, not even within the privacy of your own home. "There is a special bird that carries your voice, a special bird that reports everything you say (10:20)." Obey the laws of the realm and the commands of the king (8:2-4). A smart man will always find a way to circumvent an inconvenient law (8:5-7) or to overcome the anger of the king (10:4). "Because the penalty for committing a crime is not exacted speedily, the minds of men are filled with many schemes for circumventing the law (8:11)." Many of those whom rulers place in positions of authority are fools and knaves (10:5-7). Rulers should be wellborn, dedicated, mature individuals; but often they are not (10:16-17).

Koheles describes the truly wise man in the following manner: He fulfills his promises to God and to man (5:3-5). He is honest and incorruptible (7:7). He is patient, humble, slow to anger (7:8-9). He is kindly and conciliatory (8:1).

Koheles gives his readers some prescriptions for happy living: Avoid selfishness and miserliness (4:7-8), idleness (4:5-6) and laziness (10:18). . . . Do not be overly cautious (11:4) nor "overly righteous nor overly cunning, unless you want others to stop associating with you (7:16)." . . . Whenever you appear in public, be sure you are well groomed (9:7). . . . "A good name is more valuable than precious oil (7:1)" but do not take to heart everything people say about you (7:21). You say things about others which you do not fully mean (7:22). . . . "There is no one on earth so perfect that he always does the right thing and never does anything wrong (7:20)."

These are the teachings of Koheles. They are the teachings of a realist, a rationalist. It has been said that Koheles is a pessimist, a cynic. For those who shrink from facing reality, who cannot think rationally, who still want to believe in and to lean on their idols and their saints and their foolish folk tales, he is, undoubtedly, a most unacceptable religious teacher. But, for those who want the story straight, who do not want to be flimflammed, bull-dozed or hypnotized by the so-called teachers of the many phony religious beliefs and practices that infest the earth, Koheles is one of the truly great (and there are not many of them), a teacher who was dedicated to the basic values which an enlightened humanity will eventually accept and which a genuinely Universal Religion will eventually promote: Honesty, Reality, Truth.

TALMUDIC AND MIDRASHIC SOURCES

The classical collections of Talmudic and Midrashic materials used in the preparation of the commentary on Koheles, the nature of the materials each contains, its country and time of compilation, are as follows:

1. MISHNA, a codification of Jewish law, Palestine, 100 BCE to 200 CE.
2. SIFREY, Midrash (rabbinical comments) on Numbers and Deuteronomy, Palestine, 2nd century CE.
3. TOSEPHTA, additions to the Mishna, Palestine, 3rd century CE.
4. TALMUD, commentary on the Mishna, Babylonia, 200 to 500 CE.
5. BERESHIS RABBA, Midrash on Genesis, Palestine, 4th to 6th centuries.
6. VAYIKRA RABBA, Midrash on Leviticus, Palestine, 7th century.
7.- ROOS RABBA, Midrash on Ruth, Palestine, 8th century.
8. KOHELES RABBA, Midrash on Ecclesiastes, country of origin uncertain, 8th century or later.
9. DEVARIM RABBA, Midrash on Deuteronomy, country of origin uncertain, c.900 CE.
10. MIDRASH TANCHUMA, Midrash on entire Pentateuch, country of origin uncertain, 10th or 11th centuries.
11. MIDRASH TEHILLIM, Midrash on Psalms, Palestine, 11th or 12th centuries.
12. SH'MOS RABBA, Midrash on Exodus, country of origin uncertain, 11th or 12th centuries.

13. BAMIDBAR RABBA, Midrash on Numbers, somewhere in Europe, c.12th century.
14. YALKUT SHEMONI, collection of Midrashic materials on entire Bible, Germany, 13th century.

The Yalkut Shemoni was compiled by Simon the Preacher. The names of the compilers of the other Midrashic collections cited are not known.

A listing follows of the specific Talmudic and Midrashic sources used in preparing the commentary on individual verses:

CHAP.	VERSE	SOURCES
1	2	Bereshis Rabba 96:2
		Koheles Rabba 1:2
		Tanchuma Pikkudey 3
	3	Koheles Rabba 1:3
	4	Koheles Rabba 1:4
		Talmud Shabbas 25b
		Tosephta to Tractate Rosh Hashana, chapter 1
	5	Koheles Rabba 1:3; 1:5
	7	Koheles Rabba 1:7:4; 1:7:5
		Tanchuma Vayakhel 2
	8	Koheles Rabba 1:8
	18	Bereshis Rabba 19:1
		Koheles Rabba 1:18
		Talmud Taanis 4a

CHAP.	VERSE	SOURCES
2	2	Koheles Rabba 2:2
	12	Bereshis Rabba 12:1 Koheles Rabba 2:12
	13	Bereshis Rabba 12:1 Koheles Rabba 2:12
	14	Koheles Rabba 2:14
	15	Koheles Rabba 2:15:4; 2:15:5
	16	Koheles Rabba 2:15:4; 2:15:5
	20	Koheles Rabba 2:20 Tanchuma Kedoshim 8 Vayikra Rabba 25:5
3	2	Koheles Rabba 3:2:3
	3	Koheles Rabba 3:3
	4	Koheles Rabba 3:4
	5	Koheles Rabba 3:5
	6	Koheles Rabba 3:6
	7	Koheles Rabba 3:7
	8	Koheles Rabba 3:8
	9	Koheles Rabba 3:9
	10	Koheles Rabba 3:10
	11	Bereshis Rabba 3:7; 9:2 Koheles Rabba 3:11:1; 3:11:2; 3:11:3 Midrash Tehillim 9:1; 34:1 Talmud Berachos 43b

CHAP.	VERSE	SOURCES
	15	Koheles Rabba 3:15 Vayikra Rabba 27:5
	19	Koheles Rabba 3:19
4	3	Bereshis Rabba 28:4 Koheles Rabba 4:3 Midrash Tehillim 105:3 Talmud Chagiga 13b-14a
	6	Koheles Rabba 4:6 Mishna Avos 4:17 Vayikra Rabba 3:1
	9	Koheles Rabba 4:9 Yalkut Shemoni II:970
	12	Mishna Kiddushin 1:10 Talmud Kesubos 62b Talmud Kiddushin 40b Talmud Menachos 43b
	13	Koheles Rabba 4:13
	14	Midrash Tehillim 9:5
	17	Koheles Rabba 4:17 Mishna Berachos 9:5 Talmud Berachos 23a
5	1	Bereshis Rabba 24:1 Koheles Rabba 5:1 Talmud Berachos 60b-61a
	3	Koheles Rabba 5:4 Sifrey Ki Seytsey, section 265 Talmud Chullin 2a Tanchuma Vayishlach 8

CHAP.	VERSE	SOURCES
	4	Koheles Rabba 5:4 Sifrey Ki Seytsey, section 265 Talmud Chullin 2a Tanchuma Vayishlach 8
	5	Koheles Rabba 5:5 Midrash Tehillim 52:1 Talmud Megilla 18a Vayikra Rabba 5:5
	7	Koheles Rabba 5:7
	8	Bereshis Rabba 10:7 Koheles Rabba 5:8:1; 5:8:4 Sh'mos Rabba 10:1 Vayikra Rabba 22:1
	11	Koheles Rabba 5:11:5 Tanchuma Ki Seesa 3
	13	Koheles Rabba 5:13 Vayikra Rabba 34:4
	14	Koheles Rabba 5:14
	16	Koheles Rabba 5:16
6	2	Koheles Rabba 6:2
	4	Koheles Rabba 6:4
	5	Koheles Rabba 6:5
	8	Koheles Rabba 6:8
	9	Talmud Yoma 74b

CHAP.	VERSE	SOURCES
	10	Bereshis Rabba 8:10 Koheles Rabba 6:10
	11	Koheles Rabba 6:11 Yalkut Shemoni II:972
	12	Koheles Rabba 6:12
7	1	Koheles Rabba 7:1:1; 7:1:2; 7:1:3; 7:1:4 Sh'mos Rabba 48:1 Talmud Berachos 17a Tanchuma Vayakhel 1
	2	Koheles Rabba 7:2:1; 7:2:2; 7:2:5 Talmud Kesubos 72a Talmud Moed Katan 28b Yalkut Shemoni II:973
	5	Koheles Rabba 7:5
	7	Koheles Rabba 7:7:1 Sh'mos Rabba 6:2
	8	Koheles Rabba 7:8 Roos Rabba 6:4 Talmud Chagiga 15b
	9	Koheles Rabba 7:9
	11	Koheles Rabba 7:11
	12	Talmud Pesachim 53b Talmud Shabbas 63a
	14	Koheles Rabba 7:14:2 Vayikra Rabba 34:5 Yalkut Shemoni II:975

CHAP.	VERSE	SOURCES
	16	Koheles Rabba 7:16
	19	Koheles Rabba 7:19:1 Talmud Nedarim 32b Vayikra Rabba 4:4
	23	Koheles Rabba 7:23:1
	26	Koheles Rabba 7:26:1; 7:26:2 Talmud Berachos 8a Talmud Yebamos 63a
	28	Koheles Rabba 7:28
8	1	Koheles Rabba 8:1:4 Talmud Nedarim 49b Talmud Taanis 7b
	2	Bamidbar Rabba 14:6 Talmud Kesubos 17a
	3	Koheles Rabba 8:3
	8	Devarim Rabba 9:3 Koheles Rabba 8:8
	10	Koheles Rabba 8:10 Tanchuma Yisro 1
	11	Koheles Rabba 8:11
9	4	Bereshis Rabba 34:12 Koheles Rabba 5:10:2; 9:1:2 Talmud Nida 15a Talmud Shabbas 30b; 151b
	5	Talmud Berachos 19a

CHAP.	VERSE	SOURCES
	8	Koheles Rabba 9:8
	9	Bereshis Rabba 17:2 Koheles Rabba 9:9 Talmud Yebamos 62b Yalkut Shemoni I:23
	10	Koheles Rabba 9:10
	14	Talmud Nedarim 32b
	15	Koheles Rabba 9:15:7
	17	Koheles Rabba 9:17
	18	Koheles Rabba 9:18:1
10	3	Koheles Rabba 10:3
	4	Koheles Rabba 10:4
	10	Koheles Rabba 10:10 Talmud Taanis 7b-8a
	16	Talmud Shabbas 10a
	20	Koheles Rabba 10:20 Vayikra Rabba 32:2
11	1	Koheles Rabba 11:1
	5	Bereshis Rabba 65:12 Koheles Rabba 11:5 Talmud Pesachim 54b
	9	Koheles Rabba 11:9

CHAP.	VERSE	SOURCES
12	1	Koheles Rabba 12:1
	2	Koheles Rabba 12:2 Talmud Shabbas 151b
	3	Koheles Rabba 12:3 Talmud Shabbas 152a
	4	Koheles Rabba 12:4 Talmud Shabbas 152a Vayikra Rabba 18:1
	5	Koheles Rabba 12:5 Talmud Shabbas 152a Vayikra Rabba 18:1
	6	Koheles Rabba 12:6 Talmud Shabbas 151b

TANNAIM AND AMORAIM
MENTIONED IN COMMENTARY

The identifiable Tannaim and Amoraim mentioned in the commentary and the verses concerning which the comments of each are mentioned are:

Abba bar Kahana, Palestinian amora, 3rd generation, 280-310—1:4; 2:1-2; 6:2
Abbahu, Palestinian amora, 3rd generation, 280-310—3:10,11
Abbaya, Babylonian amora, c.280-338—6:9; 7:26
Abin, Palestinian amora, 5th generation, 335-370—3:7; 9:10; 10:20
Acha bar Jacob, Babylonian amora, 4th generation, 310-335—1:2,3
Acha ben Chanina, Palestinian amora, 3rd generation, 280-310—5:8
Akiba ben Joseph, tanna, Palestine, c.45-135—3:2; 5:1
Ammi and Assi, Palestinian amoraim, 3rd generation, 280-310—6:9
Ashi, Babylonian amora, 354-427—1:18; 8:2

Berachya Ha-Kohen, Palestinian amora, 5th generation, 335-370—1:5

Chanilai, Palestinian amora, 1st generation, 200-250—9:9
Chanina bar Pappa, Palestinian amora, 3rd generation, 280-310—2:12

Eleazar ben Pedas, Palestinian amora, 3rd generation, 280-310—3:11; 9:9
Eliezer ben Hyrcanus, tanna, Palestine, 2nd generation, 80-120—9:8

Gamliel III ben Judah ha-Nasi, tanna, Palestine, 6th generation, 200-220—7:11

Huna ben Joshua, Babylonian amora, 5th generation, 335-370—1:2; 5:1; 6:11

Ibbu, Palestinian amora, 3rd generation, 280-310—3:10
Ishmael ben Elisha, tanna, Palestine, 3rd generation, 120-140—1:16-18
Isaac Nappacha, Palestinian amora, 3rd generation, 280-310—3:10; 4:6; 9:5

Jacob ben Korshai, tanna, Palestine, 4th generation, 140-165—4:6

Jochanan bar Nappacha, Palestinian amora, 199-279—1:4; 3:10; 4:9; 6:11; 7:7,12; 9:9
Jonathan ben Eleazar, Palestinian amora, 2nd generation, 250-280—3:11
Jose bar Chalafta, tanna, Palestine, 4th generation, 140-165—1:7
Jose bar Chanina, Palestinian amora, 3rd generation, 280-310—5:7
Joshua ben Chananya, tanna, Palestine, c.40-c.125—5:1,5
Joshua ben Korcha, tanna, Palestine, 4th generation, 140-165—9:9
Joshua ben Levi, Palestinian amora, 1st generation, 200-250—5:5; 9:9
Judah bar Illai, tanna, Palestine, 4th generation, 140-165—8:1
Judah bar Simon, Palestinian amora, 4th generation, 310-335—3:15
Judah ha-Nasi, tanna, Palestine, c.135-c.205—3:11; 5:4,8,9; 7:26; 9:4,8

Levi, Palestinian amora, 3rd generation, 280-310—1:8; 6:2; 9:18
Levi bar Sissi, tanna, Palestine, 6th generation, 200-220—1:5; 3:11

Meir, tanna, Palestine, 4th generation, 140-165—1:18; 2:12,13; 4:9; 5:1,4,14; 7:1,2,8; 9:8

Nachman bar Isaac, Babylonian amora, c.280-c.356—2:12; 3:19; 8:1

Pinchas bar Chamma, Palestinian amora, 4th generation, 310-335—3:10

Raba bar Joseph, Babylonian amora, 280-352—1:18; 7:26; 10:10
Rav (Abba Aricka), Babylonian amora, 175-247—1:18; 5:1; 7:8; 9:4

Sama bar Raba, Babylonian amora, c.430-500—5:5
Samuel, Babylonian amora, 180-257—7:8
Samuel bar Nachman, Palestinian amora, 3rd generation, 280-310—1:8,18; 3:11
Samuel ben Isaac, Palestinian amora, 3rd generation, 280-310—1:2
Sheshes, Babylonian amora, 3rd generation, 280-310—10:17
Simon bar Abba, Palestinian amora, 3rd generation, 280-310—2:12; 7:2
Simon ben Chalafta, tanna, Palestine, 6th generation, 200-220—5:1; 8:8
Simon ben Eleazar, tanna, Palestine, 5th generation, 165-200—1:2; 9:4

POST-TALMUDIC AUTHORITIES QUOTED IN COMMENTARY

The post-Talmudic authorities quoted in the commentary and the verses concerning which their comments are quoted are:

Albo, Joseph (Spain, 1380-1445)—1:9-10; 3:9-14,19; 4:3,17; 7:1,20

Alfasi, Isaac (Ha-rif), (Morocco, 1013-1103)—1:18; 7:1,26; 8:1; 9:14

Ashkenazi, Baer (Matnos Kehuna), (Poland, c.1550-c.1610)—3:5

Edels, Samuel (Maharshaw), (Poland, 1551-1631)—3:11; 5:1; 7:2,26; 9:9; 11:5

Einhorn, Zev ben Israel (Maharzu), (Russia, 19th century)—1:18; 2:12; 3:5,11; 4:6

Jacob ben Asher (Baal ha-Turim), (Spain, c.1269-c.1340)—9:9

Ibn Ezra, Abraham ben Meir (Spain, 1092-1167)—1:3,4,13-15,18; 2:3-9,12,14; 3:1,2,5,8,9,10,11,15; 4:1,2,4,5,6,8,17; 5:2,6,11, 15,16,17,18,19; 6:3,5,7,8,9,10,11,12; 7:5,10,11,12,13,14,15,16,17, 18,19,20,21,22,23,24,25,26,28,29; 8:2,9,10,14,17; 9:1,2,4,5,6,7, 8,10,11,12,14,17,18; 10:1,2,9,17

Jaffe, Samuel ben Isaac Ashkenazi (Yafe Toar), (Italy, 16th century) —1:18; 3:5,19; 5:5,8; 6:10; 9:9; 11:5

Luria, David (Redal), (Bykhov, Lithuania, 1798-1855)—1:3; 2:12; 3:11; 4:9; 6:2; 7:5,7; 9:17

Obadiah ben Jacob of Sforno (Sforno), (Italy, 1475-1550)—1:13-15; 2:3-9,12,14; 3:2,11,16,17; 4:4,6,8; 5:1,2,3,5,6,10,11; 6:2,10; 7:1,5,6,8,17,18,19,21,22,23,25,26; 8:1,11,14; 9:9,16,17,18; 10:1,9,16,17

Reicher, Jacob (Iyun Yaakov), (Czecho-slovakia and France, early 18th century)—7:2

Solomon Isaac (Rashi), (France, 1040-1105)—1:4; 2:1-2,12,14; 3:2,-3,4,10,11,17,18,22; 4:8,14; 5:2,6,11; 6:3,10,11; 7:2,5,10,12,14, 19,23-25; 8:14;15; 9:5,9; 10:9,11,12-14,15,16; 11:2,4,5

Zundel, Enoch ben Joseph (Russia, 19th century)—1:18; 4:17; 5:1; 7:26